AUDIENCE OF ONE

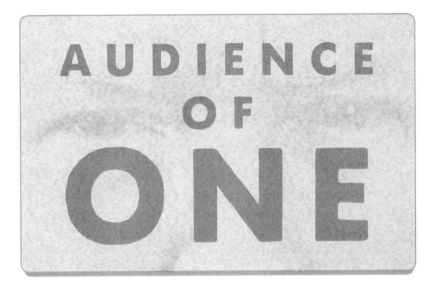

AUDIENCE OF ONE

DONALD TRUMP, TELEVISION, AND THE FRACTURING OF AMERICA

JAMES PONIEWOZIK

LIVERIGHT PUBLISHING CORPORATION

A Division of W. W. Norton & Company

Independent Publishers Since 1923

For information about permission to reproduce selections from this book,
write to Permissions, Liveright Publishing Corporation, a division of
W. W. Norton & Company, Inc., 500 Fifth Avenue, New York, NY 10110

For information about special discounts for bulk purchases, please contact
W. W. Norton Special Sales at specialsales@wwnorton.com or 800-233-4830

Manufacturing by Sheridan
Book design by Lovedog Studio
Production manager: Beth Steidle

ISBN 978-1-63149-442-0

Liveright Publishing Corporation, 500 Fifth Avenue, New York, N.Y. 10110
www.wwnorton.com

W. W. Norton & Company Ltd., 15 Carlisle Street, London W1D 3BS

1 2 3 4 5 6 7 8 9 0

For Beth,
my audience of one

For I do not exist: there exist but the thousands of mirrors that reflect me. With every acquaintance I make, the population of phantoms resembling me increases. Somewhere they live, somewhere they multiply. I alone do not exist.

—Vladimir Nabokov, *The Eye*

What is a cold child? A sadist. What is childish behavior that is cold? It is sadism.

—George W. S. Trow,
Within the Context of No Context

Man is the most vicious of all animals, and life is a series of battles ending in victory or defeat.

—Donald J. Trump, *People* magazine

CONTENTS

INTRODUCTION

THE GOSSIP COLUMNIST SAW HIM COMING FIRST.

In October 1980, Rona Barrett, recently lured away from ABC's *Good Morning America* by NBC, was putting together a one-hour prime-time special for her new network. Miss Rona, as she was called, was a morning-TV superstar, a beguiling presence with a crown of platinum-frosted hair who drove mercilessly for Hollywood scoops. She was the sort of reporter who was disdained by more "serious" (generally, and not coincidentally, male) journalists, yet who had a better understanding of the world than they did: what moved people, the narratives that shaped their interior lives, the changes bubbling up in the culture. NBC wanted to groom her as a news personality and burnish her respectable credentials.

She decided to do an interview special about rich people. "I've always felt that money, power, and sex is all that anybody really cares about," she would say years later. She realized in 1980, before the Reagan years began, before *Lifestyles of the Rich and Famous* premiered, that wealth would become a chief form of celebrity in America. And she intuited that, in the decades to come, this celebrity might ultimately lead to more than mere economic power.

For *Rona Barrett Looks at Today's Super Rich*, which aired in July 1981, she interviewed a half-dozen entrepreneurs, including fashion magnate Diane von Furstenberg; John Johnson, the founder of *Ebony* magazine; and a young New York real-estate scion named Donald Trump. He perched on a couch in his apartment overlooking Central Park, wearing a tie diagonally striped in five shades of brown, as she asked him about ambitions, connections, and family money.

In one section of the interview, which was left out of the primetime special and surfaced on YouTube decades later, the conversation took a turn—to leadership, the Iran crisis, America's stature in the world. Then something made Barrett ask a question most reporters would never think to raise with a thirty-four-year-old wannabe regional mogul: "Would you like to be president of the United States?"

"I really don't believe I would, Rona," he said. The problem, he added, was television. "Capable people"—he defined those as people who "head major corporations"—were not interested in running for office. TV had ruined the process, because it favored inoffensive nice guys.

"Somebody with strong views," he said, "and somebody with the kind of views that are maybe a little bit unpopular, which may be right, but may be unpopular, wouldn't necessarily have a chance of getting elected against somebody with no great brain but a big smile . . . Abraham Lincoln would probably not be electable today because of television. He was not a handsome man, and he did not smile at all. He would not be considered to be a prime candidate for the presidency, and that's a shame, isn't it?"

When the special aired, TV critics, already dismissive of Barrett's hire, panned it. The *Washington Post*'s Tom Shales was especially amused that Barrett introduced the Trump segment with the line, "Some say the age of Trump has just begun."

Thirty-five years later, Donald Trump, a political gadfly who had played a businessman for fourteen seasons on NBC's *The Apprentice*, called in to the Fox News morning show *Fox & Friends*, the day before he would announce what would be his successful campaign for president.

Fox & Friends was Trump's second TV home. He'd had a weekly segment, "Mondays with Trump," for four years, weighing in on national politics and recapping his elimination decisions in the *Apprentice* boardroom. It was friendly territory, but there was an obvious issue, and even *Fox & Friends* couldn't ignore it: Trump was famous for being obnoxious, and a lot of people hated the sight and sound of him.

Cohost Brian Kilmeade phrased it more gently. "Are you worried, Donald Trump, that maybe what resonates in New York and New Jersey and the northeast won't resonate in the south and the west coast, where they're maybe a little bit laid back?"

"I don't think it matters," Trump said. "I don't think this is going to be an election based on real popularity."

It was essentially the opposite of what he had told Rona Barrett half a lifetime ago. But here's the thing: he was not wrong either time.

In 1980, a person like Trump could not have won an election fought on TV. (In 1980, *The Apprentice*—a game show on which viewers cheer a businessman who lives in a golden tower as he fires his employees—could not have been a hit either, except maybe as a dystopian parody like the ones in the movie *Network*.) And Trump was not a fundamentally different person in 2016, when he ran a campaign that would not have been possible had he not spent so much of the intervening decades on TV.

What had changed in the meantime? TV had changed, which is to say, America had. This book is my attempt to describe how.

* * * *

ON OCTOBER 2, 1984—the year Donald Trump was opening his first casino, Harrah's at Trump Plaza, in Atlantic City—the media scholar Neil Postman gave the keynote address at the Frankfurt Book Fair. The fair's theme, befitting the title year of George Orwell's *1984*, was "Orwell in the year 2000."

"The choice of this theme is a mistake," Postman said. "To be precise, it is half of a mistake." Orwell's nightmare of totalitarian thought control was, he said, applicable in about half the world, particularly the Soviet Bloc. But in the West, he argued, another warning was more apt: Aldous Huxley's, in *Brave New World*. In Huxley's dystopia, the people were controlled not by force and propaganda but by pleasure—games, drugs, and phenomenally immersive entertainments. "Orwell thought we would be marched single-file and manacled into oblivion," Postman said. "Huxley thought we would dance ourselves there, with an idiot smile on our face."

For Postman, the pied piper was TV; it elevated the image over the word and thus appearance over substance. Postman's critique of TV-era politics was, in one sense, not far from Donald Trump's. Trump said that sour-faced Abe Lincoln couldn't win a modern-day election, because TV favored a pretty face and an idiot smile. "In America, circa 1984," Postman said, "a fat person cannot be elected to high political office." Things were getting to the point, he observed dryly, that "it is even possible that some day a Hollywood movie actor may become President of the United States." (Ronald Reagan would be reelected the following month.)

Postman expanded on this argument in his brilliant and prophetic 1985 study *Amusing Ourselves to Death*. It built on the ideas of Marshall McLuhan, arguing that the forms of media—the book, the telegraph, the radio—inevitably shape the ideas that they can communicate, and thus how the audience thinks. The "Age of Typography" had given way to the "Age of Television." Television spoke in image rather than text, and it engaged emotion rather than reason. "One can like or dislike a television commercial," he wrote. "But one cannot refute it." Postman laid out how this dynamic affected every area of life: education, religion, news, and politics. The ideology of television was entertainment, and what reigned in a television age was what entertained the most people.

Postman didn't know the half of it. Well, to be fair, he *couldn't* know the half of it. The electronic media of 1985, compared with the multifarious hydra of today, might as well have been two tin cans and a string. Cable TV was not yet in half of American households. CNN, launched in 1980, was the only cable news network, and Postman's analysis focused on broadcast news, which aired a relatively few hours per week. The computer modem was a thing only for researchers or hobbyists.

The distinguishing feature of the mass medium of Postman's time, broadcast TV, was that it was *mass*. Television of the mid-twentieth century was the greatest aggregator of a simultaneous audience ever invented. Postman, like other media critics of the era, was concerned about TV as a stupefying force, but related to that was the argument that TV was a *homogenizing* force, which—in the days of three TV networks that had to appeal to tens of millions of viewers at once— was true. The fear of a TV monoculture was a recurring theme of the time. Richard Hofstadter warned that electronic media could empower demagogues to whip up the mob: "Mass communications," he wrote, "have aroused the mass man." George W. S. Trow argued in *Within the Context of No Context* that broadcast TV placed the individual within "the grid of 200 million," displacing other civic communities, alienating people, and corrupting the national soul.

The emergence of cable TV, the Internet, and social media, however, would take the culture in the opposite direction: fragmenting the audience into niches instead of consolidating it into a common-denominator monolith. In some ways, TV—freed from the constraints of every show having to please a gigantic audience—got much better, more daring and diverse as an art form. But it also got much worse—it got much *more*—in ways that Postman warned about, and ways he didn't.

Postman was mortified at the implications of 98 percent of families having a TV in the living room. Now they effectively have dozens, on their desktops, in their vehicles, in their pockets. This fragmented, nichified media environment created new and different effects. It pacified the audience in some ways, but made it more heated and angry in others. It reorganized America into new subcultures, delineated not by geography but by taste and allegiance. And those divisions became hostile, replacing culture with culture war, merging fandom with ancient blood passions. The multiple twenty-

four-hour news channels became more melodramatic and sensation-
alistic. The Internet and social media, which promised to connect
the world, also divided it, allowing the efficient digital sorting of people into superfans and superpartisans, like speaking to like, affirm-
ing, exhorting, and misinforming one another. (Though Postman
dealt with computers only briefly in *Amusing*—he would expand
on them later in *Technopoly*—he was skeptical of them, predicting
that "the massive collection and speed-of-light retrieval of data [will]
have been of great value to large-scale organizations but have solved
very little of importance to most people and have created at least as
many problems for them." Or as president-elect Trump would put it,
appearing with boxing promoter Don King and dismissing the possibility of Russian hacking on his behalf: "The whole age of computer
has made it where nobody knows exactly what's going on.")

Donald Trump's career (which was, from the beginning, a media
career) began where *Amusing Ourselves to Death* left off and went
from there. So does this book.

Consider this a work of applied TV criticism, for a time when
all of public life has become TV. It tells two parallel stories. One is
about television: how TV culture changed from the era of midcentury media monoliths to the age of media bubbles, how it reflected
and affected our relationships with society, with politics, with one
another. The other is about Donald Trump: a man who, through
a four-decades-long TV performance, achieved symbiosis with the
medium. Its impulses were his impulses; its appetites were his appetites; its mentality was his mentality.

This dual story is about how TV evolved from the Great Homog-
enizer of the twentieth century to the Great Fragmenter of the
twenty-first, and how America, culturally and politically, atomized
along with it.

It's about how pop culture got louder and more abrasive, more
comfortable with cheering for the antihero.

It's about how the techniques of reality TV—conflict, stereotype, the
fuzzy boundary between truth and fiction—became tools of politics.

It's about how public fights were carried out through the pro-wrestling histrionics of cable news.

It's about how the culture war originated as a proxy for politics and increasingly became politics itself.

Through all of those changes, Donald Trump used the dominant media of the day—tabloids, talk shows, reality TV, cable news, Twitter—to enlarge himself, to become a brand, a star, a demagogue, and a president. (Whether Postman's dictum that a fat person cannot win high office in the TV era has now been overturned depends, I suppose, on how seriously you take Trump's rosy personal-physician reports.)

Because Trump so thoroughly fused himself with the pop culture of the last forty years, because he was both an omnipresence on TV and a compulsive devourer of TV, his story is its story, and vice versa. Follow the media culture of America over the course of Trump's career, and you will understand better how Trump happened. Follow how Trump happened and you will understand better what we became.

* * * *

I INTERVIEWED DONALD TRUMP ONCE, in late 2003, for *Time* magazine, when he was about to launch *The Apprentice*. When you visit Trump's office in Trump Tower, every aspect of the experience is designed, like the ballooning collar on a frilled lizard, to make him appear larger. You walk into a skyscraper with his name inscribed on the entrance, the headquarters of a Marvel-comic billionaire. You take a mirror-plated elevator, as if you're ascending to heaven.

I remember being surprised that he shook my hand. (He was notoriously germophobic.) And I remember his handing me an offprint of a *Crain's New York Business* article about the Trump Organization. He kept a stack of them out for visitors, the way you might a dish of mints. "Take one of these," he said. "When you see that, you'll know

I'm busy, right? You know, it's interesting, Jim. I'm the largest developer by far in Manhattan."

This was just a thing he said, the way a roadside diner will say it has "The World's Best Burgers." (The *Crain's* article actually repeated a different claim, apparently made by Trump's company itself, that it was the "largest privately held" company in New York.) To Trump, "large" was about looming largest in the public consciousness.

Anyway, what did I care? I was there for a half-hour interview about a reality game show. What mattered, in that field, were appearances. For that job, press clips and your name in giant brass letters over a doorway were qualification enough.

I did ask him whether he'd considered running for president in 2004. He had teased runs in 1988 and 2000, and now it was just one of those questions reporters would routinely throw at him in interviews. "I thought about it for about a week and said I didn't want to do it," he said. But someday? "Wait and see how we do this month," he said, referring to the *Apprentice* ratings.

Sure thing, Donald!

I soon forgot I'd even asked him, and the detail didn't make my *Time* feature. What I saw in that interview was a vain, show-offy glad-hander, hard to keep focused on one topic, thirsty to impress people, who would not enjoy the scrutiny or the lengthy dedicated grind that came with an honest-to-God run for president. In 2011, when he flirted with running again, I said as much. "What Trump does not like is losing, humiliation, and being made to look bad publicly," I wrote. "Once Trump were to actually get into the race, he would have to be taken seriously by the political media, his inconsistencies parsed, his business history audited, his personal foibles exhumed."

That year, I was right. In the long run, not so much. (I did not anticipate, for instance, that he could simply refuse to release his tax returns and that nearly half the electorate would happily disregard it.) But I had plenty of company.

* * * *

AFTER TRUMP WAS ELECTED, shellshocked journalists began churning out "How we got Trump" explanations. Almost always, they gave incidental attention to his life in media—his tabloid notoriety, the way *The Apprentice* made him a national star—but they usually treated it as ancillary to his business pursuits and his political exploits.

That is exactly the wrong way to see it. TV wasn't an adjunct to Trump's career. It was his career. Media celebrity wasn't a byproduct of his success. It was the basis of his success.

TV had been central to presidential politics for more than half a century. But this was different: with Trump's election, mastery of TV was now not just a political tool but a presidential qualification in itself. Even Reagan had to become governor of California first. Donald Trump leapfrogged that step. Dwight Eisenhower campaigned on TV, but he became president by winning the war in the European theater. Donald Trump became president by winning the 9 p.m. time slot on NBC.

Donald Trump made himself out of television. He treated his life as a show. He knew that it was better to *seem* like New York's most successful businessman than to actually *be* it. The seeming was something you could leverage and license and sell. He understood that if you presented the right picture within the four corners of a camera frame—glitter, competence, *über*strength—it didn't matter that the backdrop was Sheetrock or that just outside the shot was a bare soundstage and floodlights.

"For television purposes, he looked the part," I wrote in the *New York Times,* just after Trump started running. "He did it by happily creating the most vivid pop-culture cartoon of wealth outside a Monopoly box." And Trump's political rise, I came to see, was the result of changes that I had been writing about as a TV critic for twenty years without realizing how they were connected, until they converged in him.

This book is not a definitive explanation of why Trump became president. There are political factors, historical factors, cultural factors, technological factors, and demographic factors that I will cover only glancingly or leave out entirely. It's about one piece of the story, albeit in my biased opinion an important one. Without TV, there's no Trump.

* * * *

I START WITH ONE ASSUMPTION: Donald Trump is not a person.

I mean, yes, there is a corporeal human being named Donald John Trump who has walked the earth for more than seventy years. A physical body alone does not make a person—there is also memory, character, formative experiences, inner life. I assume that this private "Donald Trump" exists too, and biographers will set to figuring him out someday.

But he's not the subject of this book. I'm not sure he's of that much concern to the country that elected him. My focus is instead "Donald Trump," the multimedia character that he has honed and performed over decades, in the New York newspapers, on *Oprah*, in *Trump: The Art of the Deal*, in sitcoms and movies, on *The Apprentice*, in Fox News studios, on the Internet, in the WWE wrestling ring, in campaign rallies, and in the White House.

Maybe that Trump is a cannily constructed fiction. Maybe it's his genuine self. Maybe it's his self *as a performance*, which he amplifies whenever he feels a camera on him. I suspect the last explanation is closest, but fortunately I'm not his therapist.

Trying to sleuth out Trump's private self may have value, but it misses the point that Donald Trump is possibly the most *public* American who has ever lived. "Public" here does not mean "transparent" or "honest." Rather, it means that the Donald Trump who matters is what you see on TV and Twitter, the display model.

So if I write that Donald Trump gave his second-grade music teacher a black eye, as *The Art of the Deal* claimed, I can't say if it actually happened, any more than his coauthor, Tony Schwartz, can. ("Like so much about Trump, who knows whether that story is true?" Schwartz later wrote.) I can only say that it was important to Trump that the reader believe it. It is, as screenwriters say, part of his backstory, his character bible.

* * * *

THAT ABOUT SIXTY-THREE MILLION people voted to elect this TV character president fulfilled the auguries of an Old Testament lineage of media prophets. For a long time, I thought these critics were elitist scolds, contemptuous of TV and its audience. I still believe they were wrong about a lot, especially their consensus that television could never be art. Trow wrote of television, "No good has come of it." Postman lumped in both *The A-Team* and *Cheers*—the latter as rich and humane a comedy as there is in any medium— into the category of harmless "junk-entertainment." (He didn't care much for *Sesame Street*, either, arguing that TV "serves us most ill when it co-opts serious modes of discourse" like education.)

I've seen, over twenty years as a critic, that TV can be much more than junk. I became a TV critic in 1999, when *The Sopranos* premiered on HBO and blew television's narrative possibilities open. Since then, TV has expanded its ambitions, its subject matter, and its range of characters. A series like *The Leftovers* (about the search for purpose and meaning after a global catastrophe) or *Transparent* (which explored the nuances of identity through an elderly parent's coming out as a transgender woman) or *Parks and Recreation* (a workplace comedy set in a small-town bureaucracy that also managed to be a potent argument for the value of the commons) can be more rich with image and character than an epic movie or doorstop novel.

But Trump, though a creature of television, has never shown much interest in *this* kind of TV. Television is really two things: an art form that spins stories and an attention machine that transmits real-world images from one place to another. TV the art form imagines other worlds and lives; it shapes experience into narratives that may run for hours or years but that ultimately have an end; and those endings give you space to make sense and find meaning. TV the attention machine is the modern version of what German cultural critic Walter Benjamin referred to in 1936 as "information": the cascade of news and stimulus, item after non-sequitur item, that has no narrative, no logic, no arc, and no end.

Donald Trump belongs to the attention machine, because Donald Trump *is* an attention machine. This book is about how Trump embodies the ideologies of that sort of TV. That life is a constant, zero-sum competition, and if you are not beating someone then someone is beating you. (The lesson of sports and game shows.) That the best response to any controversy or crisis is to heighten the conflict. (The lesson of TV news.) That people perform best when set to fight against one another for survival. (The lesson of *The Apprentice*.) That there is no history and no objective truth beyond your immediate situational interests, and that reality resets with every tweet or click of the remote.

* * * *

THIS, THEN, IS A STORY IN THREE ACTS.
Part I, "Origin Story," is about how Trump made himself celebrity shorthand for "businessman" by echoing trends in pop culture (especially, though not only, on TV).

Part II, "Antihero," looks at the media forces—the rise of bad-guy protagonists, reality TV, cable news, and social media—that defined early twenty-first-century America and took Trump from tabloid curiosity to presidential candidate.

Finally, Part III, "President Television," examines how Trump used TV as a candidate and was used by it as president, and how America found out what it was like to live inside a TV show programmed for the entertainment, agitation, and flattery of, as the saying went, "an audience of one."

There will probably be people who say that treating a president of the United States as a TV character is disrespectful or trivializing, that it politicizes television criticism or reduces deadly serious politics to a show. To them I can only say: that ship has sailed, my friend. It sailed when Donald Trump took a ride down the Trump Tower lobby escalator on June 16, 2015, if not long before. It will continue sailing long after he has left office.

The best and worst leaders build themselves out of stories. They use their culture's language—legend, metaphor, archetype—to express what literal language can't. Donald Trump is the postmodern evolution of that process. He's a character that wrote itself, a brand mascot that jumped off the cereal box and entered the world, a simulacrum that replaced the thing it represented.

The character Donald Trump is as real and significant as any other creation of American fiction, as much as Jay Gatsby or Lonesome Rhodes or the performance-art personae of comedian Andy Kaufman. Like any other long-running public performance, the Trump character evolved—became more stylized, exaggerated, sharp-edged—but its constant was its understanding of the instinctual appetites and fears of its audience. It became sentient. Finally, America elected it president.

That Donald Trump is the most influential character in the history of TV. He deserves a careful review.

PART I

ORIGIN STORY

1946–1999

Episode 1

UNREAL ESTATE

DONALD J. TRUMP WAS BORN ON JUNE 14, 1946, THE FOURTH child of a big family. He had a father, Frederick Christ Trump, a real-estate developer; a mother, Mary Anne, maiden name MacLeod; and four human brothers and sisters.

He also had a fifth sibling, a phantom conjoined twin: American commercial television.

Five days after Donald was born, the first televised heavyweight boxing championship bout was broadcast from Yankee Stadium. More than 140,000 people tuned in to see Joe Louis defeat Billy Conn for the second time. Their first fight, in 1941, was considered an all-time classic. The 1946 rematch was a disappointment, a sluggish battle between two aging once-greats.

But as a cultural event, it was epochal. It was on television, available to an audience greater than could jam into any arena. *Seeing* the fight, however lousy, was a kind of magic that viewers were just learning to process, like the early moviegoers terrified that an oncoming train would drive off the screen and flatten them. According to a "Talk of the Town" item in *The New Yorker*, some Greenwich Village bar patrons watching on TV "were carried away by the illusion that they were actually at the stadium. 'Hit him, Billy!' cried a partisan spectator. 'G'wan, you think he can hear you?' retorted a realist."

The description of the viewing party gives you a sense of how alien a technology television was in 1946. The reporter describes the screen, "or what we will call the screen, though we are told that what we saw was the end of a big electronic tube of some sort." When the program switched from close-ups of the fighters to a distant panorama of Yankee Stadium, the patrons complained and the bar owner fiddled with a dial, as if believing he could change the camera angle himself.

Like Donald, TV was still a baby in 1946. Its eyes were barely blinking. Its first major pop phenomenon, *Texaco Star Theater* with Milton Berle, which would sell television sets from coast to coast, was still two years away. "Prime time" as a concept didn't exist. Only one network, NBC, aired programs at night. One of them was *I Love to Eat*, a fifteen-minute cooking show on Friday nights starring the cook and author James Beard and Elsie the Borden cow.

Donald Trump and TV would grow up together. They would be partners. They would share a temperament and a heartbeat.

* * * *

IN HIS FIRST BOOK, *Trump: The Art of the Deal*, Trump spends little time on his childhood. The last memory he shares about that part of his life recalls his mother, an elegant woman with a lofted nimbus of hair that anticipated her son's future coiffure, enraptured by the TV in 1953:

> I still remember my mother, who is Scottish by birth, sitting in front of the television set to watch Queen Elizabeth's coronation and not budging for an entire day. She was just enthralled by the pomp and circumstance, the whole idea of royalty and glamour. I also remember my father that day, pacing around impatiently. "For Christ's sake, Mary," he'd say. "Enough is enough, turn it off. They're all a bunch of con artists." My mother didn't even look up.

In his book, Trump remembers the incident as an example of the difference between his two parents: Fred, "excited only by competence and efficiency," and Mary, who was captivated by "the dramatic and the grand."

But the contrast here is also between two businesses, real estate and television.

Fred Trump's business is real estate—as ancient, concrete, and analog an enterprise as there is in human civilization. You have one physical body. You need to house it. It can take up only one space at a time. If you live in Queens, you might move from Forest Hills to Flushing for a better deal, but you're less likely to move to Arizona for the same reason, not without dramatically changing your life.

The business of real estate is the business of mastering and leveraging the availability of space. There is only so much land in New York City. There is only one Yankee Stadium.

Television is as much the opposite of that business as can be. Real estate is the business of scarcity. Television is the business of ubiquity.

Mass communication in general, and TV in particular, changes the relation of people to space. The introduction of the telegraph in the 1800s means that information is detached from the speed at which a human body can travel. Now you no longer need to be in a place to know what just happened there. The effect is both unifying and alienating. In Neil Postman's words, this change throws the "information-action ratio" out of whack: you can know about events that are happening but that you cannot witness or affect. The telegraph collapses distance; then the telephone collapses it further; and radio collapses it further still.

But television does more than collapse space. It creates a second space, visible to the eye, that exists in more than one place at once. Suddenly there isn't just one Yankee Stadium. Now there are tens of thousands—eventually there will be millions.

Actually, that's not right. There is still only one of this new Yankee Stadium, the Yankee Stadium of TV. But it exists in thousands and thousands of places at the same time, the way that God does, or Santa Claus on Christmas Eve. You and your neighbor and a guy in Brooklyn and somebody in Philadelphia are all equally in it at the same time, watching Joe Louis pummel Billy Conn. You sit in the same seat. The punches land for you at the same time and from the same angle.

From this point on, it would be as Don DeLillo later put it in *White Noise*: "For most people there are only two places in the world. Where they live and their TV set."

Before this time in history, this kind of space, distributed point by point throughout the world, existed only metaphorically. An embassy allowed you to stand on the soil of your country, step across a threshold, and stand on the soil of a country thousands of miles away. A church, that most ancient of multimedia outlets, was premised on the idea that people would enter different buildings in different places and commune as part of one entity, The Church.

Television became a kind of church itself in the 1950s, with televangelists like Fulton J. Sheen, the Catholic bishop and host of *Life Is Worth Living*, and Rex Humbard, the guitar-strumming preacher who was inspired to hold his electronic revivals by watching a baseball game in the window of an Akron, Ohio, department store in 1952. Trump later recalled watching Billy Graham's televised Crusades "for hours and hours" with his father.

And the TV show that so enraptured Mrs. Trump and so annoyed her husband was in fact a church service, and controversial at the time for exactly that reason.

* * * *

WINSTON CHURCHILL, serving for the second time as prime minister, had fought against televising Elizabeth's coronation. He appealed to the new monarch's camera-shyness, arguing that it would cheapen and undermine the monarchy to present the ancient ritual "as if it were a theatrical performance." Kings and queens derived their power, historically, from a special relationship with God. If it ceased to be exclusive, what made them kings and queens?

After a public outcry, Elizabeth and her court at first agreed to a compromise, in which the BBC's cameras would be allowed "west of the organ screen" at Westminster Abbey, so that commoners could see the processions but not the culmination of the rite. That stance—that some spaces should be eternally private and privileged—was riddled with class symbolism (the masses would be kept out by a figurative barrier at a literal screen). And it did not last long. The monarchy ultimately granted access to the entire ceremony except for the holy anointing.

The broadcast was considered the event that popularized home television in Great Britain. But it was no small show in the United States, either. This being the era before live satellite broadcasts, NBC and CBS raced to get footage back to the United States by plane for delayed viewing, editing the broadcast literally on the fly.

So the Queen's subjects watched the coronation, and so did the rest of the world, including expatriates like Mary Anne Trump, in her twenty-three-room, colonnaded mansion in Jamaica Estates. Westminster Abbey was annexed into the one-place that materialized in living room after living room. The clergy in their glittering vestments, the queen proceeding from the altar holding scepter and orb, all were public property. The show was a success, and a cataclysm.

This was, in its way, as significant a change in the relationship of governing and governed as the Magna Carta. Media professor Julia Hallam called the TV coronation "a symbolic marker of the beginning of the end of the old society in Britain, a social order based on inherited wealth and the cultural traditions and values of a small minority of the population."

But the same dynamic was shifting in the United States, whose president's campaign slogan, "I Like Ike"—derived from a song in the 1950 Irving Berlin musical *Call Me Madam*—signified the triumph of familiarity over awe. In October 1956, Dwight Eisenhower capped off his reelection campaign with a paid CBS special celebrating his birthday, or "Ike Day." American-as-apple-pie film star Jimmy Stewart narrated the story of Ike and Mamie's courtship; legendary stage actress Helen Hayes cut a slice of birthday cake for a young boy to run over to the president, who was shown watching that very TV show with his family in the White House library. The rulers could still rule, but the price of power, and eventually the means to it, would be accessibility.

* * * *

SO THIS IS THE REALITY that Donald Trump is born into, watching his mother watch the Queen. He's not quite seven years old. Like any child his age, he's coming into his awareness of the size of the world. There are the spaces he knows: his house (brand-new, with nine bathrooms), his neighborhood (Jamaica Estates, a planned slice of suburbia in Queens), his school (the private Kew-Forest college-prep institution). There's his father, who puts up buildings. It's a business a child can easily grasp. Bulldozers push dirt and men swing hammers. You make a house and it makes you money.

These are the kinds of things that any child in any era learns. But now there's also this other thing, TV—and it has the entire world inside it! (Including two of his favorite things: jewel-encrusted splendor and men beating the crap out of each other.) It does something to his mother, enraptures her, transports her somehow to the island she was born on across an ocean, to a fantastical ceremony that she and other subjects of the crown have never witnessed. It is seductive, entrancing. No one's mom spends an entire day ensorcelled by the workings of a construction crane.

Donald is among the first children to learn about this other, virtual space at the same time that he is learning about the physical world. In the 1940s and 1950s, politicians and educators knew that there was a generation coming into this dual knowledge.

To some, it was an opportunity: the home television, like the home computer generations later, was sold in part as an educational tool. "Tomorrow's children, through the great new medium of Television," said a 1945 DuMont ad, "will be enrolled in a world university before they leave their cradles." A military short film about television that same year, besides promising technical jobs in the new industry after the war for GIs (and "costume designing" work for female WAVEs and WACs), imagined that "Television can be the window to the whole world, a medium through which the united nations can better understand each other and live together in the world of tomorrow!"

To others it was a threat. The House Interstate and Foreign Commerce Committee held hearings on violent and immoral TV content in 1952. A few years later, the Senate Judiciary Committee's Subcommittee to Investigate Juvenile Delinquency took up the case, along with the scourge of comic books. Ophthalmologists worried the new machine might ruin kids' eyes. Social scientists worried that it would turn them into illiterates or sociopaths. A 1954 study cited "television addiction" as a factor in "mental apathy" and crime, with TV's "hypnotic and seductive action" detaching children from reality.

Donald Trump was born into this cultural shift like every early baby boomer. But he wasn't like just every baby boomer. He was a rich kid who lived in a mansion, with a cook and a chauffeur. His family owned a color TV set, an unusual luxury; color broadcasts had only started in the United States in 1954. (A neighbor later recalled that Fred Trump asked to put an antenna on her roof, which was higher than the Trumps', but would not agree to let her connect it to her own TV.) He was expected by his father to mature into a "killer"—in Fred Trump's binary and unforgiving worldview, the antithesis of "loser"—and raised to believe that his options were limitless.

Fred Trump had applied a rudimentary form of showmanship in his own work. When a building project was held up by red tape, he organized a photo shoot of a "groundbreaking," complete with construction equipment and models dressed in bikinis. By making the thing seem, you make the thing real.

This was learned behavior for the elder Trump, a penny-pinching, all-business type with a push-broom mustache and little taste for showboatery. He took a Dale Carnegie course—"Effective Speaking and Human Relations"—to overcome his stiffness and learn to glad-hand people. Carnegie described business relations as a kind of personal reality TV, in which you achieve authenticity through artifice: "He implored followers to use artificial means—study, practice, repetition—to cultivate a sincere smile," Trump's biographer Michael D'Antonio writes. Fred was also, as Donald would eventually be, a fan of the Reverend Norman Vincent Peale, a Christian proto-Oprah who ministered on radio and TV and whose *The Power of Positive Thinking* presented Christianity as a kind of self-help salesmanship guide.

So young Donald was being exposed to two kinds of American magic, two ways of showing people wonders and making them dream dreams. There was his father's business, which connected to the American worship of bigness—look how tall I can make this building, look at how vast the country is, how large the portions.

And then this entirely new kind of space, television, virtual but hypnotic, a space that housed people's minds the way an apartment building houses their bodies.

Real estate. Unreal estate.

What if he could combine them? What if he could use the one as a way into the other?

What if he could have the effect on other people that that coronation—all the glitter, the grandeur, the symbolism—had on his mother?

If you became a builder, there would always be other builders, other houses, other towers. But if you became a celebrity, in this new mass-media space, you could be everywhere at once. If you became famous enough, your head could be the only real estate anybody could live in.

* * * *

I'M IMAGINING THIS as a eureka moment. Most likely it wasn't. Trump's path from his inherited business to show business was gradual. But this was what he was seeing, at not quite the age of seven, as the mass media that would dominate the rest of his life were just emerging. And as Trump would later tell D'Antonio: "When I look at myself in the first grade and I look at myself now, I'm basically the same."

Certainly, the adult Trump never seemed to evolve much beyond a worldview circumscribed by the TV of his childhood. In a 1994 interview with ABC, he described a view of married life out of a '50s sitcom: "I don't want to sound like a chauvinist, but when I come home at night and dinner's not ready, I go through the roof." Jack Webb's *Dragnet* (1952), the culmination of longtime efforts by police to improve their portrayal in pop culture, presaged Trump's 2016 call for "law and order" (a phrase that had been both a slogan of Richard Nixon's 1968 campaign and the title of *Dragnet*'s longest-running TV descendant). Senator Joseph McCarthy's red-scare campaign, covered on Edward R. Murrow's *See It Now* and in the televised Army-McCarthy hearings, introduced Roy Cohn, the thuggish, bullying lawyer and hatchet man who would later become Trump's mentor in public battling. (Always attack; always deny; never apologize.) Pro wrestling, a favorite of young Donald Trump's, would figure into his casino and showbiz careers and his campaign theatrics.

But what little boys of the 1950s obsessed over most on TV was a five-part serial on ABC's *Disneyland*, starring the rugged, athletic Fess Parker as frontiersman and congressman Davy Crockett. It was one of TV's first legitimate pop-culture crazes, driving a bull market in coonskin caps. The show, introduced by a promo for Disney's Frontierland park, featuring "tall tales and true from the legendary past," was a seminal piece of populist mythmaking. In Disney's telling, "Indian fighter" Crockett, with common sense but not a lot of book learning, brings the decency of rough-and-tumble America to corrupt Washington, DC, before sacrificing himself at the Alamo. The show demonized Native Americans as savages assailing peaceful white settlers and pitted Americans against an invading horde at the Mexican border—not unlike the toxic racial imagery Donald Trump would later campaign and govern with.

It was also, not that any kid watching it at the time was aware of it, a metastory about an early American politician who had constructed his own myth, aided by the media of his day. Crockett published an autobiography and was the subject of the 1831 play *Lion of the West*, both of which exaggerated his frontier derring-do and made him into a larger-than-life hero. Disney revived the myth for a new century. The second episode of the series, "Davy Crockett Goes to Congress," ends with Parker striding into the House of Representatives—wearing the furry cap that the real-life Crockett didn't—to protest Andrew Jackson's Indian Removal Act of 1830 as unfair. An oily politician warns him he's "committing political suicide." "You know what I think about your kind of politics?" Crockett says, and punches out the smug Easterner.

Here in miniature is the political archetype that Trump would act out sixty years later: the plain-talkin' red-blooded American who cuts the crap and settles arguments like men do. The adult Donald Trump would prefer play-acted fisticuffs, like a scripted battle he fought with World Wrestling Entertainment boss Vince McMahon at WrestleMania in 2007. But violent rhetoric was essential to his campaign rallies and his presidency, such as when he tweeted a video of the staged McMahon fight, edited by user "HanAssholeSolo" on Reddit to show the CNN logo over McMahon's face.[*]

The young Donald had a more literal interest in violence. Classmates recalled him as a bully, and after Fred Trump discovered his

---

[*] Ironically, Trump was using the clip—an edited video of a phony fight—to denounce CNN as a "fraud."

son's collection of switchblades—inspired by *West Side Story*, the 1957 musical about a gang war between the white Jets and the Puerto Rican Sharks—his father sent him to military boarding school. There, Trump developed a less G-rated pop-culture influence: *Playboy* magazine.

The *Playboy* of the 1960s offered an expression of sex that was both debauched and sanitized. The founder, Hugh Hefner, described the Playboy Bunny as "a young, healthy, simple girl . . . She is naked, well-washed with soap and water, and she is happy." The columnist Katharine Whitehorn called *Playboy* "a Midwestern Methodist's vision of sin."

"That's how we learned about women," his classmate Sandy McIntosh recalled for a PBS documentary. "That's why getting out of military school was difficult. You had to realize you couldn't just follow the *Playboy* philosophy."

Or maybe you could. Maybe you could make a career out of it. Much of Trump's celebrity life—a rich man in a tux, living in a gilded pad on top of a gold tower and dating supermodels—could have been extracted directly from the imaginings of a horny fourteen-year-old poring over a nudie mag at an all-boys' boarding school.

And in a way, the later Trump persona was a kind of mash-up of the two poles of his 1950s and early '60s pop culture of choice—the lounge-lizard hedonism of his military school *Playboy*s slathered on top of the traditionalism of network TV: *Father Knows Best*, but with a little something on the side for father. All the benefits of the patriarchy; none of the boring moral responsibility.

You can see much of Trump's early life as an attempt to construct a self out of bits of pop culture, fitfully trying to reconcile the business heir he was fated to be with the fantasy of an eternal adolescent. When he graduated military school, according to *The Art of the Deal*, he considered going to film school at the University of Southern California: "I was attracted to the glamour of the movies, and I admired guys like Sam Goldwyn, Darryl Zanuck, and most of all Louis B. Mayer, whom I considered great showmen. But in the end I decided real estate was a much better business."

Notice the examples he gives. Not, say, Kubrick or Huston or Hitchcock, but the studio heads behind the directors. Even in his unrealized Hollywood fantasy, he remains daddy's boy. Notice, too, the reason he gives for not going. Another author might have used this detail as a kind of Rosebud—the story of the would-be artist, pressured into going into dad's business, who would never stop trying to recapture what might have been. This is not in Trump's self-conception. If he made a decision, it had to be because it was the right one. Real estate was the smarter choice.

And quite likely it was, for him. Trump may have loved the movies, but has not, in life, ever come off as much of a cineaste. In a 1997 profile, Mark Singer of *The New Yorker*, traveling on Trump's plane, recalled that he popped in a videotape of *Michael*—starring John Travolta as the archangel Michael come to Earth—got bored after twenty minutes, and changed to Jean-Claude Van Damme's *Bloodsport*, which he had his son Eric shave down from two hours to forty-five minutes by fast-forwarding to all the fight scenes. In a 2002 interview with documentarian Errol Morris, he concluded that the message of *Citizen Kane* was that Charles Foster Kane needed to "find another woman."

Performing himself, though: that he could do. Better to be himself, but a celebrity. Better to find a way to take the job that was handed to him and make it a performance. Better to find a way to convince people that business was as legitimate a path to celebrity as entertainment, that indeed it was entertainment, that making deals was making art.

* * * *

SO NO FILM SCHOOL. Fordham University. Transfer to Wharton. Back to New York, back to dad's office.

Even as he was starting out in real estate, Trump angled to combine his business with show business. At age twenty-three he approached

Broadway producer David Black and offered to bankroll half of his next play in exchange for billing above the title as a producer.

Paris Is Out! was a fluffy domestic comedy starring Yiddish theater star Molly Picon and Sam Levene (the original Nathan Detroit in *Guys and Dolls*) as a bickering middle-aged couple considering a trip to Europe. As Black recalled, Trump was curious about the business side of the production and how it could save money. He wasn't particularly driven by passion for the play itself.

That was just as well. The producers avoided previews to insulate *Paris* from critics. In Clive Barnes's eventual *New York Times* review after its 1970 opening, you could maybe see a glimpse of the future divide between Trump's fan base and elite opinion: "I know some people who might enjoy it more than *King Lear*. They are probably people who shouldn't go to the theater."

Paris Is Out! was itself out after 112 performances, and Trump gave up on Broadway, including a plan to coproduce *W.C.*, a Mickey Rooney/Bernadette Peters musical about W. C. Fields. ("It's a crummy business," he told *GQ* in 1984, recalling the play's failure, though in his retelling he was "sort of a semiproducer.") "I am going to go into real estate," he would later recall thinking, "and I am going to put show business into real estate."

Over the 1970s, the city fell into an economic pall, a baroque sleazy funk that would be immortalized in pop culture—Ford told it figuratively to drop dead, Son of Sam did the killing literally, and the Rolling Stones set the decline to music in "Shattered." Trump was eventually able to take advantage of the depressed economy, striking a deal in 1975 to buy the grand, in-decline Commodore Hotel near Grand Central Terminal.

And the persona of Donald Trump went into construction alongside businessman Trump—really, the celebrity lifestyle came before he had done much of anything to be famous for. Trump joined Le Club, a Euro-oriented nightclub that functioned as a basking rock for the famous and fame-hungry. Trump befriended McCarthy's former henchman Roy Cohn and Yankees owner George Steinbrenner and met a string of women.

The paradox of any club scene is that its value comes from both being exclusive and being public. A scene is worth nothing if anyone can be part of it, and it's worth nothing if no one knows that you're part of it. Donald Trump wanted the things an ambitious twenty-something in his position wanted—money, access, sex—but he also wanted to be seen to have those things.

This is what entertainment celebrities did, employing press agents and cultivating columnists to make sure that their private lives became public in ways that advantaged them. For an actress, a musician, a comedian, there was of course a direct career incentive for this: to give the audience a taste of a personal connection that they could maintain by buying tickets and albums.

For a businessman, the value of celebrity was less certain. American businessmen historically didn't make compelling superstars. Their performance was their work. They modeled seriousness and reliability, and they benefited from being a little stiff. There were exceptions—P. T. Barnum, notably—but even Barnum was in the business of selling a show, not being the show. Walt Disney depended on a public persona to sell dreams, but he distinguished between his self and his persona. "I'm not Walt Disney," he said. "I do a lot of things Walt Disney wouldn't do. Walt Disney doesn't smoke, I smoke. Walt Disney doesn't drink, I drink."

One exception was Hugh Hefner, who built the *Playboy* brand in large part by being the *Playboy* brand. He used the bunnies as a personal harem. He lived in the Playboy Mansion in Los Angeles—a fusion of the personal and commercial in his life that Trump would echo later, living above the store at Trump Tower, which like the Mansion was equal parts home, headquarters, and metonym. Hefner popularized the product, mainstreamed it, and enhanced its appeal by being its most famous customer.

Trump never lost his fascination with *Playboy*—he would make cameos in softcore *Playboy* videos, interviewing and snapping photographs of models, and once tried to convince the magazine to run a "Girls of Trump" spread featuring his female staffers. Years later, Trump recognized the connection between his brand and Hef's on season 6 of *The Apprentice* by throwing a cocktail party at the Mansion for the team that won a challenge.

Before the party, Hefner—dressed in character, in his smoking jacket—told the team a story that, but for the subject matter, could have come straight out of a chamber of commerce speech, about starting his business with "$600 that I borrowed" and a pinup-calendar picture of Marilyn Monroe. Then it was off to poolside, where the team—seven women and two men—hung out with "30 or 40" Playmates, in bikinis and bunny ears, until Trump showed up to bestow his blessing. After Trump won the Republican nomination in 2016, Hefner, by then a ninety-year-old Priapus, hailed it in an essay as the triumph of "The Conservative Sex Movement."

With Hefner as a progenitor, then, you could see what Trump was doing in the 1970s as becoming a pornographer of real estate. Early on, he saw a value in cultivating a famous image the way Hollywood starlets did in the past. And like social-media stars would in the future, he did it before he'd done much to be famous for. Whether by grand design or instinctive hunger, he acted on the assumption that another plane of existence—that holy Westminster Abbey of mediaspace—was his true home, and he needed to get there.

* * * *

THE FIRST GATEWAY was print. In 1970s New York, celebrity journalism was booming. Andy Warhol had launched *Interview* in 1969. *People* metamorphosed from a section of *Time* magazine into its own publication in 1974, and it quickly became more important to Time Inc.'s business than its parent. Rupert Murdoch, the Australian tabloid mogul who dreamt in 144-point headlines, bought the sleepy, historically liberal *New York Post*, reversed its politics, and revived the New York City gossip trade.

Trump learned to work gossip columnists, who were happy to run juicy items with a single source, which source, very often, would be Donald Trump. Former *Newsday* gossip columnist A. J. Benza said Trump would offer nightlife tips—"who said what, where was the pussy"—as long as you helped script his media character: "Regardless of what you mentioned, he never really cared as long as you said the word 'billionaire.'"

If you covered Trump long enough, you knew that he lied, but he made good copy. "Like an elephant in your bathtub, he's very hard to ignore," *New York Post* Page Six gossip Susan Mulcahy put it. He was charming and flirty and golden-boy handsome. *Daily News* columnist Liz Smith recalled being courted: "Donald would always gather me up under his arm and say to whoever might be near, 'She's the greatest! Isn't she the greatest?' This was silly and embarrassing and he did it with everybody else as well."

Trump's big early coup—the print launch of the character "Donald Trump"—was a 1976 profile in the *New York Times* that read like a write-up of a screen heartthrob. "He is tall, lean and blond," feature writer Judy Klemesrud described him, "with dazzling white teeth, and he looks ever so much like Robert Redford." (I doubt that any sentence, including any set of his wedding vows or his swearing in by the chief justice of the United States, ever gave Donald Trump as much pleasure.) His conspicuous hedonism paid off in the first paragraph: "He dates slinky fashion models, belongs to the most elegant clubs."

The article is a trove of Trump lies and flimflam. He takes Klemesrud—a society reporter who grew up in Iowa and depicted Trump's Manhattan in awed terms—around the city in a chauffeured Cadillac. (It was actually leased by his father, a detail that does not make the article.) He graduated "first in his class" at Wharton. (The school's newspaper later debunked this.) He is worth "more than $200 million." (He was claiming his dad's wealth as his own.) His ancestry is "Swedish." (His father's family was German, his mother's Scottish.) Perhaps the funniest line in retrospect is a kind of fib familiar from Hollywood profiles: Trump, Klemesrud writes deadpan, "says he is publicity shy."

Controversial! Brash! Sexy! A brand is born.

* * * *

A BRAND FOR WHAT, though? These are not attributes you'd traditionally associate with real estate, which appealed to permanence and stability and the hearth. You certainly wouldn't use this brand to sell public housing for Fred Trump in the outer boroughs. It wasn't even, traditionally, the kind of imagery you would associate with luxury real estate in Manhattan.

But by 1976, you were, increasingly, speaking to an audience of Trump's generation, who were sold products not so much on the argument of value or quality but as a means of self-expression. In their early decades, TV and TV advertising, like the culture in which they operated, affirmed the values of the community and the pleasure of belonging. You drank Pepsi, in the early 1960s, to belong to the "Pepsi Generation." You ate at Burger King, by the mid 1970s, in order to "Have It Your Way." Christopher Lasch diagnosed 1970s society, in *The Culture of Narcissism,* with a combination of self-absorption, insecurity, and craving for recognition—a kind of individualism run amok that was reflected, among other places, in marketing. "By surrounding the consumer with images of the good life," Lasch wrote, "and by associating them with the glamour of celebrity and success, mass culture encourages the ordinary man to cultivate extraordinary tastes, to identify himself with the privileged minority against the rest, and to join them, in his fantasies, in a life of exquisite comfort and sensual refinement."

To this market, it might make sense to brand a home not as homey, but sexy, exciting, special—just like you. Didn't you deserve it? Shouldn't your home be a kind of stage?

I don't pretend to know whether Trump was being prescient or a savant, whether he took the celebrity approach out of a savvy sense of the zeitgeist or simply because he didn't know how to be any other way. Maybe Trump adapted himself to his era. Maybe he was molded by it. Or maybe he was just born at the right time—a few decades before, maybe, he would have ended up Fred Trump's loud-mouthed, peacocky son, besotted with glamour, too full of himself to make a respectable go at business.

Adopting a celebrity persona to speak to an era of narcissism is something that a promotional genius might do. It's also something a narcissist might do. Either way, it's what Donald Trump did. Having failed as a producer, he made himself the production.

Episode 2

THE LEAST OBJECTIONABLE PROGRAM

"DONALD J. TRUMP," THE TELEVISION CHARACTER, WAS BORN on August 21, 1980. This is what it looked like.

Tom Brokaw is introducing the viewers of *The Today Show* to a personality who's been making noise in the New York City real-estate business. "Trying to scrape up a down payment for a little fixer-upper in your neighborhood?" he says. "This is Donald Trump, thirty-three years old, and some people think that he wants to buy the World Trade Center, the 110-story Manhattan skyscraper that anyone can pick up—if they've got the coins."*

For the audience making breakfast and dressing for work, particularly if they're not New Yorkers, it's their first introduction to a face they will see countless times again on NBC. (Trump's mid-'70s real-estate projects landed him briefly on a few local talk shows—*One Woman's New York, Here and Now*—which appear to be lost to time.)

---

* Trump was thirty-four, not thirty-three. Brokaw may have picked up the age from an August 10 *New York Daily News* feature, which referenced the rumor that Trump was interested in the WTC and also shaved a year off Trump's age.

Brokaw has a shaggy haircut and wears a suit the color of toast. The whole set is shades of toast—the desk, the curtains framing the "window." (Through it, you can see Trump Tower, or rather an artist's rendering, because the building does not exist yet.) There are flowers and potted plants. It's 1980, which is still, really, the 1970s. Jimmy Carter is still president. Everything, in 1980, kind of looks like toast.

But the 1980s are there, sitting opposite Brokaw. "Donald Trump, real estate investor," the caption calls him. His hands are clasped. He slouches a bit, like a prep-school kid at an interview for an internship he's been assured that he's going to get. Brokaw kicks off, noting that Trump has built up his father's more modest real-estate business by buying up fire-sale properties in Manhattan.

Brokaw's manner is earnest Midwest-newsman—plain-spoken, dressed like a regional bank manager, sharing his audience's wonder at the extravagances of Manhattan, like the new Trump Tower, which has just broken ground next door to Tiffany's. You can buy an apartment, Brokaw marvels, "one floor of it—one floor of that whole building, that is—$11 million altogether."

The most contentious section comes in the middle, as Brokaw asks Trump why he didn't save the renowned Art Deco friezes on the Bonwit Teller building he demolished to build his namesake tower. Trump deflects it creamily: "There was something of an outcry, but I think that's generally subsided now, and I think people like what we're doing." The friezes—delicate bas reliefs of classical nudes dancing with scarves—weighed tons, he says, and "people could have been very badly hurt and killed" if they fell into the street while being taken down.

It's transparently bullshit, of course. Trump himself will later put it more frankly in *The Art of the Deal*: "I just wasn't prepared to lose hundreds of thousands of dollars to save a few Art Deco sculptures that I believed were worth considerably less." But Brokaw's audience is not much interested in the fine points of New York preservation controversies, and he moves on. "You've said you don't care if you become a billionaire?" No; "I just want to keep busy and keep active and be interested in what I do, and that's all there is to life as far as I'm concerned."

Someone watching that interview in 1980 probably never thought twice about it again, once they polished off the toaster waffles and headed out the door. Maybe they took away a general ambient knowledge that people paid ridiculous sums to live in New York, the city they'd watched burn during the World Series just a few years ago. Trump himself, assured, subdued, unctuous, doesn't cut a memorable figure yet, beyond his mane of hair. He's still more James Spader (the oily preppy of *Pretty in Pink*) than Michael Douglas (the predator-capitalist of *Wall Street*).

But from our vantage point, there's a lot of information in it. The striking thing is Trump's tone. He sounds like Donald Trump as we would later know him, yet not at all. His manner of speaking is mild. His sentences are diagrammable. There are some familiar locutions— "very badly hurt and killed," "people like what we're doing"—but not the punching cadence, the pugnaciousness, the anger. There are no insults and little bragging. Given a chance to engage a controversy, he deflects it. He's trying to charm rather than incite.

There could be personal reasons for this, even biological ones. Trump's early speaking style could, in part, be the mannerism of the outer-borough businessman still hoping to be accepted by Manhattan society. His later manner, as a candidate and as president, could be a performer evolving his affect to his audience. It also could be a sign of cognitive decline. The science writer Sharon Begley asked neurolinguistic experts and psychologists to analyze the changes in Trump's speaking style over the decades, and they suggested the change could reflect anything from fatigue to the physical deterioration of his brain.

But there's something else you're hearing in the Donald Trump of 1980: the voice of twentieth-century mainstream media.

* * * *

THE YEAR 1980—REALLY, right about the precise moment Trump sat on Brokaw's couch—was the peak of the mass broadcast-TV audience. TV was still, essentially, a three-network medium. An American population of about 226 million had only a few programming choices at any time. A popular show could get 60 million viewers, three times as many people as would watch a number-one show in the 2010s, when the overall population was more than 40 percent greater.

In other words, the audience for each of the major networks in 1980 was about as big as it had ever been and would ever be. For several decades in the middle of the twentieth century, first radio and then television did something that hadn't been done before or since: bring together the majority of the public to have the same cultural experiences at the same time, all the time.

The mid-twentieth-century mass media took a country of regional cultures, dialects, and art forms and introduced a monoculture. At the same time that the Interstate Highway System was bypassing local byways and national chains were selling the same goods and fast food coast to coast, TV gave us national news, national amusements, and national obsessions. There was even a national voice, in the mid-Atlantic neutral-speak of TV hosts and anchors.

Today, in the twenty-first century, some commentators romanticize this period as a time when Americans shared common interests and experiences, before we were divided into bubbles.

But at the time, their twentieth-century peers denounced the same phenomenon for creating a culture of conformity and complacency: what the cultural and social critic Dwight MacDonald identified in 1962 as "masscult" and "midcult." George W. S. Trow, in the 1980 essay that became the 1981 book *Within the Context of No Context*, wrote that television divided American life into "the grid of intimacy" (one's personal relationships) and "the grid of 200 million" (mass public life, on the national scale imposed by TV). It thus obliterated "the middle distance," essentially, the intermediate institutions, between the individual and the nation as a whole, that once defined and elevated civic life.

The communal stage on which Donald Trump debuted was the broadest ever created. That created certain demands of presentation. If everyone watched the same things, then everything on TV—sitcoms, news, politicians, talk-show guests—had to try to appeal to everybody.

The ideal TV show of the time was what Paul L. Klein, an audience-measurement executive at NBC, referred to in *TV Guide* as the "Least Objectionable Program" or, charmingly, the LOP.

The LOP was a kind of programming whose chief goal was negative: *Never give the viewer a reason to change the channel.* It was fine if a show was unexceptional as long as it was unexceptionable.

Why? Television was something that flowed into your house. Rather than seek out your preferred programming—as you would choose a book at a library, or as you'd pick a show today on Netflix—you turned TV on like a tap and let gush out whatever happened to be coming through the pipes. That would be whatever channel you were watching when last you turned the machine off. The inertia of the American TV viewer was the broadcaster's best friend, the arduous journey from the couch to the channel dial a defensive moat.

The LOP—innocuous, smoothly palatable—defined the network programming of the 1950s and 1960s. (Not all of it, obviously, but we remember the exceptions—the avant-garde surrealism of *The Prisoner*, the antiwar protest of *The Smothers Brothers Comedy Hour*, the social allegory of *The Twilight Zone*—because they were exceptions.) As American life became more divided and contentious, sitcoms escaped into domestic fantasies about aliens, genies, and witches. As the carnage of Vietnam intruded into the evening news, TV offered up the chipper GI sitcom *Gomer Pyle, U.S.M.C.* and *Hogan's Heroes*, about the wacky adventures of prisoners in a Nazi POW camp in World War II.

The LOP was there to give you a break. You didn't turn on the TV to find something you loved; you turned it on to find something you didn't hate. You turned it on to have the TV on. TV aimed to be OK with everyone, to induce a kind of room-temperature stasis. It was inoffensive, unprovocative, unobjectionable.

These programming guidelines applied to politicians especially. This may have been what Trump had in mind when, two months after his *Today* appearance, he told NBC's Rona Barrett that someone "with strong views" could not be elected president in the TV culture of the time.

The mass TV audience wanted smiles and reassurances. It wanted optimism. Even if the electorate was unsettled, even if it wanted to lash out, it wanted candidates who would soothe its fury, not goad it. It wanted that cool, prime-time TV feeling of a steady hand in control. Agitator candidates, like Barry Goldwater (the 1964 Republican nominee who declared, "Extremism in the defense of liberty is no vice") and segregationist third-party candidate George Wallace, could get attention. But in the three-network-TV era, they could never win.

In late October 1980, a few weeks after Trump sat down with Barrett, President Jimmy Carter and his opponent Ronald Reagan had their only debate. Reagan had political tailwinds all year—Iran, the general American bummer Carter referred to as "malaise"—but he was hurt by the perception that he was an extremist who couldn't be trusted with the bomb.

He was, however, at home with a microphone and camera. Before Reagan was governor of California, he was a baseball announcer, a mid-tier movie star (he kept the nickname "the Gipper" from his role in the football flick *Knute Rockne, All American*), and the host of TV's *General Electric Theater.* Reagan was not a thespian of great depth—among his roles, he costarred with a chimp in 1951's *Bedtime for Bonzo*—but he knew how to disarm an audience and put them at ease. He used the debate to soften his image, famously deflecting an attack by Carter with the one-liner, "There you go again," and a smile. Message: Surely Grandpa wouldn't blow up the world!

Political analysts disagree on whether Reagan would have won the election anyway, but polling suggests that he at least widened his margin that last week. He successfully recast himself as the Least Objectionable Program.

Neil Postman wrote *Amusing Ourselves to Death* around the time of Reagan's reelection, and while his book was a study of the media over decades it was also, between the lines, very specifically about political language in the age of Reagan. (The idea that the values of show business had conquered the presidency was a defining worry of liberals at the time—at least until Bill Clinton, whom cultural critic Kurt Andersen called "the entertainer-in-chief," won in 1992.) By 1984, Postman wrote, debates were covered not as contests of ideas but as "boxing matches," albeit ones fought with velvet gloves: "how they looked, fixed their gaze, smiled and delivered one-liners. . . . Thus, the leader of the free world is chosen by the people in the Age of Television."*

Ironically, Postman's critique has something in common with Trump's complaint to Rona Barrett about election-year TV, that it gives an edge to the candidate with "a big smile." Postman was concerned that the tyranny of the cheerfully entertaining worked against intellectuals, which was hardly Trump's worry. But it also worked against bomb-throwers.

So you can see the way Trump talks to Tom Brokaw—roguish rather than threatening, urbane rather than pugilistic—as a way of reconciling himself with the voice of that media era. If he tries to reassure rather than aggravate, to soothe rather than inflame, it's because that is what 1980 required. Cool, not hot. A purr, not a scream. The least objectionable version of himself.

The journey of Donald Trump from Least Objectionable Program in 1980 to Most Objectionable Program in 2016—when he won as very much the kind of personality he said could never be

---

* In 2016, when Trump ran, CNN literally promoted the debates as a prize-fight, with a ringside-style announcer and graphics—"THIS . . . IS . . . IT . . . ROUND 3," punctuated by a boxing-ring bell.

elected in Reagan's time—is, in part, the story of the disintegration of the mass-media audience.

* * * *

TV IS A BUSINESS. What stays on the air is what makes money. In the early decades of TV, this worked simply. TV shows made money through advertising. The more viewers—young, old, urban, rural, rich, poor—the more advertisers would pay. This reinforced the idea of the LOP. If a show appealed to more kinds of people, it was better business. There was not, yet, a means of monetizing a show because it especially appealed to, say, twenty-six-year-old male extreme-sports enthusiasts.

So you offered a little something for everybody. Thus variety-show host Ed Sullivan hosted both the Beatles and Señor Wences, the ventriloquist who used a face drawn on his hand as a puppet. The television of the 1950s reflected a go-along, get-along sensibility not simply because of the social conservatism of the time, but because it kept people from changing the channel. (And, of course, the one reinforced the other.) And the television of the 1960s was much the same, even as the larger society divided.

The first fissures in the great mass-audience glacier started appearing as early as the late 1960s and the 1970s. As advertisers became more interested in more specific audiences, especially young ones ("Now it's Pepsi—for those who think young"), programmers took note.

Earlier in the '60s, TV fell hard for shows about country folk—*The Beverly Hillbillies*, *Petticoat Junction*—which appealed to rural viewers who felt represented and city folk who got to laugh at the likeable rubes. On *The Beverly Hillbillies*, backwoodsman Jed Clampett (Buddy Ebsen) struck oil and moved his family to "Californee," where their snooty neighbors looked down on them. On *Green Acres*, a New York attorney (Eddie Albert) with a fashionable, heavily accented wife (Eva Gabor), gave up the city for "farm livin'." (Trump—the Manhattan penthouse dweller with the accented wife who became president by pitching his campaign to the resentments of rural, white voters—would reprise the Eddie Albert role in a sketch at the 2005 Emmy Awards.) CBS had a lot of these shows, but at the beginning of the '70s it axed most of them in the "Rural Purge," a midlife crisis aimed at rejuvenating the network with more "relevant," and thus hopefully young-skewing, programs like *The Mary Tyler Moore Show*.

If the Clampetts were around in 2016, they'd have probably voted Trump. And Trump appealed to the Clampett in his voters, the shared grievance that they were laughed at, scorned as "deplorables," dismissed—or simply, like Jed and his kin, canceled—by an alien liberal culture.

CBS executive Michael Dann, who had programmed many of the countrified comedies, protested the Rural Purge shortly before leaving the network. "Just because the people who buy refrigerators are 26 to 35 years old and live in Scarsdale," he said, "you should not beam your programming only at them." But exactly that approach would, over a long time, become the future of television, and Dann had a hand in it. One of his last acts at CBS was to pick up Norman Lear's *All in the Family*, about an outrageous loudmouth from Queens whom millions of Americans would come to love despite, or because of, his bigoted blather.

All in the Family, which premiered in January 1971, began a few years of ferment in TV, when programmers sought to steer into the chaos of American social life rather than spackle over it. *M*A*S*H*, the antiwar comedy that launched on CBS the next year, used the Korean War as a thinly veiled stand-in for the one still being fought in Vietnam. Lear's *Maude* (a spinoff of *All in the Family*) and *Good Times* (a spinoff of *Maude*) made comedy of feminism and inner-city poverty. Even escapist TV become fashionably gritty, with violent (for the time) cop dramas like *Toma* and *S.W.A.T.* playing off the daily news of urban blight and lawlessness. (When Trump gave Brokaw his pitch about turning around the "inner city," he was referencing a narrative that prime-time TV had been giving the *Today* audience for years—even, or especially, if they lived nowhere near a city.)

But three-network TV remained a mass enterprise, and the gravitational pull of the LOP reasserted itself. By the mid-'70s, the networks wanted optimistic and upbeat, turning to nostalgia (*Happy Days*), fantasy (*The Love Boat*), and sex appeal (*Charlie's Angels*). It was as if, with Nixon's resignation, the industry saw its burst of creative restlessness as a Watergate-like fever that it had burned through. Gerald Ford declared that he was "a Ford, not a Lincoln," presenting himself as a Least Objectionable President, as anodyne and forgettable as a car commercial. TV's Ford-Carter years reached a bland détente with the aftermath of change, picking and choosing those elements of the times that were most adaptable to family entertainment. The sexual revolution became *Three's Company* (1977), feminism became single-mom comedies like *One Day at a Time* (1975), consciousness-raising became *Mork & Mindy* (1978), the sort of alien-comes-to-Earth sitcom that TV loved in the 1960s, now with a subtext of psycho-patter and cokehead mania from the improv comic Robin Williams. These shifts fit a population that was turning inward, where Lasch's culture of narcissism was taking hold. The 1970s wanted to mellow out. The LOP was happy to take the edge off.

So the population got bigger, but the number of major networks remained at three. Thus 1980, the cusp of the Reagan era, was the statistical height of mass-market television. The big fragmentation of the TV audience would come later in the 1980s and beyond, thanks to two trends that would begin to accelerate not long after Trump sat down with Brokaw.

The first was the weaponization of demographics—the idea that some people's attention was worth more to advertisers than others. NBC, Trump's future employer and partner, pursued the strategy aggressively. In 1981, the network was besieged after a string of flops, including historic stinkers like *Supertrain* (1979), about mystery and romance on a luxury locomotive. It also had one success, *Hill Street Blues*, a literate, rawly realistic police drama whose only drawback was that almost nobody was watching it.

But those almost-nobodies were young, urban, and well-off, and advertisers—increasingly focused on targeting specific consumer groups—were ready to pay a premium to reach them. As *Time* magazine put it in 1985, "Madison Avenue mavens were discovering that a rule long applied to magazines—that 1000 *New Yorker* readers are more valuable than 1000 *National Enquirer* readers—made sense in prime time as well." In the 1984–85 season, *Hill Street Blues* had an overall rating 13 percent lower than the prime-time soap *Knots Landing* on CBS, yet commanded the same rate, $200,000 for a thirty-second commercial. Advertisers preferred rich viewers for obvious reasons. They preferred young viewers for less obvious ones: they watched less TV, which made them harder to reach (thus worth paying a premium for), and, supposedly, they were developing lifetime brand loyalties.

The second thing that would break up the mainstream TV audience was cable. In 1980, when Donald Trump sat down with Tom Brokaw, CNN had been in business for only two months. MTV would go on the air a year later. As cable spread, it would transform a mass experience into a customized one. If broadcast networks began with the idea of TV for everyone, cable channels were by definition TV for some, and only some. You watched ESPN because you really wanted to see sports—because you *only* wanted to see sports.

There was a channel for music, and a channel for music for slightly older people, and a channel for country music. There was a channel for news and a channel for business news and a channel for weather. Every network-TV genre—kids' shows, cooking, game shows—became a channel, and then it became several channels, more targeted, more specific, each subdivision subdividing, and so on, like an exploding fractal pattern. In 1980, according to Nielsen, about 20 percent of American TV households had cable or satellite TV; by the end of the century it was 76 percent.

(Oh, I haven't mentioned the Internet. We'll get to the Internet, which in 1980 was barely reaching its first thin tendrils into American homes through boxy hobbyist computers and screeching modems. But suffice it to say, for now, that it would slice the already subdivided cable audience into micron-thin layers. The Internet gave us the dictum known as Rule 34: "If it exists, there's porn of it." That rule applies broadly to non-porn as well. If you exist, you are a channel, if perhaps a very, very small one.)

* * * *

BUT WE'RE GETTING AHEAD of ourselves. In 1980, these shifts were still a long way off. National TV was still in the something-for-everyone era.

And Donald Trump, it's already quite clear, was not for everyone. So say you're creating the character "Donald Trump"—a local-media creation that you're trying to get picked up for national syndication. How do you write him for this moment, the cusp of the '70s and the '80s, Carter and Reagan? What do you build him out of?

Pop culture in the 1970s did not exactly love rich guys. If you were watching a lot of TV in the '70s, you saw that prime time was filled with working-class heroes. (One of Trump's biographers, Marc Fisher of the *Washington Post*, describes '70s Trump at the end of his nights out, watching TV while eating through a bag of candy.)

The Waltons (1972) followed a rural Virginia family and community hanging together through the Great Depression. The Nielsen top 10 in the 1970s was full of people living from paycheck to paycheck, and even if the shows weren't explicitly political, they were rooted in real-life challenges. On *Alice* (1976), a single mom raised her son on a waitress's salary. In *Welcome Back, Kotter* (1975), a teacher went home to Brooklyn to teach a class of remedial learners from a range of ethnic backgrounds (one of them was Juan Epstein, the "Puerto Rican Jew"). TV's favorite characters worked in garages (*Chico and the Man* and *Happy Days*) and breweries (*Laverne &*

Shirley). When luxury was served, it was often with a side of judgment: on *Fantasy Island* (1978), guests paid to have their dreams come true at a tropical resort, but usually learned that they were better off learning to be happy with their real lives.

In the 1970s, if you were rich on TV or in the movies, you were likely the bad guy. Rich kids like Trump were the worst of all—the uptight upper-crust Omega House frat boys in *Animal House* (1978) and the snotty, entitled bullies from Camp Mohawk in *Meatballs* (1979). (The template would survive, in some form, into the Reagan era, when the screenwriter of *Back to the Future Part II* based his villain, Biff Tannen, on Trump.) On *The Dukes of Hazzard* (1979), the moonshining Duke boys, driving a Dodge Charger with the Confederate flag painted on the roof, outraced and outwitted the corrupt minions of backwoods oligarch Boss Hogg.

But by 1980, Hollywood's attitude toward rich people, heralded by the likes of Rona Barrett, was beginning to turn. The wealthy were still mainly assholes. But they were, increasingly, *our* assholes. Nowhere was this more evident than on TV's most popular show at the moment Donald Trump debuted on *Today*: a prime-time CBS soap about a lustily arrogant son of a bitch running a business handed down to him by his daddy.

Dallas, which had debuted in 1978, was in the middle of its "Who Shot J.R.?" cliffhanger, in which the audience was left hanging on the fate of J. R. Ewing, a loathsome oil tycoon who was nonetheless charismatic and compellingly watchable. In the space-besotted 1960s, Larry Hagman had played an affable astronaut who became "master" to a magical genie (Barbara Eden, in belly-baring top and harem pants) in the fantasy/female-imprisonment-comedy *I Dream of Jeannie*. As J.R., he rolled up a lusty vision of America into one sinful package: glitz, sex, and cowboy hats.

J. R. Ewing, arriving on TV during the Carter-era moral response to Watergate, offered a refreshing highball of escapist amorality. He was hungry and transparent and had a silver forked tongue: scheming against family members over an inheritance, he quipped, "Like my daddy used to say, 'Where there's a way, there's a will.' " There was nothing redeeming about anything J.R. did, but he enjoyed it so damn much—Hagman, the son of Broadway star Mary Martin, tore into the role like a plate of juicy brisket. Yes, there were good guys and less-bad guys on *Dallas*, like J.R.'s nice-guy brother Bobby, but you no more watched for them than you read *Paradise Lost* for the non-fallen angels.

When the mystery was resolved in November 1980, somewhere close to 90 million viewers watched—three-quarters of the total national TV audience. "Maybe it wasn't completely coincidental," David Bianculli wrote in *Dictionary of Teleliteracy*, "that Larry Hagman's J.R. Ewing was regaining power, and confronting his would-be assailant, the same month that Ronald Reagan was elected president: both Reagan and J.R. Ewing would spend the decade perpetuating the private-enterprise excesses of the eighties."

Dallas inspired clones throughout the Reagan years, as Ron and Nancy Reagan were reintroducing celebrity and French couture to the White House: its spinoff *Knots Landing*, ABC's *Dallas*-in-Denver soap *Dynasty* (with Joan Collins sashaying into the J.R. role), and CBS's *Falcon Crest* (essentially *Dallas* in wine country).

These shows assured you that money didn't buy happiness. And they gave you an outrageous, jackpot-winner fantasy of what you *would* buy—screw the happiness!—if you had the chance. (This was one reason that *The Beverly Hillbillies* was a hit in the populist prime-time '60s; the Clampetts were working-class and millionaires at the same time.)

Later, in a 1990 interview with *Playboy*, Trump would cite this kind of TV series as model and justification for his public flaunting: "*Dynasty* did it on TV. It's very important that people aspire to be successful. The only way you can do it is if you look at somebody who is." He realized, maybe more than most, the importance of TV in shaping people's dreams and values.

All these long-running soaps featured rich people Americans loved to hate. But love-to-hate is the first step toward love.

* * * *

WITH THIS RENEWED FASCINATION with the rich came the idea that there were gradations and categories of the rich. Maybe you could be rich and still be an outsider, a rebel.

A month before Trump spoke to Tom Brokaw—July 25, 1980—Harold Ramis's *Caddyshack* came out in theaters. It was a modest success and tepidly reviewed. But over the coming decades, it would be embraced as a classic of American comedy.

Caddyshack has a lot in common with other underdog comedies of its time (*The Bad News Bears*, *Meatballs*, *Stripes*)—namely, scrappy rebels winning out over privilege and institutions. Set at an exclusive country club, it's nominally about Danny Noonan (Michael O'Keefe), a hardworking caddy trying to make money for college by cozying up to the stuffed-shirt Judge Smails (Ted Knight). With the help of some oddball friends, Danny wins a golf tournament, and thus money for college. It's the kind of slobs-vs.-snobs story, about ragged misfits beating the system, that wove the rebellious spirit of the 1960s with the Revolutionary spirit of the Bicentennial. You can see the theme running from sports movies of the time, like *Breaking Away* (the townies vs. the college kids), to blockbusters, like *Star Wars* (the rebels vs. the Empire).

But *Caddyshack* is also a class-war story in which the richest character is the ally of the proles. Danny is drawn into a larger rivalry between Judge Smails and the boorish, crass (and much wealthier) Al Czervik (Rodney Dangerfield). Czervik, a real-estate developer, is peacocky and boisterously insulting. He wears ridiculous loud jackets rather than the Judge's ridiculous preppy nautical wear. In one of the movie's most memorable scenes, he roars up in his giant yacht, spewing wake everywhere, and swamps the dock where Judge Smails and a group of swells are christening his tasteful new sailboat.

Czervik is among the rich country clubbers, but he isn't *of* them. His wealth doesn't give him membership in high society, just the independence not to care about its rules. It's the working-class dream: fuck-you money. Judge Smails is the kind of rich prick everybody hates—superior, status-obsessed, jealously guarding the invisible barriers between himself and the riffraff. Czervik is *you as a rich person*, free to want what you want and like what you like. Watching Dangerfield—whose comic persona was of a schlub who "gets no respect"—depantsing the elitists is so exhilarating that the studio head, watching the dailies, told Ramis to rewrite the script to give him more screen time. Al Czervik was literally a scene-stealer.

This particular archetype of wealth especially served Trump later, particularly in the 2016 Republican primary, when he essentially ran as Al Czervik. (He intuited, correctly, that the Republican base was increasingly alienated from a party that continued to put forward Judge Smailses.) He sized up as his first punching bag the Smailsian Jeb Bush—soft-spoken, well-mannered, from a good family—and proceeded to spray him with yacht-wake at every opportunity. He called Bush "low-energy," suggested that Bush was sympathetic to "illegals" because his wife was born in Mexico, then refused—at a live TV debate—to apologize. The bald public insult was a straight-up Czervik move; in *Caddyshack* he tells Smails's wife, "You must have been something before electricity."

The pop culture of 1980 was on the cusp of a turn. It was betting that whatever anti-materialism had come out of the '60s, whatever populist idealism had come out of Watergate, wasn't going to stick. People were not just going to stop ogling luxury. Covetous human nature had not been repealed.

The character "Donald Trump" was that bet in human form.

Episode 3

MONOPOLY

AMERICANS DON'T LIKE REAL GOLD. A JEWELER TOLD ME THIS once, when I was shopping for a wedding ring. I didn't know anything about jewelry, but my mother grew up in Morocco, and she brought a few gold pieces over when she came to America. They were pure gold, or close to it. I loved the richness and depth of them. They looked like they had not just color but heat. I wanted a ring like that.

You don't want a ring like that, the jeweler told me. Most of the gold they sold was fourteen karat. Cost was an issue—the more gold in your gold, the more expensive it is. Practicality, too: high-karat gold is soft, it wears down, it loses its shape.

But it was also a matter of taste. Fourteen-karat gold—an alloy that's a bit more than half-gold—is brighter. It's shiny. It gleams. It announces itself. Pure gold, or near-pure gold, is different. It glows, like an ember. It looks old. Americans are used to the blinding come-on of 14K gold. When we hear the word "gold," that's what we think of.

What the jeweler was really saying is that "gold" is two different things. There is the *substance* of gold and there is the *idea* of gold. And the idea of gold is far more valuable. Without the arbitrary value we attach to it, gold is just another rock, a number on the periodic table. The more people become used to semi-gold, the kind of gold you can polish and give a mirror finish, the more it defines gold.

So for all relevant purposes—for all the reasons that make "gold" a thing to covet, to fight over, to cement the bonds of love with—half-gold is more gold than pure gold is. That doesn't make it phony. At least it makes it no more phony than the entire notion of attaching value to a piece of metal that you can't eat, can't house yourself in, can't fashion into a practical tool. What we think of as gold—the idea of gold—is simply a mutual compact to assign worth to a specific element. All gold is fool's gold.

The French philosopher Jean Baudrillard described this dynamic in his system of object value. In a consumer society, he said, there are different kinds of value that can attach to a thing. First, there's functional, or use, value: simply, what you can do with an object. (You could use a gold nugget as a paperweight.) There's exchange value, what an object is worth in terms of other objects. (An ounce of gold might be worth ten of silver.) There's symbolic value, the value that one person places on an object in relation to another person. (A gift of a gold ring, e.g., might symbolize fidelity.) Finally, there's sign value, the value an object has within a system of other objects. (Gold, unlike aluminum or lead, represents success, prestige, *class*.)

Donald Trump is a Baudrillardian by instinct, if not, I assume, by reading. He has spent a lifetime being *the idea of gold*. He understood, early in his career, that there was much more upside in *playing* a businessman than in *being* a businessman. By performing yourself to match the mental cartoons people generate when they hear the words "wealth" and "success" and "luxury," you come to represent those things. And thus, anything you're selling—an apartment, a bottle of water, a political platform—becomes imbued with those things.

If you can do that, you can become more gold than gold itself.

* * * *

THE TRUMP INTERNATIONAL HOTEL in Las Vegas is sheathed in the barest amount of gold, atoms thin, like the wrapping of a fancy candy bar at a gift shop. For the Trump International in New York,

Trump slapped gold-tinted glass on the old Gulf & Western building. Trump Castle, a planned high-rise on Madison Avenue that he
abandoned in 1984, was to be ornamented with gold leaf, and would
have a moat and drawbridge.

His most important building of all, Trump Tower, was unveiled
in 1983. It is made of the idea of gold. The outside is bronze solar
glass. This, in certain light, gives its sixty-eight stories—fifty-eight
of them real, ten of them figments of Trump's marketing plan—a
golden metallic sheen. The atrium finishes are polished brass. So
is the lettering on the nameplate over the entrance, whose height
Trump doubled, over the objections of his architect, Der Scutt.

You see the result in the descriptions of Trump Tower in the press:
"gold," "golden," over and over. Overnight, Trump—helpfully blond
himself, a handsome golden boy—became a character as closely
associated with that primal symbol of wealth as King Midas or a
Bond villain.

Before it is a building, Trump Tower is an advertisement. It is a
text. It says: This is money, this is aspiration. It says that this is luxury that must never apologize. (Brass is, literally, brazen.) It clashes
with its limestone neighbors, which are genteel, beholden to old proprieties. Architecture critics would call this a failing, but it is also
the point. It says, with its jagged angles—designed to give the apartments multiple exposures—that this is aggressive luxury, luxury
sharpened to an edge you could cut yourself on. It says, this is not
nice, but you want it anyway. It says that it is OK to want it.

It says, in three-foot-tall letters, that all these ideas are "Trump,"
and therefore that "Trump" is these ideas.

So it has to be seen, not only on Fifth Avenue but everywhere. It
has to be on TV.

* * * *

A NON-NEW YORKER coming to the city for the first time experiences, over and over, the feeling of having walked onto a TV stage.

The city is full of places you've seen since you were old enough to sit up in front of a TV set. Look: there's the Rockefeller Center Christmas Tree! There's Wall Street! There's the Statue of Liberty! They're famous places, but they're also, thanks to years of establishing shots and network news B-roll, symbols of intangible concepts. Look: there's Christmas! There's money! There's freedom!

Manhattan real estate is valuable because, if you have the right location, it gives you a space on that mental Monopoly board.

This is why Trump Tower mattered. Not just because it could be worth a lot of money. A lot of developers were bigger than Donald Trump, had more valuable holdings, but west of the Hudson, nobody knew who they were. They were rich, but who *saw* them being rich, anyway?

Trump Tower was made to be seen. Though it was mainly built and sold for private dwellings—the sales brochure touted a residents' entryway "totally inaccessible to the public"—it was consciously on display. From the beginning, Trump leveraged celebrity to promote the building. The tenants included Johnny Carson, Sophia Loren, Michael Jackson, and Steven Spielberg. He encouraged the rumor that the newlywed Prince Charles and Princess Diana were interested in an apartment, a story that appeared more real once Buckingham Palace replied with an obligatory, "No comment." Celebrity aided his business; business aided his celebrity.

Trump Tower also marked the end of whatever distinction there had been between Trump's private life and public spectacle. He moved into a triplex with his first wife, Ivana, a Czech former model with the golden tone of an awards statuette. The apartment's Versailles-theme-park décor—gold, gold, GOLD—assured more attention, and magazine photo spreads, and TV pieces, all with eye-popping images that ensured that, whoever might be richer, Donald Trump was the rich guy that you knew, the man whom you associated with the concept of being rich.

* * * *

FROM ITS '70S ALLEGIANCE with the underdog, America was developing sympathy for the overdog. Wealth was becoming a form of entertainment. The most conspicuous example was the Robin Leach syndicated program, *Lifestyles of the Rich and Famous*. The series originated as an offshoot of Leach's reporting for *Entertainment Tonight*, where Leach had squabbled with a producer who wanted his celebrity profiles to focus more on the stars' work. "Hate to tell you," Leach said, "nobody is interested in listening to Suzanne Somers stretching with Shakespeare in Central Park. They want to see Suzanne Somers in her home, in her bathtub, with lots of bubbles."

Wealth, in other words, was not just something performers had. It was a performance in itself.

Trump's early '80s TV appearances offered a soft-spoken version of his later, bellicose reality-TV character. He created a version of his aspirational self that the mass audience would accept. They would accept greedy and competitive if it was insouciant and entertaining. They would accept ostentation and arrogance if you put on a show, with a half-grin that told them you understood that it was a show. They would accept extravagance and self-indulgence if you let them share it vicariously. They'd laugh off boasting and lying if you telegraphed that you were a rascal, because that let them tell themselves they were smart enough to get the joke.

There was a synergy to the transaction. The audience, after all, wanted this kind of character—a braggart who lived large and said that it was OK to want things—and Trump wanted to play it.

Magazines profiled him like a Hollywood star. *Town and Country* said, "He thrives on challenges, and to a certain extent, controversy." In *People* magazine, he said that he wanted to "put a little show business into the profession" of real estate—friends said that "his ultimate goal" was to head up a TV network—but the piece ended with a dark quote from Trump: "Man is the most vicious of all animals, and life is a series of battles ending in victory or defeat."

* * * *

CULTURE JOURNALIST ANNE HELEN PETERSEN has written that
Trump synthesized two modes of celebrity: the "idol of production" (a term from Frankfurt School sociologist Leo Löwenthal),
which encompassed business titans like Henry Ford, and the "idol
of consumption," celebrities who get attention for their privilege and
lush lives.

Early in the 1980s, Trump posed for the kind of publicity images
you'd expect of an industrious real-estate developer, standing at a
construction site in a hardhat or looking at blueprints. These images
quickly gave way to Donald and Ivana, posing in formal wear at
home, amid chandeliers, floor-to-ceiling windows and objets d'art.
The first kind of picture is of a man whose job is building. The second is of a man whose job is *having*.

Trump merged the two with the help of new outlets like *The
Nikki Haskell Show*, a New York cable-TV society program that,
like much of the emerging media, put business and entertainment
celebrity, uptown and downtown, on the same plane. Haskell, whose
opening credits included a shot of her answering the phone in the
tub, suds clinging to the receiver, folded fashion, the downtown
art scene, and oligarchy into a glitzy whirl. (She introduced klep-
tocratic Philippine first lady Imelda Marcos as "One of the most
amazing women that I think you'll ever meet . . . the power behind
the throne, if you will.") Trump chatted up Haskell, a pal from his
'70s days at the hotspot Le Club, at his apartment, and she toured
the rough space of his new building in a fur coat and helmet. "The
location and the view are *grand luxe*," she said, "but that's part of
Donald's style."

New York real estate, in the early 1980s, embraced *grand luxe*.
Leona Helmsley, the president of the Helmsley hotel company,
starred in a series of glossy ads for her properties, styled like Renaissance paintings of decadence: Helmsley swathed in gowns and frills,
the rooms accented with gilt and crystal, a harpist in the background.
The ads touted the plush towels and bathroom phones, but also centered Helmsley as the personification of luxury and self-indulgence:

"It's the only Palace in the world," said an ad for the Helmsley Palace, "where the Queen stands guard." (It is maybe a sign of the different standards for ambitious men and women that Helmsley and Trump both became 1980s symbols of arrogance and greed, but she went down in history as the detested, bullying "Queen of Mean" while he became a TV star and president.)

In Trump Tower, Trump found an amphitheater of himself. He lived on the top, his offices were in the middle, his name loomed over the street. It was the kind of unitary dwelling/HQ/monument we're used to seeing in a comic book superhero's lair, or a supervillain's. (Trump Tower, with its jagged forbidding exterior, was used in the Batman movie *The Dark Knight Rises* as the business headquarters of Bruce Wayne, the billionaire vigilante.) So hermetic was Trump's elevator-commute existence that, when a BBC interviewer asked him in a 2010 documentary, "Don't you need fresh air?" he said, "I get it. We pump it into the building."

The most theatrical aspect of the tower, however, was the public atrium, constructed in a deal with the city that allowed Trump to build around twenty additional floors. Liveried footmen guarded the entrance; a waterfall sluiced down one of the imported marble walls. Escalators crisscrossed each other, up to high-end retail, down to a food court. Everywhere you looked, you were reflected in brass and glass. It was luxury-signifier overload, rich, rich, rich, the visual equivalent of chasing a seventy-two-piece box of chocolate truffles with a tub of foie gras.

Thrown open to tourists, the atrium made "Trump" a destination, like Disney. You could walk in and rest your feet; you might shop or you might not; but you would take home with you an impression and an association.

And if you didn't, you saw it on TV. You saw it in profiles of its developer. You saw it in Elvis Costello's video for "This Town" (starring a Donald Trump look-alike) and in Bobby Brown's video for "On Our Own," from the *Ghostbusters II* soundtrack, in which Trump walks out to see a massive projection of Brown dancing on the side of the building. You saw it in a 1988 *Saturday Night Live* parody of "Gift of the Magi"—the title, "A Trump Christmas," in gold letters—where Donald (Phil Hartman) sells his yacht to buy Ivana Trump (Jan Hooks) a set of gold-plated doors for her mansion with "TRUMP" spelled out in diamonds on them, and she sells her mansion to buy a solid-gold anchor for his yacht. You saw it in a 1980s "New York Edition" of the game Monopoly, in which Trump Tower has the most valuable space on the board, once occupied by Boardwalk.

It became added, with Rockefeller Center and the Statue of Liberty, to the permanent mental map of the average American. Look: There's ambition! There's comfort! There's everything that I want!

* * * *

THE PUBLIC-TV home-improvement show *This Old House* premiered in 1979, a bridge between the do-it-yourself, back-to-the-land, *Whole Earth Catalog* sensibility of the baby boomers' youth and their acquisitive middle years. Unlike *Lifestyles of the Rich and Famous*, it wasn't "house porn," exactly; more like house sex education. It catered to a generation of homeowners who saw a value in rediscovering neighborhoods, finding homes with good bones and history, and bringing them back to life.

During one 1983 episode, host Bob Vila takes a break from the season's project—an economically sensible, solar-powered house in Brookline, Massachusetts—to take the audience on an unusual field trip, "to a place where cost is no object."

Vila meets Der Scutt at the entrance of the newly opened Trump Tower. They walk in, and—wham, that atrium. As Scutt talks about selecting the Breccia Pernice marble from Verona, Italy, Vila is awed. "It isn't just architecture," the host wonders. "It's an experience, a feeling."

Ivana Trump takes him on a tour of some model apartments. "This is really deluxe!" Vila exclaims. "I feel like I should have black tie on." The furnishings alone, we're told, cost a cool quarter-million dollars.

The richness of the furnishings is something, as are the 1980s aesthetics: mirrored walls, sectional couches, ferns. Also striking is how gendered the sales pitch is. There's "masculine" leather throughout the unit, Ivana points out, but the master bedroom is "feminine, the woman will be very comfortable here." The bathroom has black polished stone finishes that "you can still soften up with flowers on the pattern. The man and the woman are feeling very good here."

Moving to the bedroom, Ivana asks Vila to imagine himself "lying on the bed watching your television" while across the room, at a built-in dressing table complete with shiny gold-tone telephone, "your wife can be in here using this cabinet for the makeup, answering the mail, for the reading—doesn't disturb the partner."[*]

Afterward, Vila stops in the atrium for a few words with Trump. He's more assured and swaggering than the smooth, soft-spoken Trump we saw with Tom Brokaw three years ago. He brags, not about the building's sales but its publicity: the architecture reviews and how many tourists have visited the atrium since its opening.

The episode is the early '80s in miniature, the sensibility of the 1970s yielding to something new and brazen. Watching this earnest public-TV program slaver over Trump's Mammon temple is like watching a college literature professor, freshly back from the nuclear-freeze protest, wash his used Volvo in the driveway while craning his neck wistfully at his neighbor's new Porsche.

* * * *

THE IMAGE OF THE 1980S as "the decade of greed" is well established: *Dallas*, Gordon Gekko in Oliver Stone's *Wall Street*, junk

---

[*] The image—a man who likes to recline in the bedroom and watch his television and not be disturbed by "the woman"—is purely hypothetical, I'm sure.

bonds, yuppies, BMWs, sushi. But the 1980s weren't a decade that celebrated money, exactly. They were a decade that celebrated *wanting*.

The 1980s economic boom was real enough. But it was more real for some than others. The average American household's income, in relative terms, peaked in the early 1970s. The postwar mass prosperity of the middle class was, in a way, the economic equivalent of the postwar peak of the mass-media audience—an era of common experience that had no parallel before or since. The few decades after World War II were a time of Americans more or less watching the same things and Americans (at least in the broad middle) more or less having the same things.

The income of the top one percent of Americans roughly doubled over the course of the 1980s. Everyone else? They wanted, and they stretched.

As the sociologist Juliet B. Schor observed in *The Overspent American*, people set their consumption habits by comparing themselves to other people. Once, that meant neighbors and family members— people physically close by, and thus probably closer in income. But in a TV age, the comparisons are everywhere, and they are not flattering. It's not simply a matter of seeing the Carringtons living large on *Dynasty*. It's also—as TV begins to be targeted more toward desirable advertising demographics—seeing more commercials aimed at white-collar professionals, for products they can afford.

Most people believe that all they want are the necessities. But when your references change, "necessity" changes. Beginning in the 1980s, in Schor's words, American lifestyles were driven by more "upward comparison," and "middle-class Americans were acquiring at a greater rate than any previous generation."

Two things, in other words, were happening at once. The middle class was shrinking and becoming more precarious, a trend that would continue for decades. At the same time, the aspiration to be middle class—the shared "American dream" of mere security, a house, a garage, college for the kids—was replaced by the shoot-the-moon dream of riches, or, failing that, an espresso machine, an imported car, whatever totems of class ascendance you could manage.

Thorstein Veblen identified the idea of "conspicuous consumption" at the end of the nineteenth century in *The Theory of the Leisure Class*. Once a society has prospered beyond a certain point, people spend not just out of necessity but also to establish their place in the social hierarchy. Once there is no longer an aristocracy, you get your status from what you have, and more important, what you *seem* to have. You also get your sense of self-worth from what you see others to have, which means it's possible—and as inequality rises, probable—to have more and feel like you have less.

So the "materialistic" culture of the 1980s isn't for the benefit of the world's Gordon Gekkos. Rich people never needed permission to be rich. But pop culture gave the not-rich, after the egalitarian 1960s and 1970s, permission to want.

* * * *

THERE'S A NOSE-PRESSED-TO-THE-GLASS feel to 1980s pop culture, in the movies, in soap operas, and in pop music, which, with the birth of MTV in 1981, became another aspect of television.

If the aesthetic of '60s rock was that even millionaire superstars should look like bikers, MTV was about glam aspiration. MTV videos were built to inspire coveting the same way commercials were—as short-form TV, they used many of the same devices, and after all, they were ads themselves, for artists and albums. In her close read of 1980s MTV, *Rocking Around the Clock*, E. Ann Kaplan wrote that most videos of the time "assume an upper middle-class-ambience." When they showed working-class life, it was as something to escape, a plight, an embarrassment.

The sensibility was aspirational and avaricious. It was Duran Duran cavorting with models on the deck of a yacht in the video for "Rio." It was David Bowie, who had variously adopted personae as a rock-star alien and an androgyne, re-reinventing himself as a tailored, chic dandy with a golden pompadour and exquisite pastel suits. (Yesterday glitter rock, today gold cufflinks.) Madonna's video for "Material Girl," a takeoff on Marilyn Monroe's "Diamonds Are a Girl's Best Friend" number from *Gentlemen Prefer Blondes*, sent up the gold-digger stereotype—but the song's title became Madonna's unironic MTV nickname. Even hairball Texas bluesmen ZZ Top became style icons, giving a car valet a makeover and the keys to a souped-up classic jalopy in the video for "Sharp Dressed Man." ("Silk suit, black tie / I don't need a reason why.")[*]

MTV was both niche TV—something just for the kids, as opposed to Ed Sullivan's something for everyone—and national in a way that the biggest radio station couldn't be. "We'll be doing for TV what FM did for radio," pronounced vee-jay Mark Goodman, sitting cross-legged on a table, during the channel's opening broadcast. Unlike many previous pop-music phenomena, which sprang up in cities, MTV spread first to suburbs and rural areas, where cable had reached fastest. ("Narrowcasting" to suburban white kids, the channel took years to pay much attention to genres like rap.)

MTV's commercialism always had a prophylactic dose of irony. Many of its early on-air promos were parodies of consumer culture, like a faux-beer ad that urged viewers to "pop open an MTV." It was kidding-not-kidding commercialism, self-conscious about the drug-like lure of sitting down and watching hour after hour of videos— while reminding you to keep doing it.

One of the most popular 1980s music videos was exactly in this tradition—both a repudiation and an embrace of MTV's material culture. "Money for Nothing," a 1985 single from the British band Dire Straits, is one of those '80s songs—"Thriller," "Take On Me"— that it's hard to think of separate from its video.

The song was *about* videos, actually, the feelings of awe, hunger,

---

[*] Three decades later, "Sharp Dressed Man" would be the theme song for *Duck Dynasty*, a reality show about backwoods Louisiana millionaires, one of whose stars would speak at Donald Trump's nominating convention.

and inadequacy they inspired. It opens with MTV's slogan, "I want my MTV," sung as a haunting mantra by Sting, the song's cowriter. The video combines concert footage with a story involving two 3-D animated figures. Over the opening bars, a tall, thin man watches the band on TV, entranced, his jaw dropping open, until he levitates from his chair and floats into the TV set.

Dire Straits's Mark Knopfler has said the song's lyrics came to him at an appliance store, where one of the employees was grousing about the music videos playing on a wall of TVs. The video takes us inside the store, where the narrator—a hulking Archie Bunker type with a cigar dangling from his mouth—enviously watches the same "yo-yos" we're watching on MTV: Dire Straits on stage, a rock star with his own airplane, a half-naked woman pulling up her stockings. "That ain't working," he marvels. "That's the way you do it." The chorus details his own job, hauling expensive appliances— refrigerators, TVs—for a lot less money.

The video plays, three decades later, like a concert opening act for Trumpism. There's the blue-collar white guy grumbling, not just that these entertainers have so much more than him, but that they are *valued* so much more than him. And for what? For something that's not even work. What do they risk? How much does their job hurt?

And who are you in all this, the American kid watching "Money for Nothing" in 1985? The video doesn't push you to identify with the proto-MAGA narrator, jealous, crudely homophobic. But you're not the band, either, looking down from a giant-screen TV at the delivery guys while singing about stupid poor people who don't think music is real work. Maybe you're the narrator's skinny pal, who cranes his neck around his angry friend to see the screen, while mouthing, "I want my MTV."

* * * *

THAT ATTITUDE—the yearning, wanting to be let in—was a constant of 1980s culture. The 1980 best seller *The Official Preppy*

Handbook, was a mock taxonomy of the country-club set—the same people roasted, that same year, in *Caddyshack*. Rich with charts, diagrams, and lists—the right clothing, the right schools, the right names—it was a guide to the class system of a country that purported to be class-free. The book is written in a tongue-in-cheek, pseudo-anthropological voice. (From a diagram about preppy college clothing: "For the first time they are in a community of many different types of people, and this very functional uniform helps them to identify one another in the crowd.") *Reading* it with tongue in cheek was optional, though, and it swaddled a generation in plaid skirts and alligator polo shirts.

Eventually, this winking satire of the upper class gave way in '80s culture to an unironic and unsubtle celebration. In NBC's *Diff'rent Strokes* (1978–86), a wealthy widower took in the two sons of his dying African American housekeeper as his own. ABC's *Webster* (1983) had almost the same Daddy Warbucks premise and racial dynamic, with a rich married couple adopting a cuddly black child. *Risky Business* (1983) and the movies of John Hughes popularized well-to-do kids getting in nonpermanent trouble in the upscale Chicago suburbs. (*Ferris Bueller's Day Off*—in which Matthew Broderick plays a day of hooky that ends in the crashing of his friend's father's Ferrari—is basically a reminder to loosen up and enjoy life a little before you grow up and make a pile of money like your parents.)

America's favorite not-a-preppy preppy in the 1980s was Alex P. Keaton (Michael J. Fox) in NBC's *Family Ties*. The sitcom was a kind of politics- and generation-flipped version of *All in the Family*, in which Carroll O'Connor's Archie Bunker had butted heads with his young, liberal daughter and son-in-law. In *Family Ties*, the parents were the liberals, and the establishment: he a public-TV manager, she an architect.

The show was intended, like most family sitcoms of the time, to focus on the parents. It gently mocked Alex for his conservatism and obsession with money. (In an early episode, he becomes outraged when his parents let his younger sister redo a bad dice roll in a game of Monopoly: "This is a sin against capitalism!")

But by the second season Alex had run away with the series. Alex offered an image of a young America that was running away from his lefty parents' ideals, but—because Alex was good at heart—would be fine for it. Key to his appeal was that he wasn't a rich kid himself. As the son of a liberal, middle-class, Ohio family who *wanted* to be rich, he gave the audience permission to want it too.

Permission to want came from the top as well, in the persons of Ronald and Nancy Reagan. The Carter White House had practiced a hair-shirt abstemiousness, which reflected the moralism of the president and the blue-collarism of '70s culture. The era of the Georgian peanut-farmer president had coincided with a boomlet in Southern working-class-hero culture: Johnny Paycheck's 1977 country hit, "Take This Job and Shove It," rebel trucker movies like *Smokey and the Bandit* (1977) and *Convoy* (1978), the CB-radio craze, in which homebound amateurs learned and celebrated the lingo of long-haul eighteen-wheeler drivers. After his election, Carter announced in an interview with ABC's Barbara Walters that he'd proudly wear blue jeans in the White House.

Ronald Reagan wore his denim performatively, to clear brush on his 688-acre Santa Barbara ranch. In Washington, the Reagans transformed the White House, as though exorcising the 1970s themselves with a cleansing powerwash of money. The Reagans luxuriated in black tie and designer gowns and gave the White House a $44-million-plus facelift. Nancy Reagan—herself a screen star who appeared with Ron in 1957's *Hellcats of the Navy*—became the public face of the Hollywoodization of the executive residence. She also became a target: it was she, not her husband, who was blasted for putting on nouveau-riche airs by replacing the White House china. But the First Couple successfully amplified the message of the age, that living ostentatiously was the sign you'd made it to the top.

America spent the decade craning its neck upward.

* * * *

WITH A BUSINESS-FRIENDLY government and a wealth-friendly pop culture, the idea followed that a businessman might be the best person to run the country. One of the first such pushes was the result of a best-selling, self-valorizing book by a celebrity tycoon.

The number-one nonfiction book in 1984 and 1985, *Iacocca: An Autobiography*, by the former auto executive Lee Iacocca, was in many ways a standard business bio. It opens with a Horatio Alger story of Iacocca's birth to immigrant parents in Pennsylvania, working his way up from an engineering job to the executive suite. The hero arc of the book, already mythologized in the media, was his saving Chrysler from failure in 1979, partly by arranging a bailout with Congress.

More important, Iacocca was a TV star, whom Americans knew best for his car commercials. Cars were enmeshed with American identity—"It's not just a car, it's your freedom," went a GM Mr. Goodwrench ad—and by the early 1980s, they stood for anxiety and siege. Foreign cars were swamping the market. The angst echoed in movies like *Mr. Mom* (1983), about a suburban Detroit man who loses his engineering job at Ford and—horrors—has to stay home and take care of his kids. Were we losing (not just our dominance but, as *Mr. Mom* implied, our national manhood)? Were the other guys better than us? In a 1982 Chrysler LeBaron spot, Iacocca— sounding the sort of competitive nationalism that resurfaced with Trump—defended his American cars: "I challenge you to compare their quality and technology to anything that comes out of Germany or Japan." It was a sales pitch and a pep talk: we whipped their asses in The Big War, and we will whip their asses on the assembly line!

The last section of *Iacocca* turns to politics, with a closing chapter whose title rings familiar: "Making America Great Again." By modern conservative standards it has a friendly attitude toward industrial policy: "Government planning doesn't have to mean socialism."

But its implied broad arguments are that the best kind of person to face America's challenges is a businessman, and the best kind of businessman for that job is a celebrity.

Iacocca ultimately turned down efforts to draft him for president in 1988. But his burst of fame argued that the business of America was business, and the business of businessmen, if they had bigger aspirations, was entertainment.

Donald Trump, famously, would have a book too: *The Art of the Deal*, in 1987, which claimed the penthouse floor on the *New York Times* best seller list for thirteen weeks. It built on years of headline-grabbing coups, like his feuds with New York mayor Ed Koch, to take his celebrity national. (The important thing about a best-selling celeb book, after all, is that it gets you on TV.) The book was his attempt to have his own *Iacocca*, but it was also an answer to the dutiful civic-spiritedness of books like *Iacocca*.

Trump in *The Art of the Deal*, unlike Iacocca, doesn't couch his success in homilies of responsibility. He doesn't deserve what he has because he's a good person. He deserves what he has because he has it. He says that success is not nice, a message amplified in his talk and in the Sauron's-castle aesthetic of Trump Tower. It's like reading the autobiography of a *Tyrannosaurus rex*, whose final moral is: freshly killed flesh is delicious.

The book is finally, like Trump Tower itself, a product and a brand-extension exercise. The brand that he is extending is not simply about success, though there is that. It's about always wanting more, flaunting, being shameless. If the message of *Iacocca* is that to be governed by its author would mean being governed by common sense and fiscal responsibility, *The Art of the Deal* suggests that to be governed by Donald Trump would be to be governed by an empowering shamelessness.

There is no lip service to the greater good, though there is occasionally lip service against it. By way of praising the loyalty of his mentor Roy Cohn, the corrupt legal fixer who taught him to fight dirty and never admit defeat, he adds, "Just compare that with all the hundreds of 'respectable' guys who make careers out of boasting about their uncompromising integrity but have absolutely no loyalty." The implication is not just that Trump believes loyalty is better than integrity. It's that he doesn't believe integrity is a real thing— it's just a put-on that phonies "boast about" to make themselves look good while they stab you in the back. Nobody *really* has integrity, come on! What kind of loser would want it?

Even though *The Art of the Deal* is organized, after some introductory biography, as the story of various wheeling-and-dealing efforts, it's really a work by a businessman who insists on being seen as a kind of artist. Trump's project—rebranding business as a form of creativity—was a sort of dilettante's answer to the pop art of Andy Warhol. Warhol found a beauty in publicity images and commercial objects, which he imbued with the power one gives to holy icons and symbols. In his work, Marilyn Monroe was a celebrity, and so was Chairman Mao, and so was the Brillo box. He made concrete an idea of George W. S. Trow's: "The most successful celebrities are products. Consider the real role in American life of Coca-Cola. Is any man as well-loved as this soft drink is?"

In 1981 Trump met Warhol—where else?—at a birthday party for Cohn, a fellow clubber at Studio 54. They later discussed the artist's doing a portrait of Trump Tower to hang in the building. Warhol, excited, painted eight samples, in different colors—"a mistake," he wrote in his diary, because the choice seemed to confuse Donald and Ivana, and "Mr. Trump was very upset that it wasn't color-coordinated."

But Trump kept a fond opinion of one particular Warhol quote, which he repeated in his book *Think Like a Billionaire* and, thrice, in *Think Like a Champion*: "Being good in business is the most fascinating kind of art. Making money is art and working is art and good business is the best art."

* * * *

BRANDING, AS PRACTICED BY TRUMP in the '80s, was the transformation of business into iconography. The true product was not the building but the name hanging on the outside. He boasted to *GQ* in 1984 about watching on TV as tennis champ Martina Navratilova, having won the US Open, announced that she would spend her winnings on an apartment at Trump Plaza. Whenever his name got repeated—*TRUMP TRUMP TRUMP*, like Warhol's Marilyn—it created another phantom facsimile of him in the public consciousness, slapped down another brass-plated brick on the "luxury," "money," and "winning" region of every viewer's mental map.

So his business became less about real estate and more about the idea of Trump, which was the idea of the 1980s. He bought the New Jersey Generals, a franchise in the short-lived United States Football League. Before the league died in 1985, he proposed a "Galaxy Bowl," with the USFL's champ playing the NFL's. What that really meant was creating a TV show bigger than the Super Bowl, which is the biggest TV show there is.

He opened casinos in Atlantic City, like the Trump Taj Mahal ("Where wonders never cease," as the operators were required to answer calls), whose bathrooms offered T-shaped plastic shampoo bottles. Millions of middle-class tourists would walk by, or into, Trump-branded dream palaces built like vision-board manifestations of the way they'd live if they hit the jackpot, if only, if only. He bought the Eastern Air Lines shuttle and renamed it the Trump Shuttle, a flying billboard carrying his stylized *T* up and down the Eastern seaboard. He rebuilt Wollman Rink in Central Park, which put his name in the heart of the heart of New York. He tried to sell NBC on a headquarters and studios in a massive development on Manhattan's West Side, called Television City.

Trump knew what images of gilt demanded attention, as if he learned it watching his mother mesmerized by Queen Elizabeth's coronation. He bought Mar-a-Lago, a 128-room Spanish-tiled, gold-ceilinged mansion in Florida. He bought a 281-foot yacht from the

Sultan of Brunei. They were, he told *Playboy*, "props for the show. The show is 'Trump' and it is sold-out performances everywhere."

The dividend of these investments was publicity. Jimmy Breslin, the *Newsday* columnist, described it with awed exasperation: "Trump bought reporters, from morning paper to nightly news, with two minutes of purring on the phone," he wrote. "He uses the reporters to create a razzle dazzle: there are five stories in the morning papers leading into 11 minutes of television at night."

Playgirl magazine named him to its 1986 list of the ten sexiest men in America, along with Michael J. Fox and Senator Bob Dole of Kansas. Trump became a fixture on TV, where he'd play down his reputation for getting into fights, which actually burnished it. He told *60 Minutes* in 1985 that he didn't believe that he was as "sinister" as portrayed—which was a way of saying that you *are* sinister, but with a smile. He wouldn't bring up his own worth, but his interviewers would make an estimate—$3 billion? $4 billion?—and he'd grin without discouraging it, which was a way of saying "at least that." He'd say, as he did to Brokaw, that he wasn't really in the business for the money, which was a way of getting to say "money."

Meanwhile, he found a national platform in the new breed of talk shows, which shared the tabloids' thirst for controversy and put personal issues—self-esteem, self-help—on the same level as politics. They thrived on conflict, and Trump supplied it. The same fall that *The Art of the Deal* came out, he took out a full-page newspaper ad complaining that allies like Japan and Saudi Arabia were "taking advantage" of the United States, a refrain that would become one basis for his campaign thirty years later.

Phil Donahue greeted him on *Donahue* as the perfect combination of the era's values—"You're a businessman, and you're a star." Trump also went on *The Oprah Winfrey Show*, which sounded the constant refrain—from Oprah's own story of overcoming poverty and abuse to her later endorsement of pop-philosophy books like *The Secret*—that by envisioning a thing, you can make it real.

Ronald Reagan had already established, going from movie star to governor to president, that entertainment was America's first language. The decade's culture said that money was its first objective. *Donahue* and *Oprah*—both of which raised the idea that Trump might run for president—took for granted that mastery of money and the media was a qualification for office.

* * * *

ONE OF TRUMP'S LAST brand extensions of the 1980s was Trump: The Game, released in 1989 by Milton Bradley. According to Jeffrey Breslow, the game's designer, Trump agreed to the pitch immediately—one imagines they had him at "Trump"—supplying his brand, his face, and the game's ethos. The cover of the original box features an airbrushed portrait of Trump beneath the slogan, in gold print: "It's not whether you win or lose, but whether you win!"

Trump: The Game is Monopoly with a size fetish. The lowest denomination of cash is $10 million. You buy properties and businesses (a convention center, an airline) at auction, then—the part where the game's design meets Trump's image—you sell and trade them in a "deal making" round.

The gameplay isn't especially original, but you weren't really meant to buy it for the gameplay. "A huge percentage of those games were never taken out of the box," Breslow told the *Washington Post*. "It was bought as a gift item, a novelty, a curiosity." People bought it, hundreds of thousands of copies, to buy a piece of Trump. His name is on nearly every game piece: the cash, the cards, the T-shaped tokens. (The game die also has a T in place of 6, the highest number.) In the rulebook, Trump—or whoever wrote the copy—greets you: "I invite you to live the fantasy! Feel the power! And make the deals!"

To say that the game had few creative ideas is not to say that it had no ideas. Board games are nothing but ideas. Like a reality-TV show, a board game is human experience condensed into totems, rules, and implied lessons. The game Life, launched in the postwar prosperity of 1960, invites players to get a good job, fill up your big car with children, and die with the most money. Simple games like Chutes and Ladders teach children about bad behavior and consequences.

Monopoly, the most direct inspiration of Trump: The Game, originated with The Landlord's Game, patented in 1904 by the activist Elizabeth Magie to argue the dangers of unchecked capitalism. It had two sets of rules, one in which players competed to crush one another by controlling property (and "absolute necessities" like bread and clothing), another in which everyone prospered by agreeing to an egalitarian "Single Tax."

It was a didactic utopian tract for the whole family. Its flaw, of course, was misunderstanding the ideology of gameplay. The great unwritten rule of most games is that crushing your fellow man is fun. People preferred the mean rules.

Parker Brothers developed the game we know today during the Great Depression. Monopoly took out the moral judgment and sold itself with a fanciful story of having been created by an unemployed salesman to entertain and support his family, drawing on memories of happier times spent in Atlantic City. It was The Landlord's Game de-preachified, the warnings of predatory business replaced by a backstory of scrappy boot-strapism that fit the "Happy Days Are Here Again" pep-talk spirit of the 1930s. Its mascot, Rich Uncle Pennybags, with his top hat and tuxedo, was a proto–Donald Trump: a picture of wealth in broad cartoon strokes understandable to kids of all ages.

Trump: The Game—like "Donald Trump," the 1980s multimedia character—put the predation back into the game and declared that, lo, it was good. It was one piece of a larger game, which was to place one name in every enterprise with a mainline to the American appetite: TRUMP—a horn blast, a dominant suit of cards, a verb meaning "to defeat." Its message was that wanting was good, that getting was good, that beating your enemies was good, and that all that was good was Trump. I invite you to live the fantasy!

No matter how successful you are, you can never own all the real estate in the world, or suck up all the cash. But if you can, in the unreal estate of pop culture, become the symbol for those things, you can own the idea of real estate, the idea of money.

There's a word for that. They call it a monopoly.

Episode 4

AS HIMSELF

IN A 1997 EPISODE OF *THE DREW CAREY SHOW*, DREW, AN assistant personnel director at a Cleveland department store, drives to New York City with his friends to see a Yankees game, in the old ice cream truck they use to deliver beer from their home brewing business. They end up marooned in bumper-to-bumper midtown traffic, as an impatient Carol Channing rams them with her car.

While they stew in gridlock, a businessman hails them from the sidewalk: "Hot one, isn't it? I'll have a Nutty Buddy." They tell him that they only have beer. "What are you, morons?" asks the man, whom Drew, his friends, and the home audience have all recognized by now as Donald Trump. After Drew explains the gang's predicament, Trump reaches into a pocket and offers them his box seats. "Use them, enjoy them, and welcome to New York."

By the 1990s, this was what Trump had become in pop culture: a walking, trash-talking, comical synecdoche for New York, its abrasiveness, and its sense of opportunity. He was a tourist sight, like the lights in Times Square, the window of Tiffany's, or the giant electronic keyboard at FAO Schwarz.

Or the Plaza Hotel. In the 1992 movie *Home Alone 2: Lost in New York,* Kevin McCallister (Macaulay Culkin), separated from his family in the big city at Christmastime, wanders into the Plaza— all festive trim and crystal chandeliers and chamber music—and asks a grown-up in a topcoat where the lobby is. The joke is that Kevin doesn't recognize the hotel's owner, Donald Trump.

When *Home Alone 2* came out in theaters, Trump was actually in the midst of being forced to unload the Plaza as part of a packaged bankruptcy agreement. But in the universe of the movie, it was still his. It wouldn't really work, in a kids' jingle-bell comedy, to have Middle America's favorite lost tyke ask directions of a consortium of international lenders including the Industrial Bank of Japan. You need a person. You need someone to play the character. You need Donald Trump.

Not for the last time, Trump had found partners invested in his illusion, for whom the narrative of Donald Trump was too important to let the reality of Donald Trump ruin it.

* * * *

THERE WAS AN almost impossible neatness to the timing of Trump's business downfall at the beginning of the 1990s. It was as if the 1980s couldn't end without taking Donald Trump with them— at least, the version who was the decade's love-to-hate-him business protagonist. Wayne Barrett, who investigated Trump's New York real-estate machinations at the *Village Voice*, saw a hint of the zeitgeist in Trump's late-'80s buying spree, including the Plaza. "It was as if he looked ahead on a calendar," Barrett wrote, "and decided that January 1, 1990, was the deadline: Anything he hadn't bought by then could never be his."

For years, he had made a string of debt-financed deals, his celebrity seducing lenders into offering easy money. Trump was "astonished," Barrett wrote, "that he suddenly seemed to have the same impact in a Citibank boardroom that he'd once had on the *Donahue* show." Then in 1990, those aggressive acquisitions—the casinos, the airline, the Plaza, not to mention "props for the show" like his yacht—smashed up against a recession. He ended up working out a plan with his creditor banks to restructure his loans.

But as the deal diminished the businessman Donald Trump, it made sure to preserve the celebrity Donald Trump. His role in his businesses was curtailed. But he was put on a $450,000-a-month budget, the reasoning being that he needed to keep up "appearances" in order to sell off assets at a decent price. Just as publicity made his successes seem greater than anyone's in the 1980s—they had to be greater, they were on TV!—so would it make his losses seem bigger, more devastating, more humiliating, if the media fixture with the T-shaped gold cufflinks couldn't keep up the show.

In a society where success was driven by image, a Donald Trump without his set dressing might as well be parading in public wearing a barrel. Like an actress in borrowed jewels at a red-carpet premiere, he had to present an appearance. Citibank needed him to keep playing his character the same way that *Home Alone 2* did.

Also in 1992, Trump was divorcing Ivana, a tabloid blowup that managed to belittle and inflate him at the same time. It dominated the gossip columns the crackups of old Hollywood once did, like the febrile in-and-out-of-love story of Elizabeth Taylor and her fifth (and sixth) husband, Richard Burton. There was the love triangle: Trump, Ivana, and Marla Maples, an aspiring actress and one-time Miss Resaca Beach Poster Girl. There was a feeding frenzy, a rehearsal for the later 24/7 superstories—the Nancy Kerrigan/Tonya Harding fiasco at the 1994 Winter Olympics, the O. J. Simpson murder trial, the Monica Lewinsky scandal—that culture critic Frank Rich christened "mediathons."

The real-life drama played like an episode of *Dynasty*, as when Ivana, according to *People* magazine, confronted Maples at a slope-side restaurant in Aspen: "You bitch, leave my husband alone." Both Trumps leaked to gossip columnists—Cindy Adams, Liz Smith— and the New York tabs went into red-siren mode. ("Best Sex I've Ever Had," the *New York Post* blared, a headline a *Post* reporter later said was fed to the paper by Trump himself.) The new TV entertainment magazines, with whose sensibility the straight news increasingly had to keep pace, amplified all of this. It was on ABC's *Primetime Live*, to Diane Sawyer, that Maples publicly confessed her love for Donald.

There was already, in Trump's 1980s media image, a counterimage of him as an absurdity, vain, loudmouthed, and tacky, a self-inflated gold-lamé balloon high on his own helium. The New York satire magazine *Spy*, founded by Kurt Andersen and Graydon Carter, was especially lacerating and precociously insightful. It coined the most memorable epithet for Trump—"short-fingered vulgarian," the adjectival portion of which his 2016 Republican opponent Marco Rubio extended, as it were, to imply that he had a small penis. But beyond that, it pegged him as a bloviating fraud, a Potemkin businessman; it labeled him "Donald Trump, the demibillionaire casino operator and adulterer" and mocked his pretensions of weighing in on world issues.

Now all of America could see Donald Trump as *Spy* did. The Maples publicity, on the one hand, made him a bigger name than ever. Even as Trump decried the "very dishonest" press coverage, he fed and abetted it. He could no more resist it than a flower can will itself not to turn toward the sun. But it also made him into a joke—the guy who *used* to be Donald Trump.

* * * *

BETWEEN THE BREAKUP OF his marriage and the breakdown of his businesses, 1990 tends to be considered the nadir in Trump's career. It was, if you believe, incorrectly, that he was primarily a businessman.

But if you believe that he was primarily a celebrity who leveraged his fame into business, then the 1990s were a defining period of his career—maybe more so than the 1980s. In the 1980s, Donald Trump was a businessman who used celebrity as a helpful promotional device. By the 1990s, he was a celebrity whose calling card was the ability to play the figure of a businessman. He would leverage that

performance—the self as a character, wearing the Halloween costume of a mogul—to make himself a reality-TV star in the 2000s
and a politician in the 2010s.

And the 1990s were when playing "Donald Trump" became his
full-time job.

You can understand the Trump of this period with the help of
another former big '80s sensation: postmodern theory. The post-
modernists (among them Baudrillard, Fredric Jameson, and Jean-
François Lyotard) were concerned with the "simulacrum": the copy
or representation of a thing, which, in a culture dominated by repro-
duced and faux images, comes to supersede the original. "The image
can no longer imagine the real," Baudrillard wrote, "because it is
the real." Actual nature, seen in person, disappoints next to impec-
cably shot nature documentaries. The 1950s of *American Graffiti*
replace the actual memory of the 1950s. The Piazza San Marco in
the Venetian Hotel in Las Vegas—just a stroll away from reproductions of New York City, Rome, and ancient Egypt—supersedes the
one in Venice.

And Donald Trump the simulacrum, the performance, had in
Baudrillardian fashion eclipsed Donald Trump the businessman—
so much so that the former would have to bail out the latter.

Trump had created a business whose primary product was the
idea of Trump: swagger, glitter, hitting it big. Separated from that
brand, his troubled properties would be worth less than they already
were. In the 1990s, that name became the business. Increasingly his
business ventures were like the Trump International Hotel & Tower,
where he worked with deep-pocketed partners and contributed his
famous brand. (Upon its opening, the *New York Times* described it:
"It's Donald J. Trump. All 52 stories of him.")

His job became essentially to play, on and off television, the role
of Donald Trump, mascot.

* * * *

THE CORPORATE MASCOT is one of the great American literary devices. A business invents a character to embody its image. That character has attributes, themes, even backstory and narrative. Like a comic-book superhero or a mythological figure, it personifies abstract ideals. In 1877, the Quaker Oats Company registered a trademark for "a man in Quaker garb" to symbolize "good quality and honest value." In 1890, a grain-milling company hired a former slave to play the role of Aunt Jemima—a racist caricature drawn from minstrel shows—to associate its labor-saving product with a smiling, subservient domestic worker.

Occasionally, a real person could be apotheosized into an immortal branding symbol. In 1964, when Colonel Harland Sanders sold his company, Kentucky Fried Chicken, it was with an agreement that transformed him, via TV commercials and takeout buckets, from a mere man—ambitious, demanding, with a penchant for cursing out his employees—into the personification of flavor, down-home quality, and Southern graciousness. According to a *New Yorker* profile, the new owner, John Y. Brown, saw that the Colonel's goatee and white suits were as valuable as any secret recipe:

> the possession of a symbol who was both authentic and alive—unlike Betty Crocker, Colonel Morton, or Aunt Jemima, for instance—was one of the company's greatest assets. He hired a public-relations man in New York, and the Colonel soon was popping up on the *Tonight Show*, *The Merv Griffin Show*, and other network programs, where he more than held his own with the show-business pros.

Colonel Sanders's human body died in 1980, the year the Donald Trump TV character materialized on Tom Brokaw's couch. But "the Colonel," the character Sanders played, long outlived him—stylized, ironized, polymorphous, and pangender, played in commercials by comedian Darrell Hammond and country singer Reba McEntire.

Like Jesus represented by the cross or a fish, he was essentialized in a few potent gestures: a goatee, a string tie. He was even repurposed in literature, appearing as a semimagical, sentient "abstract concept" in the novel *Kafka on the Shore* by Haruki Murakami.

Likewise, Donald Trump discovered that the abstract concept of him had a life of its own, and a potentially more successful career. He too, like the Colonel, was encapsulated in a few visual signatures: a solid-colored tie, a purse-lipped sneer, the male-model stare, and *that hair*. That impossible, Suessian tuft of hair, whatever wizardry of science and man made it possible, was like a crown that he snatched from the Pope and placed on his head, Napoleon-style. Watching his appearance evolve over the decade, become more exaggerated and stylized, is like watching a corporate logo change through successive redesigns, starting with something crude and literal—a telephone, a globe—and over the years become simpler and more glyph-like, not the thing, but, better, the abstraction of the thing, the thing that the thing makes you feel.

You have to wonder if business success was less important to Trump than becoming one of the immortal American brands, which are our undying gods, embodying aspects of the national character. Coca-Cola: a little caramel color, a little sugar, and the ideas of youth and vitality. Chevrolet: tail fins, polish, and faith in the endless possibility of the American road. Trump: a brass nameplate, aggression, and the belief that your appetites are good and correct.

* * * *

THE 1990S WERE a boom time for the businessperson as personal brand—moguls like Martha Stewart and Oprah Winfrey, whose personalities and biographies were bound up with their products. Trump, whatever his status as an actual businessman, was valuable as the easily recognizable cartoon of "a businessman." And right around the time his actual business ran into trouble, he began assembling a list of movie and TV appearances—to use the language of credits listings—"as himself."

In 1991 he won the Golden Raspberry Award as "Worst Supporting Actor" in the film *Ghosts Can't Do It*, playing opposite Bo Derek, the sex-symbol star of *10*, in a goofily seductive business negotiation. ("You're too pretty to be bad," she purrs. He pouts his lips: "You noticed.")

In a 1994 episode of *The Fresh Prince of Bel-Air*, a sitcom about a wealthy family who takes in their street-smart nephew from Philadelphia (the *Diff'rent Strokes* setup, except the benefactors are also black), he shows up with Marla Maples and a suitcase full of cash, interested in buying the family's mansion. Carlton (Alfonso Ribeiro), the family's enthusiastic preppy son, faints from excitement.

Even though he always plays himself, rather than a character—or rather, plays himself *as a character*, which he has done for his whole public life—Trump is a stiff actor. His lines sound like he's reading more than speaking them. He's not capable of forgetting in any moment that he is himself, a man standing on a soundstage and waiting for applause. But his woodenness underscores the meta-effect of his cameo appearance. You're not meant to think, "Here are the characters on my favorite show talking to Donald Trump," but rather, "Here are the actors on the set of my favorite show meeting the famous person Donald Trump." (This effect is doubled when the *Fresh Prince* studio audience cheers when Trump shows up; they're cheering, after all, for the "character" that they know from outside the story.)

On *Spin City*—the city-hall comedy starring Michael J. Fox, the 1980s' Alex P. Keaton—Trump appears as himself to plug his book *Trump: The Art of the Comeback*. On *The Nanny*, the title character introduces Trump to her wealthy employer: "Who am I kidding? All you wealthy zillionaires know each other." He flirts with model-actress Elizabeth Hurley on *The Job*; he plays poker on *Suddenly Susan* and jokes about a character's divorce; on HBO's *Sex and the*

City, he's eyeballed over cocktails by high-powered, high-libido publicist Samantha Jones. "Samantha, a cosmopolitan, and Donald Trump," says Sarah Jessica Parker's voiceover. "You just don't get more New York than that!"

In actual, brick-and-mortar New York, Donald Trump was known to readers of the tabloids as a has-been. But in the virtual landscape of TV and the movies, he was New York personified. He played the same character: a dashing, bemused man in a business suit or black tie, spending money, dispensing advice, insults, and baksheesh, creating a stir, turning heads, coming across less impressed with the characters he met than they were with him.

This had value to him, since maintaining his appearance and thus his brand was essential to keeping up the price of his assets. In the sitcom business at the time, a *Fresh Prince* director recalled, Trump "was one of those guys you would go after [for a cameo] because he was one of the few who would actually do it." In fact, filmmakers said that casting him was often a precondition of shooting on one of his properties, which was often the reason they would approach him.

The productions secured a visual shorthand for wealth and success. Trump was like a skyline establishing shot. You open a film set in New York City with footage of the Empire State Building rather than, say, Frank Gehry's 8 Spruce Street, because it immediately proclaims "Manhattan." Likewise, even if you could cast a New York mogul more successful than Donald Trump in the 1990s (Carl Icahn, say, or Henry Kravis), you'd have to explain to your audience who it was.

Trump came pre-explained, pre-stereotyped, pre-cartoonified. He was his own Colonel Sanders, a logo that told you, at a glance, what flavor to expect. When he made a TV commercial for the Big N' Tasty burger with McDonald's jiggly purple mascot Grimace, he was collaborating with a peer.

* * * *

LIKE A CHARACTER being retooled for a TV spinoff or a movie reboot, this "Donald Trump" was pitched differently than before. His character became comic-nostalgic, an unfrozen caveman Master of the Universe, walking through the world in a personal 1987 time warp, in his power suit and silk tie, in a world where young people now favored flannel and Doc Martens boots.

The 1990s were born in a recession and a screeching 180-degree turn toward suspicion of money and glitz. In 1989, *Time* had put Trump on the cover holding an ace of diamonds: "Flaunting it is the game, and TRUMP is the name." By 1991, its cover featured a bicycle and a pair of beat-up work boots, hailing "The Simple Life." ("These are the humble makings of a revolution in progress: Macaroni and cheese. Timex watches. Volunteer work. Insulated underwear. Savings accounts.") The signature doorstop novel of the 1980s was Tom Wolfe's *The Bonfire of the Vanities*, a social-realist tale of power and class conflict in a Manhattan dominated by alpha businessmen. Its 1990s equivalent—in ambition and tonnage if not in spirit—was David Foster Wallace's *Infinite Jest* (1996), a comic-surrealistic excoriation of commercial media and consumer culture that imagined "the Entertainment," a film so entrancing it killed its viewers, and that was set in a future in which years themselves were renamed for corporate sponsors. (Much of the novel takes place in "The Year of the Depend Adult Undergarment.")

You could argue that the pop-culture '80s ended in mid-1989, with Spike Lee's *Do the Right Thing*. The film, which climaxes in a riot in Brooklyn, repudiated the idea that dollar-driven real-estate development was an unalloyed good for New York. (One memorable scene in the movie involves a run-in between a white gentrifier and the black residents of the neighborhood.) It also answered the kind of race-baiting that Trump had dabbled in during the 1980s. In 1984, a white subway passenger, Bernhard Goetz, shot four black teenagers that he said had been harassing him; news reports called him "the subway vigilante" but many white New Yorkers hailed him as a hero. White fear was the kind of atavistic force that Trump was wired to pick up on; his self-promotion in the 1980s drew on his image of himself as a savior taming the fallen "inner city." On May 1, 1989, Trump took out full-page ads in four New York newspapers calling for the death penalty for "the Central Park Five," a group of black and Latino teenagers (later exonerated) accused of brutally raping a jogger in Central Park. (In 1990, Trump called the youths "one step removed from animals.") A few weeks later, Lee's film—fueled by a decade of racial incidents and depictions of black youth as predators—premiered at Cannes.

In 1991, Richard Linklater's film *Slacker* created a counter-archetype to the preppies and yuppies of the 1980s: aimless, eccentric young people seeking purpose outside a paycheck. It was the era of indie film and indie record labels, alternative this and alternative that—a bad brand environment for anyone who preferred to position himself as the default.

At the same time, TV's class dynamics were changing in the 1990s, with both working-class protagonists and fantasies of wealth like *Dallas* and *Dynasty* being pushed out at either end. An advertising structure that rewarded shows whose audiences were young, white-collar, and middle class—what saved *Hill Street Blues* in the 1980s—now increasingly produced TV characters that fit that profile.

NBC's "Must-See TV" programming bloc thrived on this sort of show. *Seinfeld*'s characters rarely seemed to work (except comically, as with George Costanza's elaborate plots to get hired and fired from jobs), yet had time and cash to hang out at restaurants. *Friends* was as well known for its ludicrously oversized Manhattan apartments as for its romantic-comedy escapades. TV turned New York from a place of struggle and aspiration—if you can make it there, you'll make it anywhere—to a pacified hangout of comfy couches and cappuccino.

With occasional exceptions like *Roseanne*, blue-collar work disappeared from television. The work that audiences did see, in the bourgie-fied TV of the '90s, was increasingly white-collar. CBS, once the home of Norman Lear's working-class comedies, refocused on shows like *Murphy Brown*, about a high-strung, high-powered TV-newsmagazine journalist who, after a day of butting heads with the powers that be, came home to a lush Georgetown townhouse.

It wasn't only working-class people (and partly by extension, minority characters) who were dwindling in prime time. The super-rich were too. The flip side of television becoming more bourgeois was that the kind of outlandishly wealthy characters popular in the 1970s and 1980s were passé. Even Aaron Spelling's teen soap *Beverly Hills, 90210*, though it was set in the toniest Southern California zip code, saw the land of plastic surgery and privilege through the lens of Brandon and Brenda Walsh, a pair of upper-middle-class transplants from Minnesota.

That soaps about the rich would dwindle at the same time TV about the working class did might seem like a contradiction. But it's really part of the same phenomenon. You didn't program a show like *Dynasty* to attract the Carringtons of the world. Like celebrity magazines in the checkout line, they're a populist medium. The sybaritism of the wealthy is escapism for people just getting by, who like their rich people as decadent and gold-trimmed as Donald Trump's triplex. Soaps of the 1980s were the class struggle dialed up to 10 and played to the groundlings.

But the kinds of viewers that networks increasingly prized by the 1990s—college-educated, with good, steady incomes—weren't as drawn to that kind of fantasy. For them, life wasn't all-or-nothing; it was something, and something a little more tomorrow. (Trump's 2016 campaign would, in part, appeal to resentment of "elites"—not the actual super-rich elite, but the comfortable white-collar class, the lawyers and managers who maxed out their 401(k)s and test-prepped their kids into selective colleges and made their money off intangible thought work, money for nothing. If Trump had a life you wanted though you knew you could never have it, these professionals had a life you needed accreditation to even know how to want.)

These viewers gravitated to network-TV characters who were, socially, more like themselves: the journalists on *Sports Night*, the lawyers on *Ally McBeal*. They liked the dry irony of David Letterman. They responded to *The Larry Sanders Show*'s depiction of the Hollywood entertainment machine as powered by cynicism, and *Twin Peaks'* vision of a cherry-pie rural American town riddled with demons, addiction, and child prostitution. They liked referential humor and series that rewarded the sort of ability to read symbol and subtext that earned you As in a literature class. You made shows like *Frasier*—the *Cheers* sequel about a wine-sipping, bon mot–dropping psychiatrist and radio host—because you wanted viewers like Frasier.

* * * *

BY THE EARLY 1990S, America had become partial to a different brand of real-life rich person. The 1992 presidential election, one cycle after Trump teased the possibility of running on *Oprah* and *Donahue*, saw the independent campaign of H. Ross Perot, a Texas data-systems billionaire with a '60s-NASA-engineer buzz cut and the voice and bearing of a rooster that a wizard had turned into a man.

Perot, who won nearly 20 percent of the vote, was the evolution of the Trump-Iacocca idea—amplified by Republicans in particular for years—that America should be run like a business. Like Trump in 2016, he was a novelty who bathed in free publicity. He essentially began his campaign by coyly telling Larry King, CNN's suspender-wearing old-Hollywood schmoozer, that if "everyday folks" put him on the ballot in all fifty states, he'd make the sacrifice of running.

He chirped out folksy catchphrases; the NAFTA trade deal, he said, would produce a "giant sucking sound" of jobs moving to Mexico. He relied on his mastery of live TV, especially the debates. He de-emphasized traditional TV ads, buying half-hour blocks to give economic lectures with cardboard charts, which out-rated prime-time sitcoms. (There was not, yet, an ecosystem of competing cable-news channels to give his insta-celebritized campaign events hours of free airtime.)

Perot was proto–reality TV, at a time when reality TV barely existed outside MTV's *The Real World*. He had an anti-slick performative populism, bolstered by his claim to simply be doing the bidding of average Americans. (His ballot challenge on Larry King was an early version of the viewer-participation model of *American Idol*: only you, America, can decide whether he returns on the show next week!) And he was an early test of the idea that a billionaire could argue that he was closer in spirit to paycheck-to-paycheck Americans than the professional classes that, in dollar terms, stood between them.

Perot was not exactly the Trump model of business mogul. His style was more Timex than Rolex. His celebrity was anti-celebrity; he commanded television by being anti-telegenic. In Dallas, the *Los Angeles Times* reported, "Locals say they see him shopping at the local sporting goods store or driving to his Saturday haircut in an '87 Oldsmobile." Donald Trump cultivated an affect that said to an observer, at a glance: "Wealthy business magnate." Perot's exterior said: "Refrigerator salesman, maybe?"

In business culture, meanwhile, the momentum was shifting away from swaggery '80s personalities like CNN's founder, Ted Turner, the mouthy Georgian who married actress Jane Fonda and competed in yacht races. The countenance of wealth was changing, in part, because the sources of wealth were changing. The face of money in the 1990s was technology wealth: America Online's Steve Case, Oracle's Larry Ellison, Amazon's Jeff Bezos, Yahoo!'s Jerry Yang, and Microsoft's Bill Gates.

There was already a template of American wealth, within which Donald Trump had situated himself: rich people made and sold concrete things you could see and touch. They built cars, extracted oil, launched airplanes, built buildings. (There was an implicit idea of masculinity and virility in the physicality of their achievements: you *erect* a skyscraper.) Technology wealth, on the other hand, was wealth from intangibles. Cornelius Vanderbilt, in the nineteenth century, made his fortune in railroads—vast physical networks than veined a continent, through which its physical riches pulsed. Networking software, on the other hand, is not a railroad but a metaphor for a railroad. Yahoo! was a place on the Internet that helped you get to other places on the Internet. Getting rich from an operating system is like getting rich by selling air.

Tech moguls built ideas. They certainly would not do anything so déclassé as to slap their name on a giant tower, like some sort of caveman.

You could understand the value of a car by going to your garage and starting it up. The tech empires created wealth out of things that required abstract thinking before you could even understand that they were things. (What is a "site" on the Internet, anyway?) There was also computer hardware, sure, but a beige work tool doesn't scream "luxury" like a gilded tower. Even Amazon—the virtual bookstore turned superstore whose raison d'être was to make "brick and mortar" an archaism—didn't make things at first but rather the means to buy things. Money for nothing!

The new money of the 1990s also redefined the aesthetic of wealth. The uniform of the tech-rich was the jeans and open-necked shirts of the engineers and programmers they often started out as. Theirs was the ostentation of anti-ostentation. Bill Gates, with the fortune of a Gilded Age monopolist and a fearsome business reputation to match, wore V-neck sweaters and oversized glasses like some sort of harmless Muppet.

It was, to borrow the name of a 1996 PBS documentary by Robert X. Cringely, the Triumph of the Nerds. (Cringely—the pen name of journalist Mark Stephens—was, in his own description, the "premier gossip columnist" of the computer business, a Liz Smith for introverts.) As Cringely describes his tech-leader subjects in *Triumph of the Nerds*, they "were, for the most part, middle-class white kids from good suburban homes," and they displayed their power and independence by continuing to dress like suburban kids.

This economic shift blossomed into a cultural one—not least because technology was an expression of culture. The 1990s was a boom time for nerdery: nerd music, nerd pastimes, nerd icons like Steve Urkel of the sitcom *Family Matters*. To be a nerd was to oppose the signifiers of a red-blooded tradition, as Benjamin Nugent writes in *American Nerd*, in which "the heroes of American popular culture are surfers, cowboys, pioneers, gangsters, cheerleaders, and baseball players, people at home in the heat of physical exertion." Nerd exertion was mental. Nerd empires were intangible. Nerd aggression was passive-aggression. And nerd consumption was inconspicuous.

There was one member of the nerdocracy who had a significant aesthetic, and it was a repudiation of 1980s polished-brass glitz. Steve Jobs of Apple would become far wealthier than Trump, but he cultivated a stylistic asceticism: black turtleneck, wire-rimmed glasses. He insisted that Apple's products be beautiful. (He originally wanted his computers to come in blond koa-wood cases.) And he defined beauty by absence: clean lines, no filigree. This eventually led to the iPhone, whose glass touchscreen was as close to a blank portal to pure idea as modern hardware could create.

Jobs was selling consumers an idea of themselves as much as he was selling machinery. Apple's computers (and later phones and tablets) were high-design status objects. They sold at a premium. But they communicated status austerely, by rejecting ornament. Jobs popularized a kind of anti-materialist materialism. It was no longer "If you got it, flaunt it." By refusing to flaunt it, you proved you were someone who got it.

* * * *

WELL, WHAT THE HELL does Donald Trump do in this world? He had managed, through his face-saving deal with his creditors, to hang on to the props of success and wealth. But being Donald Trump was never entirely about the money. It was about leaving his stamp—his golden T—on his age. The Donald Trump of 1987 was

America's gluttony artist. A decade later, he was what? A rich land-lord. A regional celebrity. A museum piece with no more grip on the popular imagination than a railroad tycoon.

Trump had been eclipsed and outbillionaired by tech and media entrepreneurs who captured the popular imagination the 1990s way, by buying and selling pieces of it. Mere solvency is small comfort to a man who—a securities analyst familiar with him told *The New Yorker*—"wants to be Madonna."

But media and entertainment still needed a symbol of flashy, richly marbled wealth that anyone could understand in a second. They still required a cartoon zillionaire who would preen and shake his moneybags the way Silicon Valley's abstemious captains didn't. The character of Donald Trump was out of fashion, but he usefully filled a niche. In a culture of minimalists, he was a maximalist. If in the 1980s he was the programming, in the 1990s he was the counterprogramming.

He was ubiquitous, for instance, in '90s hip-hop lyrics, in which "Donald Trump" was a three-syllable anapest for in-your-face riches. "Put more cash in my pockets than Donald Trump" (Master P); "Guess who's the black Trump?" (Raekwon); "I'm just tryin' to get rich like Trump" (Ice Cube); "In hot pursuit of Donald Trump rap loot" (Pete Rock); "I need a suite with the flowers complimentary at Trump Towers" (Nas, who's referenced Trump in lyrics at least eight times). By the 2016 election, after his calumnies against the first black president, hip-hop would turn overwhelmingly negative on Trump, but in the '90s, he was mostly a useful verbal ornament, a kind of human gold chain.

The man who, in the 1980s, festooned himself with luxurious "props for the show" became himself a kind of prop, a useful gim-mick to cast in TV commercials and promotions. During CBS's coverage of the 1994 Winter Olympics, he introduces coverage of moguls, before being told that "moguls" here means the skiing event. For Toshiba desktop computers, he answers an email from a twelve-year-old boy who writes him for advice on becoming a real-estate tycoon. In a Pizza Hut ad, he and his ex-wife Ivana tryst in a swanky apartment and agree to do something that she says is "wrong" but he says "feels so right": eat the new Stuffed Crust Pizza crust-end first.

If people never really change, the useful thing about fictional character franchises is that they can, adapting to the tone of the times while maintaining the core identities their creators laid down. Batman began as a stone-faced gangster fighter; then he was a campy kids'-show favorite, played by Adam West in sausage-skin tights; then he was a brooding vigilante in dark, violent films. But the essentials remained the same: lair, gadgets, justice.

The 1990s were Trump's Adam West period. His appearances "as himself" carried the seed of his aspirations and self-image, encased in a protective gel of irony, to survive until a more hospitable time.

* * * *

THIS USE OF IRONY as an impermeable defensive carapace was a particular concern of novelist David Foster Wallace. In 1993, he published an essay, "E Unibus Pluram: Television and U.S. Fiction," which sketched out some of the ideas about media that he would expand on in *Infinite Jest*. Television was not just dominating Americans' attention, Wallace wrote, but it had developed an amoeba-like ability to enfold and absorb any critique by archly laughing at itself from a posture of "hip irony." You could see this in the amount of TV that was reflexively about TV (the news-business comedy *Murphy Brown*, or the meta-referential detective show *Moonlighting*, or *Beavis and Butt-Head*, the MTV cartoon whose characters made fun of MTV videos) or that spoofed its characters' own fixation with TV (Homer Simpson spacing out staring at the tube as you spaced out staring at Homer Simpson). First TV comedy parodied commercials, as on *Saturday Night Live*, then *commercials* parodied commercials, like the Isuzu ads with the sleazy pitchman Joe Isuzu, which sold cars by telling you how much you hated people who sold cars.

Against this, literary fiction seemed outmoded, overmatched, like it was fighting off space aliens while armed with nothing but pointy sticks. Do you approach television in fiction writing mimetically, treating TV and its language as another aspect of contemporary realism, and thus affirm it as a fixture of the landscape? Or do you try to rebel against it, and risk becoming another preachy square who just doesn't get it? Either you surrender or you are impaled on your own lance. "Televisual culture has somehow evolved to a point where it seems invulnerable to any such transfiguring assault," Wallace wrote.

It's important to keep in mind that David Foster Wallace *liked* TV. He was just over thirty when "E Unibus Pluram" came out. He was no tweedy, "I don't even own a television" fogey. He belonged to the generation after Trump's, who first knew television not as a novelty but a fact of mundane existence. Unlike many intellectuals—and to be honest, TV critics—of his time, he didn't regard TV shows as dangerous objects to be held with tongs at arm's length, or folk artifacts with which to anthropologically study the great unwashed. He writes with the familiarity of a dedicated viewer. "I know I watch for fun, most of the time, and that at least 51 percent of the time I do have fun when I watch," he wrote.

But Wallace appreciated TV enough to take it seriously, and he was conscious of the ways it worked on him. Addiction—chemical and psychological—was a preoccupation of his, and he wrote with conviction on how the medium's effortless stimulation appealed to "teleholics." He also noticed TV encouraging a kind of lazy superiority in its viewer. "It's just *fun* to laugh cynically at television—at the way the laughter from sitcoms' 'live studio audience' is always suspiciously constant in pitch and duration," he noted. With that default to mockery came the danger of learning to see *everything* as fraud and artifice, deciding that everyone was phony, and thus being willing to excuse those phonies who admitted it with a wink. (As another old artificer, P. T. Barnum, put it more than a century earlier: "The greatest humbug of all is the man who believes—or pretends to believe—that everything and everybody are humbugs.")

In Wallace's view, some of the greatest carriers of this kidding-not-kidding sickness were the late-night talk shows: "[David] Letterman, Arsenio [Hall], and [Jay] Leno's battery of hip, sardonic, this-is-just-TV shticks." Letterman, for Wallace, was the Typhoid Mary of death by irony. Letterman's show, the outgrowth of a brief, surrealistic morning show he attempted on NBC in summer 1980 (it followed Trump's appearance on Brokaw's *Today*), was a kind of mad scientist's sentient monster, a talk show that knew it was a talk show. The show's mascot was Larry "Bud" Melman (Calvert DeForest), a doughy, leering martinet who was like an emcee from a twisted David Lynch dream. The bandleader, Paul Shaffer, affected a knowingly corny lounge-lizard persona. Letterman would mock and prank his own network, showing up on the set of *Today* with a bullhorn, crying, "I am Larry Grossman, president of NBC News, and I'm not wearing pants!" Wallace's short story "My Appearance" is a minutely observed rendering of a TV actress's guest spot on a 1989 episode of *Late Night with David Letterman*, which both perfectly captures the show's voice and depicts it as a kind of secret-in-the-open horror show, the absurdist gags and wisecracks masking a psychological assault of contempt and misogyny. The actress's husband, who works in the entertainment business, prepares her for the taping, warning her: "Meanness is not the issue. The issue is *ridiculousness*. The bastard feeds off ridiculousness like some enormous Howdy-Doodyesque parasite."

This criticism of Letterman, I think, is broadly accurate but not entirely right. His irony and sarcasm could be a crutch, but they weren't just nihilism. They expressed a genuine disgust for phony bonhomie and artifice, something that became clearer over the years as he aged and changed his style, becoming less of a prankster, more of a raconteur, and more straightforwardly outspoken. (It was Letterman, in 2011, who was one of the first to take Trump seriously enough to call him a racist, in so many words, for pushing the smear that Barack Obama was not born in the United States, even as serious news outlets indulged Trump as a harmless buffoon: "It's all fun. It's all a circus. It's all a rodeo. Until it starts to smack of racism.")

But of course it also says something that Letterman *did* change his style, that he found it necessary to find a voice in which he could argue what he believed to be true and not simply what he derided as fake. And the environment of his 1980s and 1990s talk shows, on NBC and later CBS, was inarguably helpful to a certain kind of guest who wanted to enter that everything's-a-joke zone to launder his own reputation.

* * * *

DONALD TRUMP APPEARED on Letterman's shows more than thirty times, over three decades. These appearances were valuable exposure, but along with his other talk-show visits, they also established a dichotomy—that Trump was both businessman and entertainer—that would be essential to him as a candidate. When you are always in a Schrödinger's-cat paradox of joking and not joking, the same message can send different meanings to different audiences: I mean it but I don't really mean it but I do. (*Wink.*)

On talk shows like Letterman's, Trump played a shock comic. Letterman delighted in prodding Trump to shoot his mouth off but also pressed him on his controversies. In a 1992 appearance, summing up how he'd sold off his assets as he faced potential ruin, Trump said, "I sold the Trump Shuttle. I unloaded my wife." The audience howled. Later, Letterman asked him about a proposal Trump had made, that prizefighter Mike Tyson should be allowed to reduce his prison sentence for rape by fighting a charity bout. "What were you thinking?" Letterman asked. "I was thinking as soon as he gets out, he's going to box at my casinos." Awkward silence. "I was only kidding when I say that, folks," Trump added.

There's a preview in this appearance of Trump the political figure, and not just because Letterman asked him to handicap Ross Perot's odds in the coming election. There's the joking-not-joking dance: I'm telling it like it is, but also I didn't really mean it—but also I'm more honest than all the phonies, because *I'm just saying* *what everybody's thinking.* (That too is an entertainer's defense, from Andrew Dice Clay to Eminem.) And you—you smart people—you're in on the joke. *You get it.*[*]

It also shows Trump participating in that most essential of celebrity-culture rituals: the comeback story. There are three elemental celebrity stories: you rise, you fall, you bounce back. For a traditional businessman, Donald Trump's 1990 might have been irreparably humiliating. But for a celebrity—Robert Downey Jr., Drew Barrymore, Rob Lowe—it's a valuable item on a résumé.

On Letterman, Shaffer and the World's Most Dangerous Band played Trump on to the theme from *Rocky* (maybe ironically, maybe half-; Rocky Balboa didn't win until *Rocky II*). Trump, like an ingenue with savvy handlers, wanted to begin the "comeback" part of his story as soon as possible. He would work that angle for much of the decade, publishing *The Art of the Comeback* in 1997. Presented as a business book on the model of *The Art of the Deal*, including a desultory list of "comeback tips" (including "be passionate" and "stay focused"), it was really a celebrity memoir at heart. The name-dropping reeked of sad '80s reverie—Michael Jackson, Madonna, Carl Icahn—and the book was plastered with more celebrity photos than a Planet Hollywood franchise. (How dare you call me a has-been! Look at me here with Sly Stallone!)

Neal Gabler writes in *Life the Movie* that the celebrity-comeback story follows the arc of Joseph Campbell's "hero with a thousand faces." An extraordinary person surmounts extraordinary forces and returns to share rewards with his fellow man. Just so, "the celebrity loses it all, a victim of his own hubris or of the public's fickleness. Only then, after he has been forced to win back his fame, does the celebrity reemerge from Hollywood, if only figuratively, in mag-

---

[*] That side of Trump would turn up more often later in the decade, when he became a regular on shock jock Howard Stern's show, rating female celebrities' bodies ("A person who is flat-chested is very hard to be a 10") and promising to change the Miss USA pageant, which he acquired in 1997, by getting "the bathing suits to be smaller and the heels to be higher."

azines and books and television talk shows, sadder but wiser, to tell the rest of us what he has learned."

The Art of the Comeback's story is not really a business story. It's a Hollywood story—a retelling of the American myth of how the secular god, the celebrity, dies and is resurrected. I got big, the story goes. I got too big. I took my eye off the ball. I crashed. I fought back. And I learned an important lesson: "I enjoy my successes much more because I realize it wasn't so easy after all." I'd been to Paradise, and now I've been to me. Trump would use that precise story as his scripted introduction, in 2004, for *The Apprentice*.

Trump's *Art of the Comeback* tour hit the same sorts of venues— TV newsmagazines, morning shows—as a Hollywood star peddling a tale of addiction and recovery. But it would leave out some typical themes of the celebrity-comeback story: humility and forgiveness. When Matt Lauer on the *Today* show asked him about his belief in getting revenge on people who wronged him during tough times— "Why not be bigger?"—he answered, "I like being small."

Celebrity comeback stories are modern-day religious parables. Showing how the lofty overcame struggles and let go of their resentments, they offer the reader or viewer a kind of New Testament– New Age inspiration—I will make it through my own troubles, I will let go the anger and resentment, and I will emerge a better and happier person.

Trump's self-authored comeback story used the same structure, but arrived at a much more Old Testament, even premoral lesson, that your bitterest fantasies are the ones you should nurture, indulge, and carry forward in life.

Someday things are going to swing back my way, and everyone who laughed at me is going to be fucking sorry.

PART II

ANTIHERO

1999–2015

Episode 5

THE DARK SIDE

WHILE DONALD TRUMP WAS IN TV-CAMEO EXILE, JIM PROFIT
was sleeping in a box.

The drama *Profit*, which was born and died on the Fox network
in April 1996, asked audiences to do something prime-time TV had
rarely done: sympathize with the bad guy. The title character, played
by Adrian Pasdar, was a cold-eyed, slick-haired young executive at
Gracen & Gracen, one of those global conglomerates so big that it
functions as a city-state. Profit was an up-and-comer who up-and-
came by any means necessary: after the company's chief died, he
began engineering his rise amid the ensuing succession intrigue by
investigating his colleagues and using their secrets to destroy them.

He had also, essentially, destroyed himself. Jim Profit was the
assumed name of Jimmy Stakowski, a dirt-poor kid from Oklahoma
whose personality had been warped by an abusive childhood. His
father—whom he eventually murdered—kept him inside a cardboard shipping box (from Gracen & Gracen), with a hole cut in it
so he could watch a constantly running TV. At the end of the two-
hour premiere, Profit returned home to his apartment, retreated to a
secret room, and curled up, naked, in that same box.

Placing a villain at the center of the action was hardly a new
device in drama (*Profit*'s creators were inspired by Shakespeare's
Richard III), film (*The Godfather*), or TV (*Dallas*). Soap operas

were fueled by dastardliness. But their villainy was set in a clearly defined moral universe—you knew who was good and who was bad and why. They allowed the viewer distance. J. R. Ewing and Alexis Carrington Colby were fan favorites, but they weren't point-of-view characters. You weren't expected to occupy their consciousness. Tens of millions of viewers could enjoy a kind of moral safari, the windows of empathy safely rolled up.

Profit, on the other hand, centered the villain's character and his psychology. You saw the world through his eyes, viewing over his shoulder as he marked the elimination of his corporate targets in a virtual-reality program on his computer. He engaged the viewer in direct-to-the-camera soliloquies, which combined acute insights into human nature and motivational-speaker platitudes. You didn't view him from a safari car; he was the ride.

You couldn't simply love to hate Jim Profit the way you did J. R. Ewing. For the show to work, you had to find him engrossing. You had to want to understand him. And you had to entertain some unsettling premises—for starters, that the best sort of person to climb the ladder of a late-twentieth-century American corporation was an icy sociopath. "Its principal conceit," wrote John Leonard, the TV critic for *New York* magazine, "was the representation of upward corporate mobility as a form of symbolic patricide."

While *Profit* had the structure and melodrama of a soap opera, there was no "good" antagonist to Jim Profit. His rivals were deeply compromised, and Gracen & Gracen's own practices were unethical. When the series began, the company was in crisis because news had leaked that one of its subsidiaries, a baby-food manufacturer, was selling sugar water as "apple juice" to boost the bottom line.

Profit didn't merely critique business. It critiqued humanity. While forging a signature, Profit tells us that copying someone's writing is not merely a mechanical act; it requires intimate knowledge of one's subject. If the worst person among us is the one who knows us best, *Profit* asked, can we be that much better?

The broadcast audience, it turned out, was not interested finding out. *Profit* was canceled after four airings.

America was not ready for an amoral, damaged businessman whose shamelessness made him powerful and whose psyche was formed by television. Yet.

* * * *

BY THE MID-TO-LATE 1990S, American culture was fragmenting and fermenting in ways that prime-time TV struggled to reflect. With the Cold War ended, the country fought the "culture war," a term that became ubiquitous early in the decade. As values of the baby-boomer counterculture became mass culture, David Friend writes in *The Naughty Nineties*, "Sex had become mainstream": Eve Ensler's *The Vagina Monologues* became a feminist theater landmark; Howard Stern, the smutty radio jock who swapped locker-room talk with Trump, appeared seminude against the Manhattan skyline, the Chrysler building deployed phallically, for the poster of his 1997 movie *Private Parts*. Social conservatives increasingly felt marginalized and supplanted, a tension that would drive politics for decades. The 1993 launch of the web browser Mosaic— which helped transform the largely text-based Internet into a visual medium—accelerated the splintering of the mass audience into web niches and online chatrooms. (Not to mention all the porn. There were no network censors on the Internet.)

And with the election in 1992 of Bill Clinton, who had a reputation for philandering long before he became president, America dropped the pretense that its president needed to be a moral paragon, or at least present a convincing pantomime of it. (Even if that principle had been most often observed in the breach, and with a wink.) In 1998, after his sexual relationship with White House intern Monica Lewinsky was exposed amid an investigation into a sexual-harassment charge, the pruriently explicit report of independent counsel Kenneth Starr had TV anchors discussing the dildonic use of cigars and the forensic import of a presidential-semen deposit on a blue Gap dress. (One of the biggest hit movies of that year, the Farrelly brothers' gross-out comedy *There's Something About Mary*, was distinguished by a scene in which costar Ben Stiller masturbates before a date and ends up, obliviously, with a dollop of his own semen on his ear. 1998 was ejaculating all over us.)

Reality, increasingly, had a hard R rating. But traditional television, constrained to a soft PG at most, didn't yet have the means to reflect this—nor to tell darker stories about morally compromised characters.

This would begin to change, late in the 1990s. Within a decade, the approach that made *Profit* a failure in 1996—what broadly speaking we call "antihero drama"—would become the default mode of some of television's best and most popular shows. The exploits of ruthless, charismatic men (with a few exceptions, it was largely men) occupied *The Sopranos*, *Deadwood*, and *Breaking Bad*. *Mad Men*'s advertising executive Don Draper, like Jim Profit, was a troubled country boy who stole a man's identity; in business, his clinical amorality allowed him to understand his market on a primal level.*

Had the medium changed, or had the audience? As is often the case, each changed the other.

* * * *

THE ANTIHERO (in literary terms a protagonist without conventional noble attributes; in layman's terms an asshole you find interesting) flourished in literature long before television. In *Anatomy of Criticism*, the twentieth-century literary critic Northrop Frye describes the progression of modes of fiction from the mythic (concerned with figures, like gods, wholly superior to the reader) to

---

* In a DVD commentary track, the creators of *Profit* said that the second season would have revealed that Profit, like Draper, took another man's identity.

the ironic (concerned with protagonists inferior to the reader). As worldly power moved from the highborn to the bourgeois and the masses, the attention of artists slid down that scale toward the ironic. In the nineteenth century, Fyodor Dostoevsky created antiheroes like the self-loathing narrator of *Notes from Underground* and Raskolnikov, the impoverished student in *Crime and Punishment* who breaks bad, St. Petersburg–style, murdering his landlady in the belief that he is above the law.

Raskolnikovs, however, were the stuff of literary rather than popular fiction. Television as a medium had to change before there could be something like literary TV.

The reason characters like Jim Profit hadn't thrived on TV goes back to the Least Objectionable Program. TV shows of the major-network era, which lasted from the late 1940s roughly until the end of the century, when cable TV began to supersede broadcast, needed enormous audiences to survive. The ratings that got *Profit* canceled—a 4.9, or about 5 million households—would have been a respectable yield for a movie and a phenomenal one for a novel. Drawing the necessary tens of millions of viewers—urban and rural, liberal and conservative, adults and children—meant not giving people a reason to change the channel.

And asking them to seek to understand cold, unrepentant evil— well, that was a reason. Before you even raise the question of whether the Americans of 1956, 1976, or 1996 were different from those of 2016, you have to confront the fact that the media's dynamics were different. Especially when there are only a few other options, fewer people will flip the channel because you reaffirm simple morality than if you question it.

TV's early antiheroes, in Frye's ironic-mode sense, came in sitcoms, which celebrated the blustery likes of *The Honeymooners'* paunchy bus driver Ralph Kramden. But TV's first great antihero, in the contemporary sense, was Archie Bunker of Norman Lear's *All in the Family.*

Archie (Carroll O'Connor), a bigoted dockworker from Queens, was based on Lear's own father, but he embodied a current dynamic of the Vietnam era: the nostalgic, working-class hardhat who felt besieged by modern life. His daughter, Gloria, was a feminist whose sexual liberation horrified him. His son-in-law, Michael Stivic, was an intellectual longhair whose politics infuriated him. And in the rest of the world Archie saw a parade of "spades" and "spics" getting entitlements denied to him. ("I didn't have no million people out there marching and protesting to get me my job," he says in the pilot. "No, his uncle got it for him," his wife, Edith, adds.)

When CBS premiered *All in the Family* in 1971—part of its "rural purge" push for relevance—it knew the show was a risk. It opened the first episode with a disclaimer ("The program you are about to see . . . seeks to throw a humorous spotlight on our frailties, prejudices, and concerns") and put extra staff on the switchboards.

It didn't need them, in part because of the show's modest early ratings, in part because the show provided so many vantages from which to view Archie. He was a buffoon, but a richly human one. Even his view of the Statue of Liberty's invitation reduced it to tribalism, but O'Connor delivered it like Walt Whitman verse: " 'Send me your poor, your deadbeats, your filthy'! And all the nations send them in here, they come swarming in like ants. Your Spanish P.R.'s from the Caribboin there, your Japs, your Chinamen, your Krauts and your Hebes and your English fags. All of them come in here, and they're all free to live in their own separate sections where they feel safe—and they'd bust your head if you go in there! That's what makes America great, buddy!"

All in the Family was driven by the small-l liberal idea that in order to conquer a social problem, you had to understand it, not simply deplore it. To Laura Z. Hobson—author of *Gentleman's Agreement*, the 1947 novel that excoriated anti-Semitism—the series went about that by dishonestly and dangerously sanitizing Archie's bigotry and language. He would say "Hebe" but never "kike," for instance. "Clean it up, deterge it, bleach it, enzyme it," she wrote, "and you'll have a show about a lovable bigot that everybody except a few pinko atheistic bleedin' hearts will love. Well, I differ. I don't think you can be a bigot and be lovable."

Lear, on the other hand, believed that you needed to see how someone could love Archie in order to see him in your own racist relatives. Which meant that—a pattern that would repeat with later antiheroes—you couldn't control how the audience received him once he was loosed into the wild. For the Michael Stivics of the world, Archie was a lasting synonym for prejudice. To other fans, he was a hero who said what they wanted to—what they believed *everyone* wanted to—but couldn't, not anymore, or not yet.

CBS anticipated this before the show premiered. It received "below average" scores from viewers at a test screening, but the network's research report suggested that this was because audience members who liked Archie "might feel required to criticize him, even if deep down they identify with him."

This was not unlike the "shy Trump effect" postulated in some 2016 election polls, and the parallels would not end there. In August 2017, Norman Lear announced that he would refuse to attend a Kennedy Center Honors reception at the White House with President Trump, whom he likened to his protagonist, but worse: "Archie Bunker was far wiser of heart." That same month, Steve Bannon—the White House strategist who had run the alt-right news site Breitbart—was quoted saying of Trump in the *New York Times*, "Dude, he's Archie Bunker." He meant it as a compliment.

ALL IN THE FAMILY became the number-one show on TV and stayed on top for five years straight. But it remained for decades an exception. The success of *Hill Street Blues* in the early 1980s moved networks to introduce, cautiously, characters with personal demons. But they needed to have tragic backstories and to work for institutions that protected the greater good. The most long-lived of these neoantiheroes was Detective Andy Sipowicz (Dennis Franz) of *NYPD Blue* (1993), a racist, homophobic, shirt-sleeved schlub, a brute and a drunk, but one who suffered enough Job-like personal woes (the death of his son, the death of his wife, cancer) to make the viewer want to hit the bottle as well.

An antihero is the sort of character who is not for everyone. Which meant that the age of the antihero would require—before artistic daring, before indelible performance—that someone develop a system in which TV that was not for everyone could thrive.

That system was cable. Home Box Office launched in 1972, focusing on boxing matches and uncensored feature films. Its most glaring distinction from mass-market broadcast TV was that, free of FCC regulations because cable did not use the public airwaves, it could air profanity and nudity. (Like many 1980s kids whose parents didn't pay for HBO, I spent my teen years straining to watch R-rated movies through the wobbly curtain of the channel's scrambled signal.)

But HBO's most *important* distinction was that people paid to subscribe to it. TV is the most Marxist of capitalist systems: the revenue stream determines the content and the ideology. Before cable, TV could only monetize breadth of interest. You made money by airing things a lot of people liked a little. The pay-TV model monetized *depth* of interest. HBO made money by airing things a relative few people liked a lot, enough to pay for them.

When HBO began creating original series—occasionally in the 1980s, aggressively by the late 1990s—its business model meant it could take chances. In fact, it had to. Why pay for something you could watch free on CBS? So HBO created what wasn't there: the inside-Hollywood satire of *The Larry Sanders Show*; the brutal prison drama of *Oz*; the sophisticated raunch of *Sex and the City*. (The second season of *SATC*, in 1999, included a prodigious ejaculation scene in a tantric-sex workshop that answered back *There's Something About Mary* like a cannon salute.)

In January 1999, HBO premiered *The Sopranos*, a show that changed the idea of who could be the protagonist of an American

TV story. Tony Soprano (James Gandolfini), a northern New Jersey Mafia captain, was an archetype of American movies but also a man of his moment. In the pilot, he began therapy after a panic attack, brought on when a flock of ducks that he'd become attached to vacated his backyard swimming pool.

Tony Soprano was both an embodiment and a critique of American masculinity. He was hulking and heavyset; he radiated a meaty, sweaty physicality, as if he were made of the slices of deli-case *gabbagool* that he would stand in front of his fridge and shove into his mouth. He was brooding and dangerous. (In the pilot, he hit a man with his car because he owed Tony money. Later in the first season he strangled a mob informant he spotted while on a college tour with his daughter.) But he was also self-pitying and nostalgic. He complained that his father, even though he had less money than Tony eventually would, had a better life, because back in the old days, people had pride and respected tradition.

On one level, Tony personified Clintonesque baby-boomer self-indulgence, the way he would compartmentalize his string of mistresses from his self-conception as a proud family man. But he was also a repudiation of the Clintonesque values of empathy and feeling others' pain—as opposed to dealing it—the way that Donald Trump would eventually be as a presidential candidate. He cheated on his wife but expected her fidelity. He surrounded himself with sycophants but convinced himself their sucking-up was genuine. He demanded loyalty but felt no obligation to return it. "This thing is a pyramid, since time immemorial," he told his captains, angry that they were not bringing in enough cash. "Shit runs downhill, money goes up."

He ruined people and went on his way, oblivious. He wanted the prerogatives of traditional manhood, but he didn't want to have to earn them. He whined and threw tantrums, yet wondered without irony to his therapist: "Whatever happened to Gary Cooper, the strong, silent type? He wasn't in touch with his feelings. He just did what he had to do." (In *Trump: Surviving at the Top*, Trump voices a similar complaint about a *Tonight* show appearance by "an actor whom I've greatly admired for years for his cool tough-guy roles," now telling a story of how he became depressed and addicted to drugs. "My reaction," Trump wrote, "is to switch quickly to the Ted Turner channel that shows nothing but old movies, made in the days when Hollywood knew how to provide the public with heroes and glamour.")

Tony was not an admirable man. *But*. He was entertaining. As Gandolfini played him, he was darkly funny, magnetic, with a feral intelligence. He was a monster and a badass. He was petty and powerful. He was a winner.

There was a push-pull to him, as there was with many antiheroes. He was an indictment of male aggression and entitlement. But he was also a fantasy of it. As Brett Martin notes in his study of anti-hero drama, *Difficult Men*, Tony and the characters who came after him tended to be middle-aged white men with power and angst— very much like the TV executives who put these shows on the air.

When *The Sopranos* portrayed civilians outside the mob— especially men—they often came across like the "regular schnooks" Henry Hill disparaged in *Goodfellas*: weak, small, envious. Tony's friend, the restaurateur Artie Bucco, was attracted to the power of his Mob connections, though his entanglements with them were ruinous. In the season 2 episode "Bust Out," Tony took advantage of the gambling addiction of his high-school friend Davey Scatino (Robert Patrick) to bleed his sporting-goods store dry. When Davey asked why Tony let him in a high-stakes card game when he knew Davey would ruin himself, Tony alluded to the fable about a scorpion who stings a frog carrying him across a river: "It's my nature. Frog and the scorpion, ya know?"

David Chase, the show's creator, was a product of, and refugee from, old-school broadcast TV, having written for the detective show *The Rockford Files* and the lighthearted *Northern Exposure*. *The Sopranos* was in part an answer to TV's tyranny of likability. Starting with *The Sopranos*, this would be a theme of many HBO dramas, which used popcorn-entertainment genres (the mob saga in *The Sopranos*, the Western in *Deadwood*, the cop show in *The Wire*) to interrogate the brutalities of American life the way that 1970s Hollywood movies had (*The Godfather, McCabe & Mrs. Miller, The French Connection*).

Chase never softened Tony, as often happens in long-running shows. If anything, he made him more reprehensible as he saw Tony developing admirers. But he also didn't feel obligated to deliver Tony his just deserts. Chase held to a dark view of human nature. People don't change. People who do evil rationalize it, and people who benefit from it—like Tony's wife, Carmela—learn to look the other way. Tony operated in an amoral universe through the end of the series, which cut to black, leaving the audience to wonder if Tony had been murdered by a mysterious man in a Members Only jacket or went on to live a long life. "The object of all these shows in the past had always been, the protagonist pays for his sins," Chase said. "Crime doesn't pay. Well, that's false. Crime *does* pay."

If there would be a judgment on Tony, God would not supply it, the guy in the Members Only jacket would not supply it, and *The Sopranos* would not supply it. It would have to come from you.

* * * *

AFTER *THE SOPRANOS*, this became a theme of many of TV's most ambitious dramas. Some antiheroes break the law, some don't. But all of them break conventions. Each of these shows reveals that the norms of moral and social behavior are not iron rules but thin tissue.

They make the same behavior seductive and repugnant: urbane Don Draper cradling an old-fashioned, sloppy-drunk Don Draper puking into a toilet. They repurpose the *Easy Rider* spirit of 1960s rebellion: the antihero won't play by your rules, *man*, and won't have his self-expression squelched. They suggest not only that immorality can be rewarded, but that the reward for a quiet life can be loserdom and bitterness.

Where conventional TV dramas generally aimed to reassure you, restoring balance and a sense of moral order by the end of an hour, antihero dramas aimed to unsettle, while you were watching and afterward. (Also in contrast to older dramas, they were usually serial stories, which put off closure until the end of the series—and some, like *The Sopranos*, refused it even then.) Who were you rooting for, and why? What's the incentive to do good in a world in which doing bad pays better? What if the thing you're best at is terrible?

That was the question of *Breaking Bad*, a series, premiering in 2008, that was constructed as an extended moral test. Walter White (Bryan Cranston), a chemist who contributed to Nobel Prize–winning research, now an Albuquerque high school chemistry teacher with a haggard face and a mustache drooping in defeat, is diagnosed with lung cancer. The treatment might bankrupt him, and his death would leave his family destitute. He hits on a desperate solution: using his scientific skills to cook the best crystal meth in the American Southwest.

His new career puts him at risk of jail—his brother-in-law is a Drug Enforcement Agency officer—and puts him in the company of dangerous gangsters. He learns to scheme, strike deals, and kill. He becomes good at it, applying his training toward better criminality through science. (In one episode, he uses a massive electromagnet to destroy electronic evidence in a police station.) He rises from cook to kingpin, eventually running the area drug trade under the pseudonym "Heisenberg."

There's a moral arc running in the opposite direction of Walt's criminal arc. As he rises in the drug trade, the creator, Vince Gilligan, dismantles his rationalizations, one by one. A successful colleague offers to pay for his treatment; he keeps selling meth. His cancer goes into remission; he keeps selling. He builds the nest egg he originally set as his target to ensure his family would be provided for, and much more. Still he doesn't stop. In the end, it's not about the money or his family, but his sense of purpose. He has, he admits in the finale, no rationalization. "I did it for me," he says. "I liked it. I was good at it. I was alive."

Gilligan, in contrast with Chase, very consciously set *Breaking*

Bad in a universe of judgment and punishment: in the end Walt loses the love of his family and dies alone, and, well, "bad" is in the title. "I like to believe there is some comeuppance," Gilligan has said, "that karma kicks in at some point, even if it takes years or decades to happen."

In the meantime, however, we're watching Walt's story. And it's incredibly exciting and audacious. The show is funny and thrilling and beautifully shot; it has the epic sweep of a Western. Walt's transformation into Heisenberg is a story of self-reinvention, a tradition of American literature that's tragic and alluring: it's James Gatz becoming Jay Gatsby, Huck Finn lighting out for the territory. Cranston, like Gandolfini, is too good an actor to make his character merely despicable. Even though—even *if*—you want Walt to pay, you wish, as a viewer, for this terrific story to keep going. Which means you want him to succeed. Just a little longer.

Making the viewer complicit—making you horrified at what you find yourself wanting—is the active ingredient in *Breaking Bad*. But it is a volatile compound. It allows for viewers who, as with Archie Bunker, decide that Walt is an unambiguous hero, who want their wishes gratified and don't want to have to feel guilty about it—what the *New Yorker* critic Emily Nussbaum calls "bad fans": "the *Sopranos* buffs who wanted a show made up of nothing but whackings (and posted eagerly about how they fast-forwarded past anything else)."

To the bad fans, Walter White wasn't a cautionary tale. He was awesome. He was a winner. His masculinity wasn't toxic; it was just being a goddam *man*. And in the words of *Breaking Bad*'s fried-chicken-entrepreneur/drug lord Gustavo Fring, "A man provides."

The gender overtones of all this weren't incidental. Antihero dramas tended to put men at the center. There were occasional well-rounded exceptions, like Carrie Mathison of *Homeland* and Alicia Florrick of *The Good Wife*, or icy villainesses, like Patty Hewes of *Damages* and Cersei of *Game of Thrones*. TV's antiheroines tended to appear in comedies, where the transgressions were more social than criminal—the soused cynics of *Absolutely Fabulous* and the self-centered hipsters of *Girls*—or comedy-dramas like *Weeds*, a precursor of *Breaking Bad*, which straddled the categories. As a whole, though, the antihero drama genre was a demonstration of the license American culture permits to men and denies to women.

These fans were especially tough on the female characters. Walt's wife, Skyler (Anna Gunn), took particular abuse from a fan base that saw her as a wet blanket and hypocrite who ruined the best parts of the show. This, critic Alan Sepinwall pointed out in *The Revolution Was Televised*, was a general byproduct of the male-antihero genre: "characters who on paper should be the sympathetic ones become hated by viewers for opposing the protagonist." In a *New York Times* op-ed, Gunn described getting hate mail and personal threats from male fans. "I finally realized," she wrote, "that most people's hatred of Skyler had little to do with me and a lot to do with their own perception of women and wives." (This was also a dynamic that female politicians were deeply familiar with.)

Unfortunately, one person's horror story is another's how-to manual. *The Sopranos* was, in part, a story of mobsters who learned how to be mobsters by watching mob movies. The characters debated *The Godfather* (Tony preferred *Part II*) and idolized Martin Scorsese. And the show's popularity added another meta-layer, life imitating art imitating life imitating art. On surveillance tapes, members of the New Jersey DeCavalcante crime family were captured gossiping about the show, trying to see if any of Tony's crew were modeled on themselves—"I'm not even existing over there," moaned one, feeling left out—and marveling at the drama: "Every show you watch, more and more you pick up somebody. What characters!" (Life imitated, or parodied, mob movies in Trump's presidency too. Roger Stone, the political dirty trickster indicted for obstruction and witness tampering in the Russia investigation, was quoted pressuring a witness to "do a 'Frank Pentangeli,'" referring to the character from *The Godfather: Part II* who is bullied into recanting his testimony on the stand.)

This is not to say that any of these dramas endorses bad behavior.

But they do require viewers, with every story, to reargue to themselves why they should behave well. This is their power, and their danger. In the same way that a joke is funnier if you get the punch line than if someone explains it to you, the moral force of a story like *Breaking Bad* or *The Sopranos* relies on your engaging with it. That's what makes this kind of drama more challenging, more complex, and ultimately more rewarding than the simply moralistic series of TV's early years.

But it's *hard*. It's much harder than simply being handed a set of moral premises and being told: you should do what is right because the opposite is wrong and you will be punished. It's hard work to reaffirm your morality in the face of stories that say, as life often does, that you may only suffer for being good, that crime may in fact pay.

These stories share, with much great art, the possibility of being read differently. They say: you can get farther in this world by doing wrong, *and yet* you can choose to do right. There is no way of ensuring that every viewer will get past *and yet*. There is a morality to antihero fiction, or there can be, but it's a complicated *and yet* one, like the morality of a religion with no heaven or hell.

These stories don't make people, in the aggregate, better or worse. But they do provide a different kind of story to tell for someone who wants to sell himself as a leader in a world where nice guys finish last, the kind of not-so-nice guy you need to get the job done.

THAT SORT OF ARGUMENT became more acceptable in public discourse after September 11, 2001. Three thousand civilians died out of the blue on a workday morning in a terrorist attack that unfolded on live TV. Americans were terrified. Rumors flew. A few media and government offices were mailed envelopes containing anthrax spores—with letters claiming a link to Islamic terrorism that was ultimately ruled out—and Americans were consumed with worries about a plague. Nor was only the public on edge. One week in October 2001, the George W. Bush administration believed that al-Qaeda had snuck a nuclear device into New York City.

Everyday life suddenly felt like an overwritten Tom Clancy thriller. Amid this atmosphere of dread and apocalypse, the philosophy of antihero entertainment—that life was a pitched battle, in which the meek and virtuous ended up dead—became more popular and feasible in both television and actual politics. (Fifteen years later, conservative essayist Michael Anton would call 2016 "The Flight 93 Election," in which he likened Republicans rallying behind the antihero Trump to the passengers who stormed the cockpit on one doomed flight—desperate people taking an act to avoid extinction.)

Five days after the attacks, Vice President Dick Cheney told Tim Russert on *Meet the Press* that we could no longer afford scruples. Beyond a conventional military response, "We also have to work, though, sort of the dark side, if you will," he said. "If you're going to deal only with sort of officially approved, certified good guys, you're not going to find out what the bad guys are doing. You need to be able to penetrate these organizations. You need to have on the payroll some very unsavory characters."

In prime-time TV, one unsavory character was about to be added to the payroll. Fox's terrorism thriller *24* was conceived months before 9/11. The first-season storyline involved a plot by Serbian, not Muslim, terrorists, and the show's intended hook was not its subject matter but the gimmick that every episode's action would take place in real time, a single day unfolding over twenty-four episodes. After the attacks, there was speculation that the pilot—which included an airliner exploding in midair—could never be broadcast.

But it was broadcast, in November, almost unchanged (the barest snippet of the explosion was clipped), and it became an instant hit, thanks largely to the protagonist, Jack Bauer (Kiefer Sutherland), a counterterrorist agent who accumulated frequent-flyer miles to the dark side.

In some ways, Bauer was a conventional hero. He suffered personal losses (his wife was raped and murdered by her terrorist captors, and the first season ends with him cradling her dead body). He was rugged, weary, his eyes icy green-blue and without illusion. He was willing to sacrifice his health and happiness for his country.

But above all, he sacrificed his morality. In the third season, he executed an innocent man to forestall an attack. In the fourth, he electrocuted another innocent to extract information. Torture was Bauer's Swiss Army knife, his universal solvent. He broke fingers and legs. He threatened to make a suspect swallow a towel, after which he'd yank it out, taking the man's stomach lining with it.

That the torture and threats of it usually worked was as much a function of the needs of hour-long drama as a political statement. A thriller—especially one that plays out in real time—needs high stakes that are resolved quickly. Here, that meant the "ticking time bomb" scenario: a nuke is going to go off, the virus is going to be released, and one bad guy has the answers. Torture yields answer yields saving the day with seconds to spare.

In real life the time-bomb situation rarely manifests and torture doesn't produce reliable results. But military officers had to deal with soldiers who now believed, because of *24*—whose DVDs were passed around in Iraq—that torture worked. The idea passed into politics and the news, where it was then laundered into living rooms as fact. In the 2008 primary debates, candidates of both parties were asked if they'd approve torturing a detainee in a time-bomb situation. "Don't we have the right and responsibility to beat it out of him?" Russert asked the Democratic candidates. In a 2016 debate, Donald Trump endorsed threatening the families of terror suspects—an idea straight from *24*, season 2, episode 12.

24 implied a larger message: that in this sick world being nasty was necessary, even noble. The show complicated the idea, often movingly: Sutherland showed how a life of brutality aged Bauer into a joyless martyr. But he was finally unrepentant. At a Senate hearing in season 7, he admitted to a sanctimonious senator that he had tortured a suspect, in violation of the Geneva Convention, but added:

"The people that I deal with, they don't care about your rules. All they care about is a result. . . . Don't sit there with that smug look on your face and expect me to regret the decisions I've made. Because the truth is, I don't."

* * * *

THERE HAD BEEN a belief in American civics, or at least a commonly accepted piety, that our leaders and protectors should be good people. If necessary, goodness was retrofitted onto them. Disney's *Davy Crockett*, in the sanitized prime time of the 1950s, emphasized its hero's fighting on behalf of Native Americans, when in real life his main focus had been the land rights of his white constituents.

This mythmaking was always complicated and a little winking. Adults understood that George Washington could tell a lie like anyone else. But after 9/11, antihero culture openly raised the question of how much goodness we required in our protectors, and how much was a liability.

"What price safety?" was a natural question for police dramas. But for decades, broadcast TV set boundaries around it. The pioneering *Hill Street Blues* ran up against hard limits. One draft script had a detective smashing a coin box at a laundry to make a phone call. The producers argued that real-life police did break laws while enforcing the law, and besides, the scene helped establish the character, a shady cop with a penchant for schemes. But the NBC standards department of 1981 forbade any "depiction of the police as being casually indifferent to the law."

In spring 2002, the cable channel FX premiered *The Shield*, another drama conceived before 9/11 that had new, greater resonance afterward. The creator, Shawn Ryan, had kicked around on broadcast-network shows like the formula cop drama *Nash Bridges*. Given a challenge/dare by a studio executive—"What would you like to write?"—he settled on an idea inspired by a Los Angeles police scandal of the 1990s: the story of a cop who was brutal, corrupt, and very good at his job.

Vic Mackey (Michael Chiklis) heads the Strike Team, an elite anti-gang unit that has become a kind of separate, unaccountable police force within the LAPD. They routinely skim the proceeds of their gang busts. At the end of the pilot, Vic shoots one of his own team members—making the murder look like a fatality in the line of duty—because the man was an informant investigating the Strike Team undercover.

Brawny and shave-headed, Vic looks like a human bullet for whom the world is a target. In a mission-statement scene, he walks into the interrogation room with a pedophile whom the competent, by-the-book detectives have not managed to crack. He unpacks a paper bag—whiskey bottle, box cutter, cigarette lighter—and says he's going to use the contents to get the man to talk. "Your turn to play bad cop?" the creep says. "Nah," Vic says. "Good cop and bad cop left for the day. I'm a different kind of cop." Vic punches him in the throat, goes to work on him with a telephone book, and comes back with the information.

The Shield was not so much a story of law and order as law versus order. In Vic Mackey's view, better to maintain order than follow the law. Innocent people lived because Vic broke the rules. If you see Vic as the bad cop, his answer is not that he's the good cop—it's that good and bad are irrelevant. You could see Mackey, confident and unrepentant, as a working-class version of an ancient tragic hero like Shakespeare's Coriolanus, the inflexible and proud Roman general who believes that his victories should put him beyond criticism by the public, which in his eyes is weak and inconstant and should shut up and be grateful to him. If police dramas are often the continuation of war by other means, then *The Shield* spoke to a war whose propagators were asking Americans to accept "dark side" tactics overseas and the restriction of liberties at home.

The Shield ultimately believed that safety did not justify thugocracy; Vic was eventually exposed and had an ignominious downfall. But where old network police dramas were designed to make a moral conclusion as easy as possible, *The Shield* made it more powerful but more difficult to reach, by making an abstract question concrete: would you rather die than be saved by a bad person?

* * * *

THE ANTIHERO ALSO THRIVED in post-9/11 comic-book movies, many of whose superheroes could be said to be superantiheroes. This was especially true of the grim, tortured, morally compromised heroes of the DC Comics adaptations. DC's chief heroes, Superman and Batman—the benevolent alien and the stealthy vigilante—date back to the 1930s, and they've changed to suit their times. In World War II, they were enlisted for the allied effort (in one *Action Comics* cover, Superman clobbers the prow of a German warship that's just sunk a passenger vessel); in the 1950s, George Reeves played an All-American, clean-cut version of the Man of Steel for TV; in 1978, Christopher Reeve reimagined him as a sensitive, introspective big-screen hunk.

The post-9/11 versions of these heroes in some ways have more in common with Jack Bauer than with their own mid-twentieth-century incarnations. In *Man of Steel*, Superman defies the decades-old dictum that the character never kill, and dispatches the villain Zod by snapping his neck. Their enemies, meanwhile, are motivated not by greed but by irrational cruelty. The quintessential modern DC villain is probably the Joker of the 2008 Batman film *The Dark Knight*, played with inchoate mania by Heath Ledger, his clown makeup slashing a red wound across his face. "Some men aren't looking for anything logical like money," Batman's valet, Alfred Pennyworth, says of him. "They can't be bought, bullied, reasoned, or negotiated with. Some men just want to watch the world burn." To foil him, Batman sets up a domestic surveillance system and employs torture. Some men, the movie says, can't be defeated by good guys.

Superman, Batman, and company have escaped countless scrapes over the decades; they have been imprisoned, tortured, dipped in acid, killed, and resurrected. But they have perhaps never been conquered so thoroughly as they were by the antihero ethos. In this era, not even Superman could be upstanding, uncompromised, and without moral complication. We are all down in the muck together, these movies tell us. Virtue is the way to extinction. People are not so good, you are not so good—even *Batman* is not so good. And if you love your family more than you do your precious moral self-regard, then you will get your goddam hands dirty and do what needs to be done—or at least get out of the way of those who are not too simon-pure and virginal to do it.

There was one figure to whom this kind of argument was irresistible, and ultimately useful: a millionaire playboy who lived atop a tower with his name on it and who would make the narrative of antiheroism another handy gadget in his utility belt. Donald Trump made the argument that kindness was a liability against enemies who wanted to see the world burn, that the world, in fact, *was already on fire*, and that someone like him, someone outside the normal structures of power, someone unencumbered by scruple, needed to be given a free hand to extinguish it.

He accessorized himself, like the Caped Crusader, with objects that carried his brand and signified power—skyscrapers, boats, planes. At the beginning of his presidential campaign, in summer 2015, he took that helicopter to the Iowa State Fair, an aerial show of force that kicked up dust and scattered the publicity hopes of his rivals in the wake of its rotor blades. The outing recalled the scene in *The Plot Against America*, the Philip Roth alternative-history novel that imagined the election of an anti-Semitic, fascist-sympathizing American government led by Charles Lindbergh (whose slogan "America First" Trump in fact revived for his own campaign), in which the flyboy president wowed the public by zooming his jet over the Potomac. (Roth's image, in turn, echoed the opening of Leni Riefenstahl's propaganda masterpiece *Triumph of the Will*, in which

Adolf Hitler arrives for the Nazi Party Congress soaring in his airplane above parting clouds over Nuremberg, framed like a god from the heavens.)

Trump took delighted children up in the air for rides, over and over, up and down, and as the Trumpcopter awaited one takeoff, an excited little boy, recording the candidate on video, asked the flashy tycoon who had descended from the sky over the cornfields, "Mr. Trump: Are you Batman?"

When the boy posted the video on Facebook, Trump's answer went viral: "I am Batman."

MONEY MONEY MONEY MONEY!

CABLE ANTIHERO DRAMAS LIKE *THE SOPRANOS* HAD A CUMU-
lative audience of millions; the dark superhero movies of the 2000s
were among the highest-grossing films of all time. But arguably the
genre that did the most to popularize the concept of the antihero is
one not generally associated with it: reality TV. Reality shows both
appealed to the thirst for authenticity—though their setups were
contrived and their stories edited—and promised a peep into real-
ities more exciting than your own. But also, unusually for broadcast TV, they featured protagonists who weren't conventionally
likeable—who echoed the notion, reverberating across the culture,
that this was not a world made for nice people.

The stakes in these shows were not life and death. But their philosophy vibed with a certain sharp-elbowed spirit of the age. It's a
cutthroat, zero-sum world, they said. For you to win, someone has
to lose, and when someone else gains, it is at your expense. Maybe
you have to cheat and lie, but aren't you doing it for the right reasons? To feed your kids? To achieve your dreams? To find someone
to love? Then get out there and do what you've got to do. Sometimes
you have to work the dark side.

* * * *

ON FEBRUARY 15, 2000, the network reality-TV era arrived with the lurid shivaree of *Who Wants to Marry a Multi-Millionaire?*, a Fox prime-time special that demonstrated that there was ratings gold in a pursuit for the affections of a man of questionably inflated wealth.

In this two-hour beauty-pageant-cum-meat-market, fifty young women—chosen from 3,000 auditioners nationwide—vied for the hand in marriage of Rick Rockwell, a jut-jawed motivational speaker from San Diego. They wore wedding dresses. They participated in a swimsuit contest, because, host Jay Thomas said, their husband-to-be wanted to be sure his lady would be "as comfortable on the beach as he is." The ten semifinalists were asked "personality test" questions, such as whether they'd mind their husband going to a strip club. Finally, Rockwell made his selection, dropped on one knee, then wed emergency-department nurse Darva Conger in a civil ceremony under a floral arch large enough to double as the funeral wreath for Western civilization.

The show was the definition of a word-of-mouth success. The Nielsen ratings built by the half hour: 10 million, 12.3 million, 18.9 million, 22.8 million. In those numbers you can practically hear the phones ringing across the country, friends telling friends, "You will not fucking believe what is on Fox right now."

By any common-sense measure, every word in the title *Who Wants to Marry a Multi-Millionaire?* was specious except the "Who" and the question mark. The "marriage" lasted seven weeks before Conger—who walked away with prizes including a new Isuzu Trooper and a three-carat diamond ring—got an annulment. (She auctioned off the ring.) And Rockwell, a onetime comedian and actor whose credits included *Killer Tomatoes Eat France!*, was a multi-millionaire only by the most generous measure. Fox contended that he was worth $2 million, with $750,000 in liquid assets. His 1,200-

square-foot house in Encinitas, California, had two broken toilets in the back yard.

But it's not as if the millions in the audience, by and large, thought they were seeing true love bloom before their eyes. They were watching spectacle: the breaking of a TV taboo, the self-satisfaction of watching what other people will do for (theoretical) money and (definite) media exposure. The marriage might be fake; the millions might be illusory. But the metadrama—the drive to appear on and "win" a TV show—was real.

Multi-Millionaire was the brainchild of Mike Darnell, a Fox executive in charge of "special programming," a category that had included *Alien Autopsy: Fact or Fiction?*, built around a hoax video of an ET's dissection. He was inspired, he said, by attending a cousin's wedding. A wedding is, after all, a staged event, complete with an audience and roles (groomsman, bridesmaid, officiant), rich with symbols of love, winners and losers (catch that bouquet!), and the hope for a prosperous future: "wish fulfillment," as they say in the biz.

Not long after the show aired, Rockwell was revealed to have had a restraining order for alleged domestic abuse, a scandal that killed *Multi-Millionaire* as a franchise. But the ratings incited interest in reality TV as a genre. Darnell would go on to bring more and less respectable reality hits to Fox, from the lust-on-the-beach bacchanal *Temptation Island* to the aspirational singing contest *American Idol*. The special's producer, Mike Fleiss, would create ABC's *The Bachelor*.

And the gross, captivating two hours of *Who Wants to Marry a Multi-Millionaire?* contained within it the kernel of the entire reality TV genre to come. Shock. Greed. Pumped-up drama. Zero-sum competition. Sex. And above all, the relentless challenging of norms: the feeling that you were watching a thing that you were not supposed to be able to see on TV—and yet here it was.

* * * *

REALITY TV IS almost as old as TV itself. In 1948 Allen Funt brought
his radio prank show, *The Candid Microphone*, to television, where
it became *Candid Camera*. As important as the practical jokes—
e.g., a woman would ask passersby to help with a broken-down car,
which turned out to have no engine—was the "reveal," in which
Funt would tell his marks: "Smile! You're on *Candid Camera*."

It was a simple gag comedy, but like many later reality shows, it
had a layer of social experiment. You were also seeing how people
would respond to someone in distress, or how they would handle
being duped. (The show's training of its audience was so successful
that in 1969, when hijackers took control of an airplane Funt was
flying on, his fellow passengers assumed they were being pranked.)

Cheap nonfiction entertainments—game shows, dating shows,
variety shows, talk shows, *The Gong Show*—were TV staples for
decades, evolving with the times. In the 1950s, *You Asked for It* presented dangerous live stunts at the audience's request. At the tail end
of the populist '70s, NBC's *Real People* valorized unsung Americans:
turkey callers, senior-citizen disco dancers, and Tom "Wrong Way"
Wooten, who pedaled a bicycle backwards across the United States.

There were also occasional standouts of ambition. In 1973, PBS
aired *An American Family*, a twelve-episode cinema-verité narrative
about the Louds, of Santa Barbara, California. It was meant to chron-
icle ordinary middle-class life; it ended up capturing the breakup of
Bill and Pat Loud's marriage and the coming-out of their gay son,
Lance. The show was criticized as intrusive, destructive, and manipulated for drama—but it was also a national obsession, a stunning document of American society's *All in the Family* moment of upheaval.

You couldn't re-create the found drama of a series like that. But
you could create the conditions for drama, which was the idea behind
MTV's *The Real World* in 1992. Inspired by *An American Family*,
producers Mary-Ellis Bunim and Jonathan Murray devised a format
in which a group of young strangers would live in a house, cameras
would roll, and what would happen would happen. What happened

ranged from hookups to alcohol abuse to violence to various brands of interpersonal friction.

The third season, set in San Francisco, had its own Loud Family moment of social relevance, with the story of Pedro Zamora, a gay AIDS activist who had the disease himself. Zamora was not only a rare gay personality on national TV, he would for some viewers be the first person they knew living with AIDS—and, the day after the season finale aired, he would be the first person they knew to die from it.

The story was not happenstance. Zamora was intentionally cast, as was David "Puck" Rainey, a belligerent bike messenger who provided much of the rest of the season's drama by traumatizing his housemates. But *The Real World* promised, and often delivered, something beyond just drama. Its introduction promised to show what happened "when people stop being polite and start getting real."

In other words, the promise of *The Real World*, and decades of reality TV that followed it, was authenticity. It argued that there was something genuine in human interaction that TV didn't show you, because TV was too bound by commercial pressures, the mores of its audience, the artifice of genres like sitcom and cop show.

But it was more than that, *The Real World*'s slogan implied: *actual people* didn't show you their real selves either. They were socialized to be "polite," which, the show's introduction implied, meant fake. In *The Real World*'s progressive formulation, this was small-c conservative inhibition, but in the early 1990s political conservatives were making a parallel argument. In 1991, I sat in a packed crowd at the University of Michigan's football stadium, where the commencement speaker, president George H. W. Bush, made his first public attack on "political correctness"—which he said "declares certain topics off-limits, certain expression off-limits, even certain gestures off-limits"—to an audience of students who would watch the premiere of *The Real World* a year later.

By a few seasons into its run, an appearance on *The Real World* was a highly sought-after résumé item—a basic-cable Rhodes scholarship, drawing over 35,000 applicants a year. One housemate, Sean Duffy, parlayed his fame from season 6 to become a Republican congressman from Wisconsin. His wife, Rachel Campos-Duffy—a conservative who struck up an unlikely friendship with Zamora in season 3—became an omnipresent commentator on Fox News.

Young people knew *The Real World* was a construct; it acknowledged that, which played to the Generation X impulse to be suspicious of mediation, not to be a sucker. Reality fans might not know exactly how their shows were manipulated—how participants were plied with alcohol on dating shows, or how scenes filmed at different times were stitched together to seem like a real-time interaction. ("Frankenbiting" was the term of art.) But they knew that something like *The Real World* was a created environment, like a workplace, which in fact it was. Reality TV required a stance that was simultaneously credulous and skeptical: the awareness that you were being manipulated was part of the entertainment. The "reality" that reality fans were watching, then, was that of people authentically responding to a fabricated environment—the real experience of being on a TV show.

* * * *

SO WHO WANTS TO MARRY A MULTI-MILLIONAIRE? was nothing new, per se. But it was in a new place: on a major TV network, at the top of the ratings.

In 2000, traditional broadcast TV was in a commercial, artistic, and existential crisis. First, the fragmentation of media—all those cable channels—meant that even the most popular shows now had lower ratings. But hit shows with celebrity actors, like *Friends* and *ER*, weren't getting any cheaper to make. Second, *The Sopranos*, which had premiered the year before, was the kind of pop-culture sensation that the broadcast networks couldn't create. HBO wasn't policed by the Federal Communications Commission, because it didn't use the public airwaves, so it could air as much profanity and show as many naked strippers at the Bada Bing as it cared to.

But even if you suspended the FCC content rules, the old networks couldn't make an equivalent to *The Sopranos*. It was too demanding. Like a literary novel, the show had a dense serial plot, explored moral gray areas, and required close attention to details and subtext. Because HBO's viewers paid to watch, *The Sopranos* only needed those viewers who were *really* into *The Sopranos*. The big networks couldn't afford that.

Next to cable, network entertainment was simply . . . boring.

Who Wants to Marry a Multi-Millionaire? was vile, reductive, exploitative, outrageous, caricaturing, sexist, and stupid. But it was not boring. Reality TV had its own version of the HBO value proposition: here is something TV didn't used to give you. It challenged the norms and pieties of traditional TV storytelling.

Survivor, which premiered on CBS in May 2000, combined the voyeuristic shock appeal (and bikinis) of *Multi-Millionaire* with the stakes of a game show and the pretensions of, as its executive producer Mark Burnett grandly liked to call it, a "social experiment." Sixteen contestants, living as a "tribe" in Borneo, had to work together for food and shelter, while also voting members off one by one until the last one standing won a million dollars. Nominally, the show was about humans against nature. The real game, and the real attraction, was human against human.

The first season's master of the "social game" was corporate consultant Richard Hatch, who would become the first of many reality-TV antiheroes. He was openly gay—a rarity on network TV in 2000—and he stood out early on for his habit of striding around the beach naked, his torso pale and fleshy, his nethers pixellated for prime time. But above all he was first to crack the idea that the key to this game was not wilderness skills but shamelessness and the will to flout social norms: to lie, to make alliances and break them, to convince people that it's in their interest to hold their nose and work with you until you no longer need them. In the finale, his vanquished opponents awarded him the million bucks in spite of this, or rather because of it. They recognized that he outplayed them.

Early on, there was a moral panic around *Survivor*, its critics arguing that it was spiritually corrosive and celebrated bad behavior. This was simplistic. (I speak as someone who's watched the show religiously since the first season.) A level of moralism was built into *Survivor*—as with a soap opera, you couldn't really enjoy it without judging the "characters." If anything, the show was didactically moral; one season, featuring returning players, was subtitled *Heroes vs. Villains*. Going into the season 1 finale, most audience members polled were rooting not for Hatch but Rudy Boesch, a seventy-two-year-old former Navy SEAL—as was the host, Jeff Probst. "Everybody on the crew wanted Rudy to win," he recalled. "The only outcome nobody wanted was Richard Hatch winning . . . [It] would be a disaster."

In fact, the audience shrugged it off. What *Survivor*, and shows like it, did do when it came to their antiheroes was to invite you to compartmentalize morality from outcome. The logic of a Tribal Council vote isn't, "Richard is not really bad." It's: "Richard is bad, but he's entertaining, and he played a great game."

Many reality shows would invite the same logic: Maybe *American Idol*'s Simon Cowell was cruel when he destroyed another off-pitch singer scratching the nails of her ambition down the chalkboard of her limited ability. But he was *right*—he was just willing to say what the rest of us would be afraid to. Would you want your kids to be like Richard Hatch? Maybe not. But did he deserve to win? Hey: it takes a crooked guy to win a crooked game in a crooked world! Courtney Robertson, after winning *The Bachelor*, wrote a memoir whose title could well be the motto of the genre, if not of this entire era of American history: *I Didn't Come Here to Make Friends*.

But *Survivor* was more than a soap opera, a man-vs.-nature story, a sporting event, and *Lord of the Flies*. It was also a masterpiece of applied postmodernism, a faux reality built entirely from simulacra of the real world, an imitation of life more satisfying and pliant to the creator's will than reality itself could ever be. It was laden with enough signifiers and signs to keep a semiotician occupied for years. And though it was created by a British man (Mark Burnett) using the template of a Swedish series (*Expedition Robinson*), it was, in its determination to tame actual nature into a submissive, stylized replication of itself, thoroughly American.

For his 1975 essay "Travels in Hyperreality," Umberto Eco traveled across America exploring the country's fascination with simulations and reproductions, "instances where the American imagination demands the real thing and, to attain it, must fabricate the absolute fake." He visited a re-creation of Lyndon B. Johnson's Oval Office in Austin, Texas; a re-created nineteenth-century farm on Long Island; and—of course—Disneyland, where he rode a boat down a simulated wild river.

An animatronic crocodile in the river at Disneyland, Eco argued, is more satisfying than an actual crocodile in the wild, because it conforms to our *idea* of a crocodile better than the real, living thing does. "A real crocodile can be found in the zoo, and as a rule it is dozing or hiding," he writes, but through Disney's reliably menacing robo-crocs, "faked nature corresponds much more to our daydream demands."

Survivor took place on the daydream of a desert island. What does that mean? Well, what would you draw in a cartoon? What had you seen on *Gilligan's Island*? (In the first season, contestant Greg Buis, intuiting that *Survivor* was a TV concept of an island built out of previous TV concepts of islands, pretended to talk on a "coconut phone" like Gilligan had.) There needs to be sand. There need to be palm trees and coconuts. There need to be machetes and bamboo huts and treasure maps—all the accoutrements stored in your subconscious in a trunk labeled "Desert Island." On *Survivor*, nature wears itself as a costume, like a celebrity walking on set for a sitcom cameo "as himself."

Burnett deployed iconography as if designing a religious liturgy. Each contestant was given a tiki-style torch, which was extinguished when he or she was eliminated. "Fire represents life," host Jeff Probst intoned. The show loved nature allegory: it intercut scenes of contestants scheming with footage of insects preying, rats scuttling, snakes slithering. Life, the visuals said, is a struggle red in tooth and claw, and—even if this was a show about people "surviving" while trailed by camera crews—it was giving you the real-deal version of mankind's true state. In the season 1 finale, Susan Hawk, a truck driver from Wisconsin, endorsed eventual winner Richard by comparing him and runner-up Kelly Wiglesworth to feral creatures: "I believe we owe it to the island spirits we have come to know to let it end in the way that Mother Nature intended: for the snake to eat the rat."

* * * *

SURVIVOR WAS ACCOMPANIED that same summer by CBS's *Big Brother*, another European import, which applied the same crabs-in-a-barrel approach to contestants sequestered together in a house wired with cameras. In the eighteenth century, the English philosopher Jeremy Bentham proposed the panopticon, a prison in which any inmate might be under surveillance at any time, so that all prisoners would constantly have to mind their behavior. *Big Brother* and its followers were the panopticon in reverse. Continuously being watched meant continually acting out, the better to make it into the final edit.

There was a short-lived sentiment, after the 9/11 attacks, that a new, more sober era of wartime would be the end of reality TV. Surely, in dark times, people would turn to more wholesome entertainment. Surely, a series called *Survivor* would seem glib, insensitive, out of touch at a time when towers were collapsing and the country was preparing for two wars, in Afghanistan and Iraq. Like so many literal-minded attempts to bet against the unkillability of the American entertainment impulse, this one was dead wrong. Reality TV did not just survive 9/11. It became the defining entertainment form of the 2000s. Like the sci-fi B movies of the Cold War, reality shows, with their themes of constant strife and competition, were a palatable way of processing the angst in the daily news.

Reality shows had, on the one hand, a socially progressive streak:

series like Bravo's makeover show *Queer Eye for the Straight Guy* reflected and encouraged diversity, and reality shows were often more inclusively cast than sitcoms and dramas (even as they played with and against stereotypes). But reality TV also reflected a conservative sentiment: that life was a social-Darwinist competition and that people had gone soft in what was still a hard world. Only you, the individual, could rely on yourself to advance your own interests; the community was an illusion. (If Ayn Rand were born later, she might have conceived *The Fountainhead* not as a novel but an architecture reality show: *Project Skyscraper*.)

Hanging over all this was the populist argument of reality TV, that it represented *you*. TV, it promised, was no longer a velvet-roped club only for the celebrities and the elect. You, or at least someone like you, could get onto the other side.

* * * *

THUS THE GENRE MULTIPLIED. There were dating shows, quiz shows, home-renovation shows and talent shows. There was *Chains of Love, Rock of Love, Flavor of Love*, and *Conveyor Belt of Love*. *American Idol, American Candidate, American Gladiators*, and *American Inventor*. *Design Star, Nashville Star, Rock Star*, and *Dancing with the Stars*. *Joe Millionaire, Average Joe*, and *The Joe Schmo Show*. *Shark Tank, Whale Wars, The Mole*, and *The Swan*. *Fear Factor, The It Factor, The Benefactor*, and *The X Factor*. Some reality shows cast celebrities, like *The Osbournes*, the MTV "reality sitcom" about the home life of Ozzy Osbourne—a heavy-metal terror reinvented as a dotty rich dad. Others created celebrities, like *The Simple Life*, about the exploits of socialite Paris Hilton and her friend Nicole Richie, which premiered weeks after a sex tape of Hilton and her boyfriend was released to the public.

Survivor, meanwhile, was a staggering hit, not simply by the standards of a fragmented media era but by any era. Its first season finale had 51.7 million viewers. The second season was the number-one show on TV. It became such a consistent and established success that its live finale episodes became events in themselves, demanding a dramatic setting.

For the fourth season, that setting was New York's Central Park. On May 19, 2002, an invitation-only crowd squeezed past post-9/11 security to watch host Jeff Probst announce the winner and Rosie O'Donnell emcee a reunion special at Wollman Rink. It was there, on a tiki-beach set constructed atop the park's skating center, that Mark Burnett noticed the signs, in all-capital letters, commemorating the rink's renovation by Donald J. Trump, who, as any Hollywood professional knew, had spent almost a quarter century playing a businessman on TV.

Trump had been approached before by producers about starring in an *Osbournes*-type reality show, but he turned them down. After the *Survivor* finale, Burnett came to him with a different idea: *Survivor* in the business world, an extended "job interview" whose winner would be hired by the Trump Organization.

Burnett made the deal the way contestants would later win out on the show: flattery. "He told me all the right things," Trump said, among them that he had been Burnett's idol since he read *The Art of the Deal* as a young, hustling entrepreneur, selling T-shirts on Venice Beach. It would be a few hours' work a week. It would be convenient: the "boardroom" set—where Trump would meet with and judge contestants—would be built on a floor in Trump Tower.

Above all, it would give Trump, whose job was largely to be famous, the chance to reintroduce his TV character to a new audience. Every week, on national TV, contestants would leave footprints on their rivals' skulls for the chance to win his favor. He would be spoken of reverently. He would be feared and desired. Other reality shows might have a host (Jeff Probst) or a judge (Simon Cowell) or a star (Paris Hilton). Donald Trump would be the host, the judge, the star—and the prize.

Trump brought something more to *The Apprentice* than the ability to offer a job. Reality TV is the art of symbol, and Trump had been amassing signifiers of wealth his entire image-obsessed career. His airplane, a Boeing 727 that he picked up used and plastered with the name TRUMP. The silhouette of a giant "T" standing outside the Trump International hotel. His apartment, an orgasm of gold and chandeliers that outdid the palatial love lairs of *The Bachelor*. The casinos, the helicopter, all branded with his name. Above all, his foundational brand symbol, Trump Tower, which *The Apprentice* would use lavishly.

Trump's set dressing would flash the same signal on *The Apprentice*—"Rich Guy"—that it had on *Lifestyles of the Rich and Famous*, on *60 Minutes*, in *Home Alone 2*, instantly establishing the show's atmosphere and cachet. And Mark Burnett would not have to pay a dime to create them.

Donald Trump had essentially been building a reality-TV set for decades before reality TV existed. His life's work was creating Umberto Eco's daydream simulation of "business," something that, like Disney's mechanical crocodiles, more closely matched the popular fantasy of success than the bloodless, boring machinations of actual business did. He had been playing himself as a character for years. He embodied a lifestyle that was enviable yet accessible. His life looked like the last five seconds of a commercial for scratch-off lottery tickets.

The author Fran Lebowitz would later say that Trump was "a poor person's idea of a rich person." But that's exactly what reality TV is about. *The Bachelor* is a lonely person's idea of love. *Survivor* is a shut-in's idea of nature. *The Apprentice* didn't need a businessman. It needed the *idea* of a businessman. That was Donald Trump. It was the entire point of him. He had spent a lifetime in symbiosis with television, adopting its metabolism, learning to feed its appetites. Now, finally, he would merge with it.

* * * *

THE OPENING SHOT of *The Apprentice*, which premiered in January 2004, places you hurtling toward Manhattan over the water. It is a ride-of-the-Valkyries assault of images of wealth, narrated by Donald Trump:

> New York. My city. [*Video of a teeming Times Square.*] Where the wheels of the global economy never stop turning. A concrete metropolis of unparalleled strength and purpose [*overhead shot of the Chrysler Building*] that drives the business world [*floor of the New York Stock Exchange*]. Manhattan is a tough place. This island is the real jungle. If you're not careful, it can chew you up and spit you out. [*Homeless man, sleeping on a bench.*] But if you work hard [*construction workers toiling on a building*], you can really hit it big, and I mean really big.

Trump didn't just bring his own props to *The Apprentice*. He brought his own stories: the self-aggrandizement of *The Art of the Deal* . . .

> [*Interior of Donald Trump in his limo.*] My name's Donald Trump and I'm the largest real-estate developer in New York. [*Pan down 40 Wall Street, to the lettering "THE TRUMP BUILDING."*] I own buildings all over the place. Model agencies. [*Trump watches a model strut down the catwalk.*] The Miss Universe pageant. Jetliners. Golf courses. Casinos. [*Exterior of the blindingly lit Trump Taj Mahal.*] And private resorts like Mar-a-Lago, one of the most spectacular estates anywhere in the world.

. . . and the face-saving narrative of *The Art of the Comeback*, which the show retold as prologue to its narrative of strivers climbing the jagged glass wall of success:

> But it wasn't always so easy. About 13 years ago, I was seriously in trouble. I was billions of dollars in debt. But I fought back and

I won, big league. I used my brain. [*Trump talks on the phone in his office.*] I used my negotiating skills. [*Trump shakes hands with men in suits.*] And I worked it all out. [*Liveried doormen at the gleaming entrance of Trump Tower.*] Now my company's bigger than it ever was, it's stronger than it ever was, and I'm having more fun than I ever had. [*Trump poses with boxing promoter Don King.*] I've mastered the art of the deal. [*Still-life of Trump: The Game.*] And I've turned the name Trump into the highest quality brand. [*Rows and rows of Trump Ice water bottles.*] And as the master, I want to pass along my knowledge to somebody else.

In barely two minutes, the opening communicates a message that Trump had spent most of the 1990s trying to send: that Donald Trump is not a has-been or a trivia question—he's everywhere and everything. The terms of his survival, his transformation into a figurehead—the introduction glides past all that. (That "I own" in the monologue ignores, for instance, that the Taj Mahal was by then owned, following a prepackaged bankruptcy, by the publicly traded Trump Hotels and Casino Resorts. And "largest real-estate developer"? Well, who's to say what "large" means!)

Like his creditors past, *The Apprentice* is interested in preserving Trump's brand value. Donald Trump's name is on things, the introduction says, on fabulous things—and now it is on NBC, on your TV, the most important real estate in the world.

The opening ends with Trump seated, hunched over, in his helicopter: "Who will succeed? And who will fail? And who will be . . . The Apprentice?" Then, through the magic of editing, we're sucked out of the chopper as it tilts toward the skyline, TRUMP on its side, its passenger lofted above it all.

* * * *

LIKE **SURVIVOR**, *The Apprentice* has a liturgy, every episode following a sequence as ritual as the Catholic mass:

The Opening Hymn. "What if . . . you could have it all?" the opening titles ask, over a golden cross of Manhattan sky and a fisheye shot of a private jet. On the logo, Trump looms over the Manhattan skyline, tall as the Empire State Building, as a man with a briefcase runs toward him desperately. He, or his body double, walks through a doorway, a black silhouette drenched in light (the same way he would walk on stage at the 2016 Republican National Convention). He struts from a limo, a model's pout on his face, hand on his silk tie. The contestants' names run by on stock tickers, amid a dizzying montage of Trump branding. Trump Tower's sharp corners reflect golden light. You hear the heartbeat bassline of "For the Love of Money" by the O'Jays. If you remember only one lyric, it's the infectious chorus: "Money money money money—Money!" For decades, Donald Trump had been a brand. Now he has a jingle.

The Introductory Rites. We join the contestants in their Trump Tower suite, where they get a call on a gold-toned phone—like the one Ivana Trump showed off on *This Old House* two decades before— summoning them to meet "Mr. Trump." (It is always "Mr. Trump.")

The Presentation of the Host. We happen upon Mr. Trump busying himself with business: inspecting a construction site, visiting a golf course, taking a phone call ("Be a hardass, Scott . . . OK, so long"), getting upbeat reports from underlings. ("So Barry, I hear we're killing the competition." "We are!")

The Weekly Text. The two teams, modeled on the competing "tribes" in *Survivor*, get the episode's task, which might involve drawing up an ad campaign or operating a restaurant. The challenges, triumphs, and backbiting, all overseen by Trump's associates, fill the middle of the show, interrupted by—

The Homily. Like Trump's books, *The Apprentice* is pitched as self-help. Each week, Trump delivers a bit of canned wisdom that foreshadows the conflicts that will play out in the challenge. "Don't negotiate with underlings." "Nobody else is going to fight for you."

"The leader that wants to be popular, that leader is never going to be successful." Having listened as a boy to self-help minister Norman Vincent Peale preaching the power of positive thinking, he is now assuming the pulpit.

The Offering of Gifts. After the task, the winning team collects a reward, which is usually Donald Trump. They dine with him at the 21 Club's "Fred Trump Table" and jet off to his Florida palace, Mar-a-Lago. In the first episode, they visit his apartment—Heaven, if Liberace were God—the camera lingering on the statuary, fountains, and gilded ceilings to the swell of synthesizer strings and a chorus. The apartment was made for this kind of public display, even if Trump tells the winners, "I show this apartment to very few people. Presidents. Kings." And now, by Nielsen's estimate, around 18.5 million Americans.

The Confession of Sins. The losers repair to the boardroom, where, Trump warns, "somebody will be fired." The soundstage corporate lair is inky-dark as an old master painting. (Producers designed the set after the room where Ned Beatty gives his "The world is a business" speech in the movie *Network*.) It oozes cigar-club masculinity, even when Trump is flanked by a female sidekick: the steely Carolyn Kepcher ("There are many men buried in her wake") or his daughter Ivanka. It's what you would produce if someone handed you a crayon and told you to draw what "business" looks like. Gold door handles. Stiff chairs. A stack of note paper that no one ever uses. And the massive wooden table, where Trump sits in a red-leather throne.

The Prayers for Forgiveness. Now, the free-for-all begins. It's a reverse communion, designed to sunder the congregation rather than bring it together. Players assign blame and plead innocence. They cajole, they attack. Above all, they suck up, reminding Trump that they've studied his biography and worldview—like Sam Solovey, who appeals to Trump's often-repeated belief that success is genetic:

"I've got genetic pool big-time, Mr. Trump, just like you got from your father, Fred Trump, and your mother, Mary Trump."* Often, Trump ignores what happened in the challenge altogether, basing his decision on what happens in this room, which leads to—

The Concluding Rite. The most politically significant two-word catchphrase in TV history, a verbal execution that tells you Mr. Trump is decisive, that someone must lose so that you can win, that life is harsh and dark and thrilling, with salvation for the elect but wailing and gnashing for those who displease the Father and are cast from the garden: "You're fired."

The mass is ended. Get your ass outta here.

* * * *

OVER SEVERAL SEASONS of *Survivor*, Burnett had learned how to produce a tight, riveting TV competition, and the first season of *The Apprentice* shows it. The casting aims at giving everyone in the audience someone to see themselves in: racially and geographically diverse, evenly split by gender. For red-state Americans, there's Troy, the "country bumpkin" with a high-school diploma, pitted against elite-educated city slickers. (All the contestants are introduced with broad symbolism: a player from Los Angeles is pictured in front of the Hollywood sign, a real-estate agent at the gates of a mansion, and so on). The challenges and close living quarters maximize conflict. (As well as, fingers crossed, romance—although that can be implied in editing if Cupid doesn't cooperate. The first season milked a flirtation between Nick and Amy for all it was worth.)

Above all, Burnett knew how to push buttons. Reality TV, from

---

* In *The Truth About Trump*, Michael D'Antonio writes that the Trump family believes in "racehorse theory," the notion—a form of eugenics, the quack theory embraced by pseudoscientific racists and the Nazis—that a talented father and mother will produce genetically superior offspring. The belief in "good genes" recurs on *The Apprentice*. "Negotiation," Trump says in the third episode, is "almost innate. It's in the genes. A negotiator is born."

The Real World on, thrived on divisions that people recognized from life. A big one was gender. The first season of *The Apprentice*, and some later ones, divided the candidates into teams of men vs. women, which had worked for Burnett earlier on *Survivor: The Amazon*. This allowed the show to toy with stereotypes while ostensibly disavowing them. ("Women have a tougher time in the workplace— or so they say," said Trump, who would later suggest that a female debate moderator who was tough on him was having her period.) The show encouraged the women to use sexuality (they pitched a phallic ad campaign for an airplane-leasing company to win the second episode) while shaming them for it (a contestant was fired for dropping her skirt to sell candy in the second season).

The biggest, shiniest button was race. *Survivor* established that a breakout reality show needs a villain, and *The Apprentice* found its first in Omarosa Manigault, a former aide to vice president Al Gore and the only black woman in the cast. Tall, intense, and imposing, Omarosa (her monomym is the true mark of her fame) recognized that *The Apprentice* was a psychological game first and a business challenge second (if that). She used calculated drama and cutting remarks to destabilize her opponents and wreak turmoil—for instance, accusing a competitor of racism for using the phrase "calling the kettle black."

This was gold for reality TV: people getting "real" about race, the ultimate topic sublimated by polite society. This guaranteed her screen time: "When I was a good girl, there were no cameras on," she said. "The minute I started arguing, there was a camera shooting me from every angle." It also allowed her, as media critic Jennifer L. Pozner pointed out, to be edited according to a TV template dating back to *Amos and Andy*: the Angry Black Woman. She was a troublemaker, overbearing and strategically irrational—and, to white viewers inclined toward such messages, an example of an African American cynically deploying the "race card" for her advantage.

Omarosa was playing the most Trumpian game: *Always foment conflict. Chaos creates opportunity. Divide your opponents with irrationality.* Above all: *Bad attention is better than no attention.* She would not win the season, but she won celebrity, and would have the longest association with Trump. In 2010, he appeared with her on *Donald J. Trump Presents The Ultimate Merger*, a dating show in which she was the bachelorette. ("Is there anybody that can tame you?" he asked, sliding her a metal briefcase with dossiers on prospective suitors.) She appeared in a string of other reality shows and published a self-help book, *The Bitch Switch*. After his election, Trump hired her to a $179,700-a-year White House position as communications director for the Office of Public Liaison.

* * * *

BUT THIS TIME, the star of the reality show was not the villain. It was Donald Trump, or rather the television character "Donald Trump," birthed on Tom Brokaw's couch in 1980 and now revised again, a quarter-century later, on NBC. *The Apprentice* could use Trump as a shorthand for wealth because he had made himself one—insouciant, cocky, boastful—on *60 Minutes* and Robin Leach and Phil Donahue. It could present him as amusing and accessible because he later played himself that way on *The Fresh Prince* and *Drew Carey*.

Like movie producers rebooting Batman, Burnett and Trump made the new, updated character a palimpsest of the previous versions. Yes, Trump was all those things, *The Apprentice* said, but he's also a very serious businessman. His heavy-browed scowl, his jowls, his parodic puff of hair—these recast the 1980s tabloid playboy as a leonine captain of industry. He had the brand; he looked the part.

TV had changed in the twenty-four years since Trump charmed Brokaw on *Today*—become brasher, more confrontational, less soothing. In a fragmented media market, TV shows didn't aim to be "for everyone"; to stand out, they had to be willing to alienate someone.

TV, in other words, was ready for the 100-proof version of Donald Trump. His character was, essentially, an antihero: the blunt, impolite apex predator who knew how to get things done. And he was—because the show's format required it—instinctive and quick and a shrewd judge of character.

His catchphrase, that curt "You're fired," combined the ethos of reality TV and Trump's mythmaking as the man with the golden gut who cut through the crap in his drive to have the best. Maybe it wasn't nice, maybe he wasn't nice, but then, success wasn't nice. Was being *nice* going to get you a job in the miserable post-9/11 economy? Were we going to whip al-Qaeda's asses by being *nice*? No; we had to choose. With every firing, the show's premise told us, we got closer to perfection, closer to Trump.

Was his instinct actually that unerring? The producers—mindful of how the season's story arc and logic would play on TV—consulted with Trump on who did well and poorly in the challenges. Still, editors on the early seasons told the journal *Cinemontage* that Trump would often make "arbitrary decisions which had nothing to do with people's merit . . . based on whom he liked or disliked personally, whether it be for looks or lifestyle." The producers would then have to go to the tape and edit the episode to rationalize his decision. Clay Aiken, a former *American Idol* finalist who appeared on a later *Celebrity Apprentice* season, claimed that Trump would get firing instructions from producers through a device disguised to look like a phone.

For *The Apprentice* to sell itself as the best reality show, its contestants had to be competing for the best prize. That meant Trump had to be the best businessman. Jonathan Braun, a supervising editor on the early seasons, described the show's mission as "Make Trump look good, make him look wealthy, legitimate." Mark Burnett was as invested as Trump's 1990s creditors in maintaining his façade.

So the crew constructed that majestic boardroom set, bypassing the shabby rooms and "chipped furniture" of the actual Trump Organization offices. Episode after episode staged visits to Trump-branded enterprises, where lackeys reported good news and swollen coffers. Some of his associates were famous in their own right, like Jean-Georges Vongerichten, chef at the four-star restaurant Jean-Georges at the Trump International Hotel. Business is "amazing," Vongerichten says, "everybody's coming in, all the stars, everybody."

Trump's portrayal also borrowed from a less-conventional business archetype. Braun described the music the editors played when Trump would be shown riding down the Trump Tower escalator as "this funk, pimp-walk . . . like the head pimp in charge." When winners of a season 1 challenge stay in the penthouse of the Trump Taj Mahal, gorging on caviar and shrimp, contestant Kwame Jackson marvels, "This is some pimped-out, rap-video shit."*

What is a pimp? In pop culture, going back to 1970s blaxploitation movies like *Super Fly* and *The Mack*, with their richly begarbed heroes—and more broadly, to Hugh Hefner and his celebritized harem keeping—he's a man defined by sexual potency, mastery of women, a hint of danger, and a shit-ton of flash. He may not be a role model, but he lives large in such an entertaining manner that the audience accepts him. He doesn't hide his fortune, he displays it—he even wears it. That strut, that vicarious spectacle, is his kickback. He gives us a show.

Mack daddy Trump, in *The Apprentice*, is an object of fear and desire. He's shown in power positions: riding in a helicopter, working the phones in his limo, announcing a challenge by video from his private plane like a spymaster in a secret-agent movie. He's shot from below, to appear larger. He announces the first episode's challenge—running a lemonade stand—from the balcony of the New York Stock Exchange, like the Pope delivering the *urbi et orbi* at St. Peter's. A visit to Trump Model Management shows him surrounded by beau-

---

* Jackson, the other African American in the first season's cast, would lose in the finale; Trump's lawyer, Michael Cohen, later told *Vanity Fair* that Trump had said, "There's no way I can let this black fag win." Randal Pinkett, the first black contestant to win an *Apprentice* season, told *The New Yorker* that Trump asked him if he would share the title with another contestant, a white woman.

tiful women who must cater to him. ("Are you doing well?" he asks one. "Yes, I'm really, really happy," she says.)

He must be courted, appeased, emulated. He is spoken of and worried about even when he's not around. Contestant Tammy Lee says that she's doesn't care whether the other candidates like her, because "the only person I really need to be concerned with liking me, ostracizing me, is Donald Trump." A candidate lunching with Trump takes care not to touch her shrimp cocktail "until Mr. Trump does." When he arrives at the Taj to oversee a challenge, he glides stone-faced down the escalator like a golden god, as guests crane their necks for a glimpse. *The Apprentice* used a version of this shot over and over, and then he heisted it for his campaign announcement in Trump Tower.

As edited for TV, Trump does everything better. No: Trump does everything *the best*. (Trump is never accompanied by a comparative when a superlative is available.) His preferred method of self-promotion—the un-checkable brag—is perfect for the stage-crafted exaggerations of reality TV. The Taj, he says in an episode, is "the number one hotel in Atlantic City." Well, sure . . . maybe. What does "number one" mean, exactly?

When he and the week's winning team visit the New York Mets at Shea Stadium, he throws a baseball, and there's an editing cut to a fielder catching a ball with a satisfying *smack*, as if Trump had thrown a perfect clothesline. Did he? Was that even the same ball that Trump threw? It must have been. Trump succeeds. Trump is success.

Above all, there is the name, everywhere. "TRUMP" is in giant gleaming letters outside the boardroom where candidates enter to answer for their sins. "Trump" is a noun ("They like Trump") and adjective ("This is Trump luxury"). Sometimes it's both in the same sentence ("Largest windows. Highest ceilings. You see why Trump is Trump."). Watching *The Apprentice* is like watching the scene in *Being John Malkovich* where the title actor goes inside his own consciousness and every phoneme in the language is replaced by his name. ("Malkovich?" "Malkovich!" "Malkovich.")

The show builds on Trump's media character—braggart, shark, showboat—but expands it. Now, Donald Trump is fun! "Where else do you get a good time like with Trump?" Trump asks an employee, a female lawyer he's just introduced to America with, "There's Miss Universe, right there!" He pokes fun at his multiple marriages, like Johnny Carson did: "I know a lot about weddings—unfortunately." He jokes about his impossible floof of hair, inviting players to pull it to prove it's not a wig.

He even plays Cupid, spiriting Nick and Amy off to Mar-a-Lago late in season 1 with their parents, as on an episode of *The Bachelor*. They eat caviar and goggle at the surroundings, including an oversized Trump portrait hanging in the library bar. This romantic-getaway segment is opulent and frankly bewitching. The message, repeated over and over on the show: *Some day, you could live like this, if you follow the way of Trump.*

Trump is luxury. Trump is love. Trump is what every parent wants for their children.

(Trump would deploy the same props as president. Mar-a-Lago, the "Winter White House," became a symbol for a kind of privatized public sphere, the palace of a CEO-president-king, done up in the opulent dictator-chic favored by Third World kleptocrats, where Trump would hobnob with the president of China or order military strikes over a fat slab of chocolate cake while the members of his private club snapped selfies. As he prepared for his inauguration, he posed for a Twitter photo "Writing my inaugural address" at the Mar-a-Lago concierge desk in front of a wall of Spanish tile— Sharpie in hand, staring into the middle distance, corner of his notepad pulled up so we couldn't see if it was blank or not. It was a picture of statesmanship as Mark Burnett might stage it for B-roll footage; it looked like "writing" the same way a scowling man at a boardroom table looked like "business.")

The Apprentice also casts Trump as magnanimous and selfless, qualities he has rarely been accused of. When contestant Heidi Bressler learns that her mother is sick, Trump offers her permission to quit and go home. "I felt like I was talking to a friend," she says in a sit-down with the camera.

In season 3, a contestant asks Trump if it's true that he once paid a New Jersey couple's mortgage after his limousine broke down and they assisted him. This is an ancient, apocryphal tale, told about celebrities from Nat King Cole to Perry Como. Trump's office had denied it to the press years ago. But this time, after a pause, Trump says, "That's true." (Or, at least, the editors intercut Trump saying, "That's true" after footage of the question. Either way, "Never happened" would not have made good TV.)

In the boardroom, he's witty, with a cutting sense of humor and quick ripostes to the candidates' excuses. He's meritocratic, despite having been handed a business—and hundreds of millions of dollars—by his father. Season 3 divides the candidates between a highly educated "book smarts" team and a "street smarts" team of high-school grads, burnishing the "blue-collar billionaire" image of a man who, in real life, referenced his bachelor's degree from Wharton business school almost as often as his surname. ("I love the poorly educated!" he crowed on the campaign trail, referencing his poll numbers among that demographic.)

All the theatrical power of TV is invested in making one aging man look desirable, one skinflint look generous, one lucky rich boy look self-made, one checkered business career look flawless, one accumulation of set dressing look like reality.

* * * *

DO AUDIENCES BUY IT? The common slur on reality-TV fans is that they're suckers who watch uncritically. But that misses a key point: no one more strongly believes that "reality TV isn't reality" than its fans. Part of the pleasure of watching a reality show is looking out for the artifice. How is the editing trying to fake you out—building tension, leading you to believe that one player is going to be voted off instead of another? Are the *American Idol* producers trying to give a singer a boost by giving her a better performance slot? The true connoisseur of reality shows knows how to look for the "loser edit"—that is, to judge, from how a contestant's story is framed, whether he or she is about to get the boot.

If anything, dedicated reality fans may watch more skeptically than most TV viewers. A 2006 *Time* magazine poll, taken in *The Apprentice*'s heyday, found that only 30 percent of respondents believed that reality shows largely reflect what actually happened. A quarter of them believed the shows were almost totally fabricated. But they still watched and enjoyed. Arguably, they were attracted by the appeal to their savviness. *Other* people are suckered by the editing, you tell yourself, whereas *you* see through it. Trump would rely on this same dynamic as a candidate and president: His devoted followers would write off his obvious, provable lies as "jokes" they could see through, or as empty rhetoric that only their enemies were uptight enough to care about.

But *The Apprentice* also performs a kind of magician's misdirection for Trump. As a reality viewer, you're trained to look for artifice when it comes to the *contestants*, not him. Is Omarosa really crazy, or crazy like a fox? Are the producers showing you the screw-ups by the men's team so you'll be surprised when they win the challenge?

You're looking, in other words, for deception and sleight-of-hand on the part of the game. But in *The Apprentice*, Trump isn't the game. He's the game board, the premise. His success, his wealth, his celebrity are all presented as a given, manifest in all those weeping chandeliers in his triplex. As a viewer, you don't question the extent of his business holdings, because they're what gives the game the idea that contestants are competing for a prize of value. If *The Apprentice* is *Survivor* for the business world, then Trump is the island.

* * * *

AND WHAT IS THE GAME? Ostensibly, it's about business. But as the season goes on, boardroom after boardroom, it becomes clear that it is mostly about the ability to sell one's self.

The challenges, which take up most of the episode, determine which team goes into the boardroom. But once the doors shut, it's often as if the challenge never happened. The boardroom becomes a pressure-cooker game in itself, where the object is to please the boss, undermine your colleagues, and find a more vulnerable teammate to sacrifice.

Facing Trump in the boardroom is like being trapped in a cage with a capricious monster. You don't know what he wants, what will anger him, or why, but it's your job to make sure he eats your adversary instead of you.

The boardroom is like a platonic visualization of Trump's mindset. There is the idea, which he practiced in business and politics, that conflict, especially among teammates, is the most productive state of humanity. He loves to put contestants in prisoner's-dilemma situations, asking them in turn, "Who should go?" You could get in trouble for naming your opponent simply because they named you. You could get in trouble for *not* doing it.

But it is important to fight. Boardroom Trump loves a fighter. "I know a lot of people who are overly aggressive," Trump says in one episode. "But they do very well."

In season 1, he fires a player for turning the other cheek toward Omarosa, who'd attacked her: "To me, that was a form of weakness," he says. Ceding a personal advantage, whether out of confidence or principle, is stupid and he hates it: he fires a season 2 contestant for giving up the immunity he'd gained by winning a challenge.

Over and over, candidates seal their fate simply by saying one damn thing too many. In the season 5 premiere, he's lengthily dressing down a player who failed at a challenge, when a seemingly safe candidate, Summer Zervos, interjects. "Why should you interrupt me when I'm knocking the hell out of him?" Trump says. "How stupid is that?" He fires Zervos instead. (Years later, Zervos would accuse Trump of sexual harassment and sue him for defamation, claiming that he groped her when she approached him about job opportunities after the season ended.)

There is always a wrong thing to say to Trump, and that thing changes every episode. A candidate who compliments an opponent is "not very smart." A candidate who criticizes an opponent is "nasty." He criticizes even-keeled competitors for lacking fire in the belly. He criticizes others, especially women, for losing control of their emotions. Women who use sexuality to win challenges are undignified. But when a candidate says she thought it would be undignified to wear a chicken suit for a fast-food promotion, Trump takes offense: "I wore a chicken suit on *Saturday Night Live*. Did anybody see *Saturday Night Live*?" What, are you too goddam good to wear a chicken suit like Donald J. Trump?

You get the sense that the boardroom is the real game for Trump. The challenges are a formality—blah blah salesmanship, blah blah teamwork. In the boardroom, there is no team. There is only the self. There is you in relation to Trump, attempting to commune with the mind of Trump, to anticipate his moods and needs. There is no long-term strategy, only the moment. It is a dark vortex of chaos and opportunity. Everything is situational—you must react in the moment and be attuned to sudden, microscopic shifts in the mood of the boss. There is no being happy for your teammates. The success of another is a wound to be nursed and avenged.

The boardroom would be a direct blueprint for Trump's administration, a dogpile of competitors, cronies, and relatives throttling one another daily for survival. During one astounding week in summer 2017, he brought in communications director Anthony "The Mooch" Scaramucci—the East Coast loudmouth, a favorite reality-show type—who promptly precipitated the resignation of press secretary Sean Spicer and the ouster of chief of staff Reince Priebus, then denigrated top adviser Steve Bannon to *The New Yorker* as an egomaniac who was constantly "trying to suck [his] own cock." Scaramucci was gone ten days after he was named to the job, and Bannon left a few weeks later, the White House equivalent of a special quadruple-elimination episode of *The Apprentice*. What seemed like bedlam from the outside—because it was—invigorated Trump, who believed, like a born reality-TV producer, that warfare and distrust were the most productive and entertaining modes of existence. If his team of suck-ups, throat-cutters, and toadies were constantly fighting among themselves, it meant that they were fighting *for his favor*—and that meant that *he* was the one who mattered, *he* was the sun who gave every flower life, and every day would be the Who Loves Father Best contest that he craved.

Above all, the *Apprentice* boardroom embodies the highest value of reality TV and a key to Trump's persona: being "real," which is different from being honest. To be real is to be the most entertaining form of your self; he encouraged people, Omarosa later wrote, "to exaggerate the unique part of themselves." To be real is to be willing to offend, to tell someone off to their face, to "say what's on your mind," even if what's on your mind happens to be a lie.

This code of conduct is crystallized in an exchange in a season one boardroom. When a contestant accuses a teammate of acting unethically, she turns to Trump: you wouldn't want to work with an unethical person, would you? "I would like to tell you the answer is no," he says, "but it doesn't always work out, because you don't know."

Trump isn't really answering the question. To the extent that he's implying an answer, it's that if his colleagues are shady—his construction associates, say, or Russian partners on a development deal—he doesn't want to know about it. But in the framing of *The Apprentice*, Trump has the high ground. He's the one being real.

THE APPRENTICE ENDED its first season with its finale atop the week's Nielsen ratings, a one-week accomplishment that led Trump, for years after, to call the series "the number-one show on TV." That claim was a lie, but his gifts as a reality host were real enough. He had a genuine ability to improvise—in the live finale as well as the taped episodes. He knew instinctually what the camera wanted, the kind of conflicts and drama that hook an audience. And he showed that he could maintain this kind of performance for an extended run rather than a single TV appearance here and there.

Donald Trump, the boy with one of the first color television sets in Queens, the young man who dreamed of running off to LA to go into the movie business, was finally a star.

NBC, which had envisioned *The Apprentice* with different businesspeople hosting each season, changed its mind. It wanted more Trump, and so, as always, did Trump. He threw himself into the performance. He had been notorious in the media for decades, but this was different. Said Jim Dowd, NBC's public-relations rep for *The Apprentice*, "He was a hero, and he had not been one before."

The show's fans especially loved his catchphrase, "You're fired." Which is to say, they loved the antihero who embodied the dream of living like a king and telling people that they sucked without worrying about hurt feelings or repercussions. This was always a key part of the Donald Trump character. Now it defined him.

Trump took to the publicity circuit like a Hollywood ingenue. He swelled with the attention. The man who was once Tom Brokaw's soft-spoken guest now went on the *Today* show weekly, holding forth on that week's *Apprentice* and on topics in the news. He ate up his celebrity, launching short-lived brand extensions—Trump University, Trump Steaks—and hanging up a fake cover of *Time* magazine ("Donald Trump: The 'Apprentice' Is a Television Smash!") in his golf clubs. He did skits on *Saturday Night Live* and at the Emmys. He got a star on the Hollywood Walk of Fame. He tried to develop a scripted TV drama, *The Tower*, about a ruthless businessman loosely based on him—basically Fox's *Profit*, this time as autobiography.

He had a character he was expected to produce—the You're Fired Guy—and he obliged. He developed a go-to pose for publicity stills: eyes furiously narrowed, mouth opened as if in mid-scream, thumb cocked and index finger pointing straight at the camera. On red carpets, he would wheel around and shoot the pose at camera after camera: *You're fired you're fired you're fired*. He was a "You're fired" delivery machine.

You can see this in the second season of *The Apprentice*. Like a breakout sitcom character, the Trump character becomes exaggerated: tougher, more insulting, determined to give the crowds twice as much of what they wanted, twice as hard. The general tone is harsher, sharper-edged. Speaking to Bill Rancic, the season 1 winner now assigned to a Trump Organization project in Chicago, he signs off, "You'd better do a good job, Bill, or your ass is grass." A poor team performance in a challenge is "disgusting." When he reshuffles the team rosters at the beginning of an episode, he wraps up: "That's life. And that's business. So deal with it."

Trump's season-3 *Apprentice* introduction begins: "My name is Donald Trump. You know everything about me." The show was, at this point, still lucrative for NBC, partly because of its aggressive product placements. (The challenges were by now almost exclusively built around non-Trump brands: Best Buy, Pepsi, Mattel, UPS, QVC, M&M/Mars.)

The ratings, however, never matched their season-1 peak. One problem may have been burnout. Most reality competitions spotlighted their contestants rather than the host, so they generated new stars and new stories every season. Some, like *American Idol*, aired only once a year, the better to make their seasons seem like an event. *The Apprentice* lived and died by Trump, and NBC ran two seasons a year.

On average, 20.7 million people watched the first season. That number drifted down steadily to 9.7 million by season 5. Trump—always one to fixate on numeric measures of worth—obsessed over the ratings and lied about them to reporters. (He would carry this numbers fixation to the presidency, lying about his popular-vote loss and the size of his inauguration crowds. He would even taunt action-movie star and former governor of California Arnold Schwarzenegger on Twitter for the weak ratings of his brief-lived revival of *The Celebrity Apprentice*: "Wow, the ratings are in and Arnold Schwarzenegger got swamped [or destroyed] by comparison to the ratings machine, DJT.")

Trump blamed NBC's scheduling for the ratings drop; he blamed the network's decision to air a spin-off, starring lifestyle magnate Martha Stewart, concurrently with season 4. He did not, heaven forbid, blame himself; he just made his performance shoutier and more belligerent. NBC and the producers tried various twists to revive interest. There was another men vs. women season; there was the book smarts vs. street smarts season; the episodes focused more on the emotional backstories of contestants. Finally, for the sixth season in 2007, *The Apprentice* did what so many flagging TV series do: it took the show on the road.

The Apprentice: Los Angeles is a magnificent work of tacky desperation, an attempt to salvage a lucrative franchise with gimmicks. It opens with Trump riding in his limo through rainy New York City, talking on the phone to his third wife, Melania, who's with their baby son Barron in California, where, Trump announces, he's decided to build a house. Cut to a *Tonight*-show style big-band theme and Trump driving a sun-kissed freeway in a convertible ("I love L.A.!") and pulling up to the mansion that will double as his Los Angeles office. Melania—the most Trump-like of Trump's wives, with a model's glower that matches his own—joins him in the driveway with baby Barron, and the Trumps fix the camera with a dead-eyed stare.

The season lards up the game with twists and clichés, the biggest being a *Survivor*-style gimmick in which the losing team sleeps outside in a tent encampment, drawing water from hoses and cooking over a fire, filmed with night-vision cameras. The vibe is chintzy and mean; despite the glitzy setting, the season misses the aspirational glamor of the New York edition.* Trump, meanwhile, has gone from tough to grumpy, barking at contestants to "shut up" and snapping when a team walks into the boardroom wearing promotional caps

---

* The visit to L.A. did allow Trump to come full circle on his teenage worship of Hugh Hefner's *Playboy*, hosting a reward party at the Playboy Mansion for the team that won a challenge to design and market bathing suits, with the contestants as models. One player on the winning team, Surya Yalamanchili, recalled Trump telling Hefner, "It's hard for me to tell which of these girls are yours, and which ones are mine."

that they were given for the challenge: "Take your hats off. You're inside. Take 'em off."

No one was having any fun, on that side of the screen or this one. The viewership dropped to 7.5 million, making it the seventy-fifth-most-watched show on network TV.

*   *   *   *

THAT MIGHT HAVE BEEN it for *The Apprentice*, if Ben Silverman— a producer who made the short-lived culinary-world reality show *The Restaurant* with Burnett—had not become programming chief of NBC and been strapped for content by the 2007–08 TV writers' strike. The strike took sitcoms, dramas, and late-night comedy shows off the air—but not reality shows, whose story editors (writers in all but name) were not covered by the union. Silverman scheduled the revival of *The Apprentice*, with another gimmick that would prove permanent.

The Celebrity Apprentice was a shadow of the original phenomenon. Many of the celebrities were barely recognizable, and they were competing for charity rather than for a job, which diminished the stakes. In the arc of Trump's career, however, *Celebrity Apprentice* is a fascinating document. It is to the original *The Apprentice* as 1990s Trump was to 1980s Trump: a diminished, winking self-parody of something that used to be a mass phenomenon.

Like the Trump of his sitcom-cameo years, his show turns into a metafictional construct, a simulacrum of itself. The theme of the show becomes, like the theme of Trump's career, less about business acumen and more about how to monetize celebrity. The contestants are encouraged to "use your star power" and to call in their famous friends to lend publicity to their business challenges. In the first episode, former *Playboy* Playmate of the Year Tiffany Fallon gets a scolding for not phoning Hugh Hefner.

Because the celebrities are playing for charity, *Celebrity Apprentice* also becomes less cutthroat and more sentimental. Not all of the contestants play the game sweetly, however, which sets up an angel-vs.-devil first-season finale between country star Trace Adkins, who exudes aw-shucks humility, and British journalist turned American newscaster/reality host Piers Morgan, who plays the sneering heavy. (Both stars, of course, are playing roles that benefit them in their real, off-show careers.) Morgan's charity is the Intrepid Fallen Heroes Fund, which provides treatment to wounded soldiers, allowing Trump to appear somberly on stage in the finale with decorated veterans—looking very much like a president—an American flag billowing on a giant flat-screen TV behind him.

The finale builds to a strikingly meta finish, an interrogation of the very values of television that's simultaneously moralistic and cynical in a way that only reality TV can be. Morgan, making his case, demands that Trump make a decision, not just as to whom to hire, but about what the core priorities of his show are.

"It would be very helpful to all of us, Mr. Trump, if you would just clarify absolutely what the purpose of this game was," Morgan asks. "Was it to be the nicest guy in the boardroom, or was it to be the most efficient, effective businessman-stroke-charity fundraiser?"

For the first four decades of American television, the answer would have been: nice guy. The era of Tony Soprano and Richard Hatch said otherwise, and Piers Morgan walked away the winner.

* * * *

THE CELEBRITY APPRENTICE did its job well enough. About 11 million people watched that first season, and the later seasons stabilized in the high seven figures. It was, for NBC, OK—not a top-40 show, but a decent performer that didn't cost too much and had a nice income stream of product placements.

But for Trump, it meant, again, having had a taste of being a phenomenon and looking forward to a lifetime being . . . just OK: the guy who used to be the You're Fired Guy hauling out his shtick with a cast of other used-to-bes. He would be the broken statue of Ozymandias in the pop-culture desert, his once-towering ratings clipped off at the shins.

It was about this time that Trump revived his old interest, as a political gadfly. But this time—in a fragmented media age, with specialty audiences looking for personalities who superserved their interests—he did not position himself as a moderate appealing to a bipartisan audience who wanted to hear from a no-nonsense businessman. Instead, he found a receptive audience for his angry, abrasive character in the angry, abrasive sphere of conservative media, especially Fox News.

There, he was a hit. In March 2011, Fox's morning show, *Fox & Friends*, aired an ad for a new regular segment: "Mondays with Trump." It plugged the weekly call-in guest as "Bold, brash, and never bashful," with an interview clip of him declaring, "My message is a better message than anybody else." Against a bright blue background with "TRUMP" in capital letters, he stood, eyes narrowed, teeth bared, pointing his finger-gun dead at the viewer.

The You're Fired Guy was back.

THE PARANOID STYLE IN AMERICA'S NEWSROOM

REALITY TV AND CABLE NEWS WERE MARRIED ON OCTOBER 15, 2009, after a long courtship.

That afternoon, every cable channel was locked onto news-chopper video of a silver, Jiffy Pop–shaped weather balloon 8,000 feet above Colorado. The balloon, anchors said, had come untethered in the backyard of Richard Heene, an unsuccessful actor and amateur scientist. Unbeknownst to Heene, his six-year-old son, Falcon, had been hiding inside a hatch in the balloon when it broke its leash. Now we were watching the vessel in which a terrified child might be hurtling to his death.

It was horrific. And it was great TV. Suspenseful, emotional, cheap—just air the video feed and have anchors blab while office workers and stay-at-home parents across the country stare, literally distracted by a shiny object. It even had a happy, if confounding, ending. The balloon descended and was found empty—Falcon was safe at home. Shepard Smith, anchoring the afternoon coverage on

Fox News, called it "one of the strangest things in the history of my television career."

The Heene family's cover story was that they had found Falcon, quickly nicknamed "Balloon Boy" in the press, hiding in their garage. It didn't make sense—why wouldn't he have come out sooner, if his parents were screaming for him in terror? And as the family launched on a media tour—*Larry King Live, Today, Good Morning America*—the story fell apart. Falcon was under stress, vomiting twice during live TV interviews. On CNN, he blurted out to his father, "You guys said that we did this for the show."

The Heene family was no stranger to shows. They had twice appeared on *Wife Swap*, an ABC reality show where families traded spouses to experience living under another parent's rules. And at the time of this Icarus-meets-*Up* escapade, Richard Heene had been unsuccessfully pitching a TV version of his YouTube show, *The Psyience Detectives*.

Heene pled guilty to a felony charge (though he maintained for years that the incident was not a hoax). He never got his show. But you can understand the strategy. If you were redesigning the seal of the United States for the twenty-first century, "We Did It for the Show" might as well be the motto.

The incentive systems in reality TV and TV news had become much the same. Outrageousness paid. The same year as Balloon Boy, TV discovered "Octomom," a California woman who was purposely impregnated with octuplets. She became the subject of a two-hour special on Fox. A month after the Heenes' escapade, Michaele and Tareq Salahi, a socialite couple hoping to get cast on the Bravo reality show *The Real Housewives of D.C.*, breached White House security to crash the Obamas' first state dinner, camera and makeup crew in tow. Piers Morgan, whom Donald Trump named the winner of the first *Celebrity Apprentice*, had earned the "celebrity" portion of his title as a British tabloid editor who was fired in a 2004 hoax-photo scandal, then found a second career as a TV loudmouth on *America's Got Talent* and *You Can't Fire Me, I'm Famous*. Later,

CNN hired him to replace talk host Larry King. Donald Trump was one of his first guests.

The same rewards for notoriety applied in politics. The conservative-cultural backlash against new president Barack Obama had already begun to simmer. It took its name, "the Tea Party," from a February 2009 rant by CNBC reporter Rick Santelli, who fulminated on the floor of the Chicago Mercantile Exchange against the administration's aid to homeowners in danger of foreclosure after the financial crisis of 2008, which to Santelli rewarded the "bad behavior" of deadbeats. "We're thinking of having a Chicago Tea Party in July," he shouted, as the traders on the floor whooped against the idea of saving broke people from a disaster unleashed by Wall Street.

That Tea Party kettle came to a whistling boil, and conservative media stars rose aloft on its steam. Republican representative Joe Wilson of South Carolina yelled "You lie!" at Obama during his 2009 address to Congress, a televised breach of decorum for which he was punished with over a million dollars in campaign donations. Sarah Palin, the 2008 vice presidential candidate and culture warrior—she once contrasted liberal cities with what she called the "pro-America areas of this great nation"—went from Alaskan Agnew to Fox News commentator to the star of multiple reality shows. ABC's *Dancing with the Stars* cast a stream of downfallen politicians to tango in prime time, including Tom DeLay, the former GOP majority leader indicted in a campaign-fundraising scandal, and Rick Perry, the Texas governor who later became Donald Trump's secretary of energy, heading a department he had failed to recall the name of during a live 2011 presidential primary debate.

Everyone was doing it for the show. And TV news, especially cable news, was the heaving lung of this corpus: it breathed in scandal and breathed out celebrity, which in turn fed its continual need for content. You want to break out? Act out.

* * * *

ELECTRONIC MEDIA HAD NOT always been like this. On April 18, 1930, nothing much of note happened, so that was what the BBC reported. "There is no news," said the evening announcer, and the radio returned to Wagner's opera *Parsifal*.

But as media outlets proliferated, a news vacuum was a problem to be solved, and for those with something to gain by filling it, this created an opportunity. In 1962, the historian Daniel Boorstin identified the "pseudo-event": news stories engineered by public-relations artists and snapped up first by newspapers, then electronic outlets with yawning appetites.

"We used to believe there were only so many 'events' in the world," Boorstin wrote in *The Image*. "If there were not many intriguing or startling occurrences, it was no fault of the reporter. He could not be expected to report what did not exist." But over the twentieth century, this changed. "We expect the papers to be full of news. If there is no news visible to the naked eye, or to the average citizen, we still expect it to be there for the enterprising newsman. The successful reporter is one who can find a story, even if there is no earthquake or assassination or civil war."

The imperative for constant excitement and novelty didn't just create expectations. They created an agitated style, a staccato syntax, a hummingbird metabolism. In *Amusing Ourselves to Death*, Neil Postman called it the "Now . . . This" sensibility, for the two words news anchors would use to transition from one story to an unrelated one. With it, "the newscaster means that you have thought long enough on the matter (approximately forty-five seconds), that you must not be morbidly preoccupied with it (let us say, for ninety seconds), and that you must now give your attention to another fragment of news or a commercial."

The style of TV news is the opposite of narrative. There is no arc, no causality. It's not one thing, therefore another, therefore another. It's: thing thing thing thing. The audience becomes a school of tropical fish, swimming in one direction for a minute, then pivoting en masse to another, their previous object of attention already forgotten.

Postman was writing in the mid-1980s, which today already looks like an Athenian age of quiet reflection. He focused on the broadcast TV networks, which devoted a mere half hour an evening to the news. But already another force was working to hasten the now-thisification of America: twenty-four-hour cable news, as pioneered by CNN.

Cable News Network was founded in 1980—the year of Reagan's election, the year Donald Trump sat down in Tom Brokaw's toast-colored *Today* studio—by Ted Turner, a publicity-hungry billionaire with a talent for self-inflation. The network was meant to change the world, or else why would Turner bother? In a sign of his monumental expectations, he launched CNN with a plan to voice the last expression of human civilization. He prepared a "doomsday tape," a video of a military band playing "Nearer My God to Thee," which producers would roll in the event of apocalypse. CNN would bring you the world, and it would take you out of it.

In the early days, CNN operated in a spirit of commercial-tinged idealism, or ideals-tinged commercialism. No longer would you need to wait for the *thunk* of the newspaper on your porch or the 6:30 news to find out what was happening: you would know *now*. People would be *more* informed, so it was assumed they would be *better* informed. (This was a dubious assumption, but as the Internet would later prove, this was not the last time someone would make it.)

Reese Schonfeld, the veteran TV journalist who cofounded the network with Turner, wrote that while CNN was a business, it had a higher goal: "to offer information and understanding of current events, to place them in historical context, and to illustrate them with arresting images. It was created to permit its viewers to talk back to CNN. It was created to provide, for the first time, timely financial news, sports news, entertainment news. It was created to offer news from 6 a.m. to 6 p.m. to 6 a.m. again."

That was a hell of a lot of time. Actually, this is an understatement. It was *all the time that there was*, forever, until and unless the brass notes of that military band finally stilled mankind's troubled consciousness. It is a big world with much to learn, but even a well-funded global news organization has only so many resources. How do you fill up forever?

In the most ennobling telling of CNN's myth, its defining event was the first Gulf War in 1991. Its correspondents, holed up in a hotel in Baghdad, reported a view no one else had of the city's bombardment. *New Yorker* writer Ken Auletta wrote in *Three Blind Mice*, his study of how the major networks lost their cultural monopoly, that the war signaled a permanent shift in TV news. "For as long as the war held their interest," he wrote, "viewers could choose for themselves when to watch the news as easily as they could choose to flick to an HBO movie, an ESPN basketball game, or a Disney cartoon." CNN would become as ubiquitous as light and air, available in every hotel room, playing in airport terminals around the world, every screen a little embassy.

But arguably what truly established CNN and set the model for 24/7 news came in 1987, four years before the Gulf War, when eighteen-month-old Jessica McClure fell into a backyard well in Midland, Texas. It was the most elemental of human stories, the child in peril—a pop-history template that the Heenes would repeat as farce more than two decades later. It was the complete formula for tantalizing terror: the ability to see a horrible event while being powerless to affect it.

Reporters converged on the site, where "Baby Jessica"—without knowing it, she'd become a celebrity—was trapped for sixty hours. But only CNN could put the story on all the time. Relatives and volunteers and firefighters were interviewed. Cameras trained on drills boring a shaft into the earth. A rescuer wriggled into the tunnel (yes!), nearly reached Jessica (hooray!), and had to come back out (oh no!). America prayed; CNN was the church. When she was finally brought out alive, 3.1 million households were watching the network.

The best story was the longest story. This effect repeated manifold with the O. J. Simpson murder trial in 1994 and 1995. The trial of Simpson, football star turned actor and rental-car pitchman, cleaved black viewers from white viewers, who divided not just over Simpson's guilt but over the very question at stake in the trial. To one group, the trial asked if O.J. was guilty; to another, it asked whether to reward a legal system that had persecuted black men for years and was now trying to put away one of the most famous black men in the world. Simpson's legal team used that division to question not just the evidence but the idea that there could be objective truth—a stick-with-your-team approach that worked, first in this trial and later in political campaigns like Donald Trump's. It was a national trauma. But trauma keeps people tuned in.

* * * *

MOST OF THE TIME, of course, the news gives you neither Baby Jessica nor O.J. nor the Gulf War. Most of the time, today's news is yesterday's news continuing to happen. But the proposition of twenty-four-hour news is that something is always happening, and you need to be watching to know about it.

In the quaint days of the Kennedy administration, Boorstin worried about the pseudo-event. Cable news brought the pseudo-report: the "breaking news" that really broke hours ago, the debates that went on while we were waiting for events to happen, and the coverage of the coverage of the events and the debates. The point was to communicate constant excitement. If pseudo-events were staged by flacks to sell a product or an ideology, pseudo-reports were generated by the news outlet to sell itself.

The strongest emotions to incite were fear and sadness and anger, and those could be found anywhere. Somewhere there was a war, a crime, a murdered child (like JonBenet Ramsey, a *Larry King Live* obsession in the 1990s). If you were a heavy cable news consumer—for instance, a retiree spending a lot of time at home—this was what the world became to you. (The cartoon *Daria* on MTV immortalized this kind of tabloid-TV mentality in the fictional news show *Sick, Sad World.*)

Like other developments in TV around the time—the rise of HBO, for instance—the change in tone was driven by a change in business. The old evening newscasts were artifacts of the mass-audience era. Like everything on TV, they strove not to alienate anyone enough to change the channel before the game shows, entertainment newsmagazines, and hospital dramas that followed. They cultivated fatherly anchors like Walter Cronkite and David Brinkley, who could assure the mass audience of millions that a broadcast-TV model required.

But CNN and its followers had different needs, just as HBO did. With dozens or hundreds of other channels available, they needed a smaller but more intense audience of news junkies. They needed to agitate their viewers, not settle them.

The most versatile form of pseudo-report for this purpose was the good old-fashioned argument. Two people set against each other in a studio would generate the emotion-fuel that kept viewers glued to the screen, without costly reporting. (It could do this even better than an actual news report, since you could count on debaters to cast the facts in the most apocalyptic, and thus entertaining, terms.)

From this standpoint, CNN's true coming of age was in 1982, with the launch of *Crossfire*. It borrowed the format of segments like *60 Minutes*' "Point Counterpoint"—a battle between the commentator "from the right" and the commentator "from the left"—and made it the substance of an entire show.

Crossfire paid fealty to a particular mainstream-media idea of objectivity, that it was more important to arrive at the *center* of a controversy than at the *truth* of it. And the most entertaining way to arrive at the center was statistically—by finding two people on far opposite sides to have at it. Both sides needed to be represented, always and equally, even if both sides did not have an equal share of the evidence or of informed opinion.

Crossfire was not only a hit but also influential. The show's original "from the right" host, the nationalist demagogue Pat Buchanan, ran for president twice. His Republican primary challenge in 1992 (which Trump more successfully emulated) was the first wound to George H. W. Bush's reelection bid. His Reform Party run in 2000 (which Trump briefly contested) shifted enough votes in Florida—in part because of an inept ballot design that led some Al Gore voters to select Buchanan by mistake—to help make George W. Bush president.

How else do you fill up forever? With noise. With repetition. Also sharks: sharks were terrific. They came to the rescue in the summer of 2001, a torpid moment after the Bush-Gore legal battle when the country had seemed to settle into psychic hibernation. (As a writer for *Time* magazine at the time, I remember being called into the editor's office and assigned to come up with a list of pop-culture covers, because it seemed there might never be big geopolitical news stories again. This was a week or two before September 11. None of my hastily conceived ideas ever ran.)

But one day in July 2001, a shark did the news media the favor of biting off a boy's arm near Pensacola, Florida. This launched "The Summer of the Shark," in which newspapers, magazines, and above all cable news networks turned into *Jaws* marathons. Only later did researchers find that there were only seventy-six unprovoked shark attacks in 2001, down from eighty-five the year before. What created the news was the need for news. The sharks were us.

Then came the clear blue morning of September 11 and, columnist Frank Rich wrote, "the great shark scare of 2001 was consigned to the dustbin of history when *People* magazine scrapped its shark cover." The terrorist attack was a genuine calamity, and one that, with the wars in Afghanistan and Iraq, would be news for years. But it would be covered by a cable-news business that had learned that its ratings depended on generating constant fear and passion.

* * * *

ROGER AILES HAD BEEN manufacturing fear and passion through television since 1968. Ailes started as a producer on *The Mike Douglas Show*, whose glad-handing host interviewed Hollywood stars and athletes, as well as politicians—who, Ailes realized, were now employed in show business too. One day the show booked Republican presidential candidate Richard Nixon, and the twenty-seven-year-old Ailes, long interested in politics, offered the candidate his services as a media adviser.

Nixon's performance against John F. Kennedy in a televised 1960 debate, in which he came across shifty and unattractive with a pencil-shading of dark stubble, was the seminal legend of a candidate being killed by TV. Ailes believed TV could bring Nixon back to life.

Ailes studied media guru Marshall McLuhan, who believed that broadcast TV favored the "cool"—the relaxed, improvisatory, and vaguely defined—and set about to give Nixon a meticulously engineered air of casualness. (Watching Nixon tinkle the piano on *The Jack Paar Program* in 1963, McLuhan said that the performance "would have quite altered the result of the Kennedy-Nixon campaign.") Ailes sent his candidate on *Rowan & Martin's Laugh-In* to say the hipster sketch show's catch phrase, "Sock it to me." He prepped Nixon with one-liners for political events, because, Ailes wrote in a memo, "The general public is just not sophisticated enough to wade through answers."

Ailes sifted through Nixon's video clips and realized that he was most likeable in one-on-one exchanges. So Ailes staged some: genuine manufactured events, reality politics. He created *The Nixon Answer*, a series of TV panels where Nixon took questions from selected citizens in front of an audience recruited by local Republican organizations. Nixon was placed heroically on a platform. A "warm-up man" worked the crowd before the event just like at a talk-show taping. Ailes handpicked the panelists, who might include a housewife, a black questioner—always one, and only one—and a blue-collar racist whose crudeness Nixon could disdain while endorsing its spirit. The press was not invited. "It's a television show," Ailes said. "Our television show." If the media was not your friend, you created your own media.

Nixon won, wrapping the fears and prejudices of the daytime talk-show audience into a daytime talk-show package. Ailes spent the next decades toggling between politics and TV, working on campaigns for Ronald Reagan and George H. W. Bush and founding the short-lived America's Talking Channel for NBC. When Rupert Murdoch, the conservative head of Twentieth Century Fox, asked him to launch a news channel, Ailes brought his interests together.

Fox News Channel was fueled by cultural resentment even before it went on the air. It was built into the branding. Its slogan, "Fair and Balanced," was classic advertising sleight-of-hand, sneaking in the assumption that competition is unfair and unbalanced. That this argument was being made by Ailes, a professional partisan, would bother no one that it was meant to appeal to. A second slogan—"We Report. You Decide."—was dreamed up by Republican ad consultants. *We* will give *you* the power, it said, meaning *they* have been keeping it from you.

Among the team Ailes assembled was Chet Collier, his old boss from *The Mike Douglas Show*, whom Ailes's biographer Gabriel Sherman quoted as telling producers: "Viewers don't want to *be* informed; they want to *feel* informed." Collier's aphorism was one word too long. Viewers wanted to *feel*, period. Feel angry. Feel scared. Feel gleeful. This was what Fox delivered.

CNN had one solution to the question of what to do when there wasn't enough news: make the news more exciting. Fox News had another: Make the audience more excited. It didn't have the global reporting staff of CNN, so it homebrewed its content. Fox applied to TV the principles of right-wing talk radio, where rageaholics like Rush Limbaugh became superstars in the 1990s by flogging the Clintons and fanning conspiracy theories (including one that Bill and Hillary had a deputy White House counsel, Vince Foster, murdered).

It hired a prime-time lineup of conservative opinion hosts. It would often book more stridently left-leaning guests than CNN would, because—like the stereotypes cast to strike sparks on a reality show—they made for more cartoonish foils and better fights. Its daytime "straight news" shows, with titles like *America's Newsroom*, focused on the same culture-war topics that Fox's conservative opinionators would tee off on at night: "Has P.C. changed our view of the Founding Fathers?" "Will [Bill] Clinton's focus on race make existing problems worse?"

The topics changed, but the argument was constant and existential: *they* were giving *our* stuff away to *them* and taking away from *you* and *your kind*. A favorite Fox perennial was "The War on Christmas," a crusade promoted by John Gibson, a pale, melting snowman of an anchor, who claimed that PC secularists were engaged in "a liberal plot to ban the sacred Christian holiday."

It didn't matter that anyone with eyes could see the annual avalanche of Christmas music, Christmas specials, and Christmas advertising pouring from the same TV sets on which Fox declared the "war." The point was a message of cultural nostalgia for besieged conservatives. Every time someone said "Happy Holidays," it was an existential threat, a reminder that your traditions used to be the default in America, and now they weren't. Now you had to say words that acknowledged that other people in the world were different from you and that they deserved consideration. The future was slipping away from Christian Americans, and the culture was devaluing traditional morality.

The great irony was, much of that devaluing was being done by . . . Rupert Murdoch's Fox broadcast network, home to the liberal satire of *The Simpsons* and the gleeful raunch of *Married . . . with Children* and *Temptation Island*. Murdoch's media empire was a self-powering perpetual outrage machine: the Fox entertainment network produced the same pop-culture Gomorrah that Fox News would bemoan.

Fox News didn't just have an ideology. It had an aesthetic. It was loud, flashy, bedazzled with blinding graphics. Thundering martial drums played as 3-D captions—"WORDS OF WAR"—swooshed toward you on the screen. Watching Fox was like living inside a patriotic video game. The flashy packaging—brazen, déclassé—subliminally echoed the network's philosophy of conservative class resentment. This was not, the visuals said, tasteful news for snobs. This was NASCAR news: loud, fast, and made for the red states. (The divisive shorthand "blue state" and "red state," for liberal and conservative America, was itself a creation of TV news. In 1996, the network election-night maps settled on red to represent the Republican party and blue to represent Democrats, as if the states themselves made up bitterly opposed teams, complete with squad colors. Before 1996, the colors had been used interchangeably, with yellow occasionally thrown in.)

Fox treated the news like ESPN treated sports: as an exciting, bracing contest with conflict, a little jocularity, and rooting interests. CNN told you the news was important. Fox told you the news kicked ass.

Even the casting sent a visual message. The hosts were generally white, for starters—super white, country-club white, Oktoberfest white. The men looked like '50s sitcom dads. The women were young and blond and—on Ailes's orders—dressed in skirts. The meat-market presentation of Fox's women, in particular, hearkened back to Hugh Hefner's heyday and forward to Ailes's ouster from the network in 2016, when he was exposed as a serial sexual predator of his female employees. Ailes had a type, apparently, that was eerily reflected in Fox's on-air look. For decades, viewers had been living virtually in a dirty old man's libido.

* * * *

FOX LAUNCHED a few months after MSNBC, a cable-news partnership of NBC and the software giant Microsoft. MSNBC's style was . . . different. It had an upscale, tech-world aesthetic. Its studios were accented with exposed brick, desktop computers on display everywhere, as if it were the headquarters of a Silicon Valley startup, or a chichi Internet café with a white-collar clientele. Its tech-oriented news hour, *The Site*, paired host Soledad O'Brien with Dev Null, a digitally animated "barista" who chatted from behind a coffee bar.

As much as they offered two different approaches to television, the Fox and MSNBC of 1996 presented two opposed ideas of the future. MSNBC suggested that in prosperous, post–Cold War America, an educated, comfortable public would download and rationally problem-solve the news of the day in a coffeehouse of the mind. It was the end of history, with scones.

Fox replied: Fuck you. Human nature had not been rewritten. No social or economic change would erase tribal differences. Life was and would always be a fight, with winners and losers, to be engaged lustily.

Fox's vision may not have been more heartening, but it was, for TV purposes, more accurate. (MSNBC would come to realize this, morphing for a while into a conservative Fox clone, then more successfully into a liberal Fox competitor.) On 9/11, this vision became ratified. Fox responded instinctually. It added an American flag to the corner of its feed, a gesture CNN and MSNBC matched like politicians stabbing obligatory flag pins into their lapels. Fox was the first cable network to deal with the flood of news that morning by adding the "zipper," the crawl of news headlines at the bottom of the screen.

The zipper became the anxious EKG of the next decade, a visual manifestation of the fire hose of constant information, terrifying (*WHITE HOUSE EVACUATED . . . FAA HAS SHUT DOWN ALL DOMESTIC FLIGHTS . . .*) and eventually bathetic (*IPHONE 4 IN SHORT SUPPLY FOR CHINA LAUNCH . . . LINDSAY LOHAN COULD ENTER REHAB THIS WEEK . . .*). The zipper carried a message; it was a message. The emergency is permanent. The warning lights are always on. Keep watching.

After the attack, Fox topped the cable-news Nielsens. Its anchors taunted CNN on-air with the glee of a point guard who just buried a three-pointer. The thrill of besting one's rivals was part of Fox's brand identity. Conservative politicians would rise and fall, but conservative grievance had no term limits. Fox told its viewers they were oppressed by liberals whether they were in power or out, whether winning or losing.

When Barack Obama rolled toward election in 2008, it was galvanizing. Reaching back to Ailes's tactics in Nixon's 1968 election, the network played to its white viewership's sense of siege by the black candidate with the Kenyan father, Arabic middle name, and African surname. When video was discovered of Obama's former pastor Jeremiah Wright, preaching "God damn America" in a sermon decrying government-propagated racism, Fox practically made Reverend Wright his running mate—playing over and over for its white viewers the clip of a black minister voicing black rage in front of a black choir. When Obama affectionately bumped fists with his wife on the campaign trail, Fox anchor E. D. Hill called it a "terrorist fist jab."

* * * *

OBAMA'S LANDSLIDE VICTORY launched a baroque and lucrative era of Fox News persecution theater. In his 1964 essay "The Paranoid Style in American Politics," Richard Hofstadter anticipated a refrain that would become common on Fox and in Republican politics (which were becoming increasingly indistinguishable): "I want my country back."

"The modern right wing," Hofstadter wrote, "feels dispossessed: America has been largely taken away from them and their kind, though they are determined to try to repossess it and to prevent the final destructive act of subversion." Hofstadter argued that the right was more susceptible to this ideation because of its continual sense that the country was moving away from it. But he was not describing an ideology so much as a leitmotif. America was always inches away from the apocalypse in this recurring tune, whose notes were "heated exaggeration, suspiciousness, and con-spiratorial fantasy."

Fox's maestro of paranoia was Glenn Beck, whose show began the day before Obama's inauguration. A buzz-cut former CNN *Headline News* host, he turned the 5 p.m. hour into a daily seminar of the sort of ideas you used to have to get from hand-printed pamphlets handed out on street corners. Sure, he argued that Obama's recession-fighting policies would lead America to tyranny and blood-in-the-streets disorder. But that was just the warm-up. In Beckland, America had been on a long march to big-government fascism since Woodrow Wilson, which contention he supported by pointing out the fasces on the reverse of the 1916 Mercury dime.

In 1993, the Fox broadcast network premiered *The X-Files*, a long-running sci-fi serial involving a vast plot by aliens and their human quislings to subjugate mankind. The surface storyline drew on a long history of fantasies about alien invasion, from H. G. Wells's *The War of the Worlds* to the Cold War parable *Invasion of the Body Snatchers*. But it added refrains from such counterculture sci-fi authors as Philip K. Dick and 1970s conspiracy thrillers like *The Parallax View*: that the creatures from beyond were working with a cabal of our own leaders and elites against, that what you perceive as reality in the news and daily life was a scrim hiding a horrible truth. (This was the essence, for instance, of the 1988 John Carpenter sci-fi horror film *They Live*, whose protagonist dons a special pair of sunglasses that allow him to see that advertising slogans hide secret commands to conform, and that many human leaders are actually hideous aliens.)

The X-Files' entertaining paranoia echoed, if unintentionally, the 1990s right-wing militia members who believed that a globalist world government used black helicopters to patrol the skies on behalf of the United Nations. But it also looked back, to the disillusion of the 1960s and 1970s (the creator, Chris Carter, cited Watergate as a formative influence), and forward, to the theorists who

would insist that the 9/11 attacks were an inside job. The series' slogans—"I Want to Believe," "The Truth Is Out There," and "Fight
the Future"—anticipated a coming wave of political conspiracists,
gobbling up weird tales from online forums and *InfoWars*, who
wanted to believe some out-there truths, driven by the lust to fight a
future that they believed would not include them.

Beck was like the daytime-TV *X-Files*, the missing link between
politics and talk-radio ufologists like Art Bell. His shows were part
sermon, part performance art. He'd riff a seventeen-minute defense
against critics who called him "dangerous" and "crazy," then lay out
his objections to a bailout of toxic bank assets while pulling sticks
out of a teetering Jenga tower. His premonitions of doom rivaled a
medieval religious ecstatic's. The AmeriCorps volunteer plan "indoc-
trinates your child into community service." Mexico would soon collapse and send millions of refugees over the border. America would
devolve into civil war by 2014. Sometimes he would weep.

Beck soon had an audience of over two million, astonishing for
late-afternoon cable. For an audience to whom the inauguration of a
man named Barack Hussein Obama seemed like the opening of the
seventh seal, Beck's prophecies were both more exciting and more
sensible than the humdrum actual news.

And he backed them up with so many facts! Well, at least, so
much *data*. He used charts, and diagrams, and a chalkboard, cited
historical texts and trivia and, always, numbers. ("Conspiracists,"
as Kurt Andersen wrote, "love learning the names of little-known
government programs, especially if they contain numbers—the air
force's Area 51, CIA's Operation 40, Special Ops' US war games in
2015 called Jade 15.") It was the theater of education, like admission
to an occult college whose syllabus revealed long-suppressed truths.

This was pure Hofstadter, who in the era of the John Birch Society and Barry Goldwater saw an impulse that applies just as well
to the conspiracists of the Web era. "A final characteristic of the
paranoid style is related to the quality of its pedantry," he wrote in

1964. "One of the impressive things about paranoid literature is the contrast between its fantasied conclusions and the almost touching concern with factuality it invariably shows. . . . It is nothing if not scholarly in technique. McCarthy's 96-page pamphlet, *McCarthyism*, contains no less than 313 footnote references."

Beck became too successful, too quick: he clashed with Ailes and left Fox to start his own media company. But he left a message behind on his chalkboard: there was a stunningly passionate following out there for anyone willing to offer up an ambitious enough conspiracy.

* * * *

IT WASN'T ALL JENGA and tears on Obama-era Fox News. A cable-news network had to have its version of fun, and that was where *Fox & Friends* came in.

Fox & Friends was the network's twist on a TV staple, the morning talk show. It had been on the network almost since its beginning, with three amiably shallow hosts on a curvy couch: Steve Doocy, a onetime kids'-TV host; Brian Kilmeade, a former sportscaster; and a succession of female cohosts. Doocy and Kilmeade's chucklehead banter, and their tendency to talk down to the women paired with them, gave the show a feeling of a Greek Week mixer at a party-school frat house. In its early days, it was a frothy morning smoothie of headlines, weather, and showbiz news. (In 2000, I appeared on it to talk about—what else?—reality TV.)

But it was also, especially in the Obama years, a go-to spot for towel-snapping, if not in-depth, conservative commentary. In 2007, the hosts spread a bogus story that Obama had attended a "madrassa" as a child in Indonesia. John Moody, Fox's executive vice president of news editorial, deflected the controversy by calling the show "an entertainment show that does some news."

That description might apply to the entire network (Beck called his own show "the fusion of entertainment and enlightenment"), but

Fox & Friends existed in its own brackish transitional zone between infotainment and politics. That zone was where Donald Trump, host of *The Celebrity Apprentice*, happened to live.

Politics had been important to the Trump business since before Donald Trump ran it—political connections and favors were essential to Fred Trump's New York enterprises, and Trump continued that family tradition. For decades he used his celebrity prerogative to weigh in on politics. His positions were mercurial: he praised the Clintons before attacking them; denounced Pat Buchanan's "intolerance" before he trebled it; endorsed single-payer government health systems before he disparaged Obamacare. His few consistent themes reflected his brand and self-image. We needed, generally, to be "tough." We were being taken advantage of by other countries, both competitors—Japan, since the 1980s, was a favorite target—but also allies, who didn't pay what they owed us. Everyone owed us. But we were being cheated, because our leaders were stupid. The other constant was racism, going back to his 1989 crusade against the Central Park Five, the black and Latino teenagers wrongly accused of a brutal rape. The five were exonerated on DNA evidence, but Trump not only did not apologize or recant, he likened the youths to "animals," a term he would later apply to terrorists and accused criminals who were minorities—and only to minorities.

Trump could count on ravenous media interest when he teased a run for office. But mainly he was a familiar type: the celebrity kibitzer who likes to shoot the shit about politics. On Howard Stern (with whom he once joked about having sex with Princess Diana, but only if she'd take an HIV test), Trump would handicap elections, showing the conventional-wisdom awareness of a TV news junkie but always hedging his bets. "Would you fire [George W.] Bush?" Stern asked shortly before the 2004 election. "Well, I love his tax policy and I hate his war, so I guess, you know, we'll have to see what happens," Trump answered. On the syndicated-TV entertainment magazine *Extra*, he had a semiregular segment, "World According to Trump," in which he'd promote his brands (like the cologne "Success by Trump," sold at Macy's), weigh in on Hollywood gossip, like actress Halle Berry's love life, and expound on the political scandals du jour, like Secretary of State Hillary Clinton's having been caught on camera downing a beer. ("I think that was just fine. She's relaxing.")

Trump was hardly on Fox News's radar before *The Apprentice*. He'd occasionally show up to speculate on the real-estate market or to defend his former tenant Michael Jackson, who'd been arrested for child molestation. ("Rita, I will say this. It's very, very dangerous today to be a celebrity. It really is, especially if you're a rich celebrity.") He hedged on whether he supported the Iraq invasion on Neil Cavuto's show in 2003, then returned to the same show in 2004 saying that he'd felt all along that the war—which by then had become a quagmire—was a mistake.

With *The Apprentice*, Trump became part of *Fox & Friends'* entertainment-news universe. They made "You're fired" jokes. They covered his public spats, like a feud with Rosie O'Donnell, who called him a hypocrite for judging the morals of a Miss USA contestant. They covered his 2005 remarriage and his daughter Ivanka's 2009 wedding and his casting of disgraced former Illinois governor Rod Blagojevich on *Celebrity Apprentice*. They covered him, in other words, like a celebrity.

On February 19, 2010, the hosts had him on "to talk about some of the politics in Washington, D.C., which he wants to do." Trump had recently said that former vice president and environmental activist Al Gore should be stripped of his Nobel Peace Prize, because the capital was experiencing its coldest winter in years. Now *this* was relevant to Fox's interest: "The Donald taking on former V.P. Al Gore!"

But was Trump joking about Gore's Nobel? Yes and no, depending what you preferred. "Yes, I was kidding," he said. "I was being sarcastic. But when I get down to it, was I really kidding?" What about the difference between the weather in a particular place and the global climate? "Well, they always have an answer," Trump said. "Then they get caught sending e-mails around saying it's a con from the scientists."

Trump's response was like a secret handshake to the base: he was referring to a controversy, much covered in conservative media, in which a trove of climate researchers' e-mails were hacked, then quoted out of context to make it appear as if they were arguing in favor of distorting data. The honest explanation was complicated. The smear was easy; and here was the You're Fired Guy saying it in Fox's own language.

Fox & Friends invited Trump back throughout 2010, just as the Tea Party rhetoric against Obama was growing febrile and theatrical—grown men cosplaying in Revolutionary tricorn hats at rallies, incited by leaders like Palin, who claimed that the Obamacare health legislation would lead to "death panels" ruling on how long Grandma was allowed to live. When the US commander in Afghanistan, General Stanley McChrystal, was quoted in *Rolling Stone* mocking Obama administration officials, the hosts asked Trump if the general should be "fired"—his pundit character merging directly with his reality-boardroom character. How about the collapsed drilling rig that had been spewing oil into the Gulf of Mexico for weeks? "We should blow it up." On an appearance to plug the lineup for the next *Celebrity Apprentice*—"Dionne Warwick, Gary Busey, José Canseco"—he admitted that he was thinking about a political run "for the first time." "So what you would say to Congress is, you're fired!" said Doocy.

The recurring theme: there were easy answers to our problems, ones you probably thought of yourself, and the pointy-heads were just too befogged to see it. Not Trump. *Blow something up! Get China on the phone! You're fired!* The intellectuals, like Obama, loved to tell you the world was more complex than you assumed. No: Trump, like the broad strokes symbols of a reality-TV show, told you that the world was *exactly as simple* as you thought it was, and you were the smart one for seeing that.

"It sounds like we might need Donald Trump in charge of a heck of a lot of things!" said cohost Gretchen Carlson.

(Trump, for his part, would show little reciprocal loyalty to Carlson, the former Miss America 1989, when in 2016 she sued Ailes for sexual harassment, having recorded him telling her, "I think you and I should have had a sexual relationship a long time ago, and then you'd be good and better and I'd be good and better." Trump, by then a presidential candidate, defended Ailes, saying that he "felt very badly" for him and pointing out "how much he's helped" women like Carlson.)

Trump became like an adopted Fox family member. The hosts talked about him even when he wasn't on the show. (A report about a shark infestation near Palm Beach managed a reference to Mar-a-Lago: "Look out, Donald Trump!") And Trump seemed to be paying attention to Fox while he was away, taking an interest in controversies the network was whipping up, such as the "Ground Zero mosque," a plan to build an Islamic community center a few blocks away from the World Trade Center site, which conservatives called a "victory memorial" for terrorists. Trump offered to put up money to relocate the center, prompting favorable coverage on *Fox & Friends*.

It was like a brand merger. Trump and *Fox & Friends* traded favors, each invested in the other. A few days after the Ground Zero report, Trump's wife Melania came on the show to promote her jewelry business—"Melania Timepieces and Jewelry," peddled on shopping network QVC. ("Fun & Affordable," a Fox caption read.) The hosts asked her how she managed to juggle motherhood and business, an odd question for a woman wealthy enough to hire an army of jugglers. The next day, Trump came on *Fox & Friends* to argue for extending tax cuts for the rich. ("Aren't the rich the ones who spend and hire everyone else?" Carlson asked. "Donald Trump will answer that. He's rich.") In October, news broke of a mysteriously funded poll testing Trump's chances in a presidential run. "I hear the results are amazing," he said. "I don't know what they were."

In the fall of 2010, as Fox's Republican home team was marching toward a midterms victory that would give them control of the House of Representatives, Fox began airing a promotional intro clip recorded by its favorite guest: "I'm Donald Trump, and you are watching *Fox & Friends*. And if you turn the channel—*You're fired!*"

* * * *

FOX SERVED AS a kind of test-market for Trump's political opinions, a real-time feedback mechanism to see what best unleashed the gut passions of the audience and kept the camera rolling. Conspiracy theory: good. Xenophobia: good. Laying into Obama: very, very good.

There was one particular, potent claim that rolled all these into one, multiplying their power. Since Obama had been elected, fringes of the right had embraced the theory that the president had been born not in Hawaii but Kenya and therefore was constitutionally ineligible to be president.

How and why exactly someone would have engineered a conspiracy with medical and government officials in the belief—in the segregation-era America of 1961—that a black baby would grow up to be president fifty years later required some logical gymnastics. But the emotional evidence, to the fervent believers, was that a black man whose name rhymed with Osama bin Laden's, with the middle name *Hussein* for God's sake, was running the goddam United States, and it was not normal, he was not *a regular American president*, something had gone crazy. In Hofstadter's words, America had been "taken away from them and their kind."

It was all so volatile, and so nuts, that for all its catering to its viewers' passions, Fox News steered clear of it in 2009 and 2010. Even Glenn Beck, the man who saw fascism on the back of a dime, dismissed it. And yet it was out there, spread on Facebook and in chain e-mails and the radio shows of Rush Limbaugh and Lou Dobbs. It was potent—the pure, black-tar, straight-to-the-artery speedball version of Fox's usual intoxicant—and hanging out there for anyone to use if only they were unencumbered by shame.

Trump had already learned a lesson from his Central Park Five crusade: What stirs people up? Racial issues. What *really* stirs them up? Actual racism!

On February 10, 2011, Trump spoke at the Conservative Political Action Conference, a proving ground for Republican presidential candidates. His speech was standard Trump—China is killing us, America is a laughingstock, our leaders are losers—with a new variation: "Our current president came out of nowhere. Came out of nowhere! In fact, I'll go a step further. The people who went to school with him, they never saw him. They don't know who he is. Crazy!"

Crazy! The crowd indeed went nuts. On Valentine's Day, *Fox & Friends* reported that Trump had been the "star" of CPAC. The wider media was abuzz too, both with the outrageous birther claim and the possibility that that guy from TV might be an honest-to-God candidate for president the next year. The *Tonight Show*, on Trump's home network, NBC, aired a bit with politicians' heads superimposed on contestants in an *Apprentice* boardroom, Trump telling House Speaker John Boehner, House Minority Leader Nancy Pelosi, and Vice President Joe Biden, "You're fired!"

As it happened, the fourth season of *Celebrity Apprentice* was premiering on March 6, 2011. This provided the perfect, mutually rewarding peg for *Fox & Friends* to announce its new guest feature, "Mondays with Trump," making Trump's association with the show official. The motivation for the segment lay—like Trump and *Fox & Friends*—at the intersection of right-wing politics and infotainment. The segment was on Mondays, because *Celebrity Apprentice* aired Sunday nights. So "Mondays with Trump" would be in part a morning-TV staple—the "morning after" segment about the weekly elimination on a reality show—and part commentary by the new darling of the right, who had just suggested that their viewers' most-despised president should constitutionally be ejected from the boardroom.

Trump's celebrity self and political self were fused on "Mondays with Trump." One minute he'd be asked his opinion of the US military action in Libya. ("The stupidity of our leaders and politicians is unbelievable.") The next: why did he fire supermodel Niki Taylor, after the *Celebrity Apprentice* challenge to create the perfect outdoor experience for the Camping World R.V. company?

In the rest of the media, Trump's birther claims raised his political profile. *Good Morning America* introduced him as a potential challenger to President Obama, and sent reporter Ashleigh Banfield on his plane—"Trump Force One," host George Stephanopoulos called it, laughing—to ask him about the birth-certificate theory (mostly unchallenged), as well as piracy off the coast of Africa ("I would wipe them out of the sea so fast") and the recent public meltdown of actor Charlie Sheen, fired from the sitcom *Two and a Half Men*, who'd appeared on a Beverly Hills rooftop drinking red liquid from a bottle labeled "tiger's blood" and waving a machete. To CNN's Anderson Cooper, Trump claimed, without evidence, that one of his "investigators" in Hawaii had reported the birth certificate missing.

The birther conspiracy, now that Trump had raised it, was suddenly an acceptable topic on Fox. Sean Hannity waded in during his prime-time show: "Produce the birth certificate, and it's all over." On *Fox & Friends*, Trump denied that he was a racist. "Frankly, I think it's insulting," Trump said. "People are calling me from all over and saying, 'Please don't give up on this issue.'" Later, he fumed at former Bush adviser (and Fox contributor) Karl Rove for calling Trump a "joke candidate" over birtherism. "You're more fired up than usual this morning," Carlson said, "and that's why you're a great guest."

* * * *

ON APRIL 27, 2011, three days after Trump fired LaToya Jackson in the boardroom, President Obama released the long-form version of his birth certificate, a document that birtherism argued could not exist. (At a press conference in New Hampshire the same day, Trump tried to spin the release as a victory, beginning his remarks, "Today,

I am very proud of myself.") On April 30, as a guest at the White House Correspondents' Dinner in Washington—a ritual commingling of showbiz and political stars—Trump was viciously roasted both by comedian Seth Meyers and President Obama himself: "He can finally get back to the issues that matter—like, did we fake the moon landing?"

The popular narrative was that this was a disaster for Donald Trump, an abject humiliation. Maybe. It may have factored into his decision, later that month, not to run for president in 2012. (The corollary, advanced by political reporters, biographers, and Omarosa, was that he ran in 2016 for revenge: "Every critic, every detractor, will have to bow down to President Trump," Omarosa said.) There was no denying the TV footage of Trump paralyzed at his table, rictus-faced, laughed at, gradually turning into a tomato.

But on *Fox & Friends*—where it mattered to Trump in the long run—it was no defeat at all. The roasting was a compliment, he said. After all, the whole evening was about him! More important, the show continued to treat him as a serious presidential contender, if not in the Republican primary, then as an independent.

The message was as much about serving the audience as about serving Trump. That message was: Donald Trump did nothing wrong, and neither did you. Donald Trump is smart and competent, and so are you. If you had believed in birtherism, if you wanted to believe—if you *still believed*, as Trump would soon make clear he did—then you are smarter than all of them. That was, after all, the implicit promise that Roger Ailes made back in 1996. "Fair and balanced," "We report. You decide"—all that messaging said that only Fox was fair, only Fox could be trusted, and if the liberal media— i.e., everyone else—said that you had been factually disproven, that was only more evidence that you are right.

With *The Celebrity Apprentice*'s 2011 season ending, Trump announced, at NBC's gala fall-schedule presentation for advertisers in New York, that he would not run for president in 2012. But "Mondays with Trump" continued during the *Apprentice* off-season.

Trump bashed Obama on the economy, then took questions about his new, $100-million jet, with gold faucets and suede ceilings. ("LIVIN' THE HIGH LIFE," said the chyron at the bottom of the screen.)

The show, whose audience if anything had been polarized onto Trump's side by the birther humiliation, became more deferential, even obsequious. "Donald Trump is confident, he's successful, he's a wonderful family man," said Kilmeade. (To which of his three families, Kilmeade did not specify.) The hosts taped a special segment for Christmas morning with Trump's grown children in the lobby of Trump Tower. (This bit itself played to the networks' "War on Christmas" theme: the messaging said that the Trumps celebrated *real Christian Christmas*, goddammit, not "holidays"—although Ivanka had converted to Judaism before marrying her husband, Jared Kushner.) They called him "The Trumpster." Doocy and Kilmeade even promoted Trump's menswear line, announcing that they would wear "Trump ties" every Monday.

As *Fox & Friends* went, so went the Republican party. That is, it went prostrate. In 2008, political observers noted a "Fox primary," in which the party's candidates made the rounds of the network's shows to court its hosts—and hopefully, its management and its viewers. In 2012 that became the "Trump primary." Candidates flattered Trump and visited him at Trump Tower—even Mitt Romney, who found him coarse and potentially alienating to the general public, bent the knee (doing his best not to be caught on camera) and eventually secured Trump's endorsement. Romney too badly needed what Ailes had created, and Trump had captured.

Romney lost. Trump persisted. For the next two and a half years, he had a second TV career on *Fox & Friends*, which you might have been entirely unaware of even if you were a fan of *Celebrity Apprentice*. On NBC, he rode herd on C-listers like former basketball star Dennis Rodman. On Fox, he weighed in on North Korea—because Rodman had struck up a friendship with the nuclear-armed, hoops-obsessed dictator of North Korea, allowing Trump to cast himself as the antithesis of "bad negotiator" Obama.

Cable TV's mentality paralleled Trump's almost perfectly. It was anti-narrative, a series of excitements and explosions without an arc, more like a movie trailer than a movie. Cable, like Trump, sought out conflict, rewarded provocation, framed life as a continual win-lose struggle, in which someone was always up and someone always down. What Fox took to as a calculated strategy—the appeal to ugly, atavistic emotion—he took to by instinct. Which is why he was not simply a cable-news guest, but a voracious consumer. He pushed the drug, and he got high on it.

Fox therefore provided material for Trump as much as he provided material for it. It was perfect symbiosis. What was the base going nuts over? What would the next birtherism be?

In 2014 Fox, which had moved from one sensation to another under Obama—Benghazi, Obamacare, Trayvon Martin—became fixated on the "border crisis." There was an increase in migrants crossing the border with Mexico, especially unaccompanied children fleeing gang violence. But in conservative media, it was sinister, criminal, brown adults pouring over the border to rape, murder, and steal jobs. It was the combo: crime, liberal weakness, and a foreign, specifically racial, threat to their America.

For decades, Donald Trump had harped on Japan, China, OPEC—never much Mexico. A former aide said Trump was originally "indifferent" to using immigration as an issue in a potential run for president. But Fox was providing ample evidence that its base was enflamed over the border and immigration. And Trump knew, since his days demagoguing the Central Park Five, that fear and racism were powerful. He just needed to shift his target. In February 2015, he again spoke at CPAC, and again, test-drove a new line: "As far as our borders are concerned, we need strong borders. We need a wall. If I run, I will tell you, the king of building buildings, the king of building walls."

Or at least, the king of building symbols. His same lizard-brain postmodernism—the salesman's intuition that the cartoon of a thing was more powerful to people than the thing itself—could be applied to politics as well as real estate and reality TV. What does wealth look like? A gold tower. What does business look like? A paneled boardroom. And what does border security look like? A solid, giant-ass wall. (The concept of the wall itself, it was later reported, was a "memory trick" hit upon by Trump's advisers to remind him to talk about immigration.)

The symbiosis of the Republican Party and the Fox News base was complete, and Trump was enmeshed in it—much more so than the actual politicians, who felt compelled to wink and nod at the base while holding the truly wild stuff with tongs. For the viewership, this was dissonant, and no fun. They were used to getting the straight-heroin nightmare fuel from their shows, like Glenn Beck had given them: a Manichaean, operatic struggle in defense of their guns, their values, their Western Christian culture. And then they got the old bait-and-switch: they were asked to vote for a John McCain or a Mitt Romney, who treated them like crazy cousins.

But not Trump! He was everything they got from Fox—the anger, the racist dog-whistling, the alpha-male sexism—and he owned it. He didn't act ashamed of it. Trump gets mad! Trump tells it like they tell it on TV! Fucking Obama! Fucking Mexicans!

By 2015, Trump's family at *Fox & Friends* seemed to sense that he was on the verge of ascending to the next level. They began speaking to him like an eminence grise, even as he began hosting another season of *The Celebrity Apprentice*, with Fox reporter Geraldo Rivera and reality star Kate Gosselin of *Jon and Kate Plus Eight*. On March 2, 2015, as the season closed—congratulations, champion Leeza Gibbons—the hosts asked if he would sign another contract, and he answered: "I'm looking at something much more important. I think you understand what that is."

* * * *

THAT AN NBC GAME SHOW host could sit on a national news pro-gram and soberly intimate his plans to become the leader of the free world would have seemed parodic in 1980, when Donald Trump first emerged as a TV personality. In 2015—well, it still seemed parodic, but now the parodic had become the possible.

A lot had happened since 1980, when Trump presented the easy-listening version of himself in Tom Brokaw's beige-on-beige studio, when he told Rona Barrett that "somebody with the kind of views that are maybe a little bit unpopular" could never win a TV campaign. Fox News had happened. Reality TV had happened. The fragmentation of the audience had happened. The embrace of the antihero had happened. All of this happened in the world of celebrity, where Donald Trump began playing the character of rakish billionaire playboy, evolved into a comic self-parody, and evolved again into the caustic You're Fired Guy. It happened as well in the world of politics, into which he had spun off that character. This meant that, maybe, where a presidential candidate once had to make a majority comfortable, he could now discomfit an intense enough minority to carry him over one rival, then another, and take their followers with him.

The last "Mondays with Trump" aired June 15, 2015. *Fox & Friends* was buzzing about the big announcement Trump would make, the next day, about his political future. In the larger media, there was skepticism—Trump, pundits suggested, was just grabbing headlines, like in 1988 and 2000 and 2012—but in the Fox studio, it sounded like a done deal. There was a valedictory feel to the interview, wistful and proud, like a goodbye party for a coworker who'd landed a top-level job at another company. Doocy made one more reference to Trump ties, for old times' sake.

Finally, the new female cohost—Elisabeth Hasselbeck, conservative commentator and fourth-place finisher on *Survivor: The Australian Outback*—noted that the day before had been Trump's sixty-ninth birthday. (The screen showed a picture of a smiling Trump with a "HAPPY BIRTHDAY!" graphic and balloons.) Doocy asked, "What does Donald Trump get for his birthday, just out of curiosity, gift wise?"

"If you folks came to my party," Trump said, "I would want really beautiful, expensive gifts."

Of course, *Fox & Friends* had been giving him a priceless gift for four years straight. The next day, gliding down an escalator to the pink-marble-lined food court of Trump Tower, he would open it.

Episode 8

THE MOST OBJECTIONABLE PROGRAM

Be sure to tune in and watch Donald Trump on Late Night with David Letterman as he presents the Top Ten List tonight!

—@realDonaldTrump's first tweet, 2:54 p.m., May 4, 2009

EVERY NEW MEDIUM GOES THROUGH A PHASE WHEN PEOPLE figure out what it's really for. When television first emerged, people guessed that it would be an educational tool. A university lecture, right in your living room! But for entertainment, they assumed, it could never replace radio. "The problem with television is that the people must sit and keep their eyes glued on a screen," the *New York Times* explained in 1939. "The average American family hasn't time for it."

Just so, when Twitter emerged, most celebrities, like Donald Trump, saw it mainly as a promotional tool for their appearances in more important media. Trump's first-ever tweet plugged a CBS *Late Show with David Letterman* appearance (mistakenly using the title of Letterman's old NBC talk show) before the *Celebrity Apprentice* season finale. It referenced him in the third person, as if he were a product, not the author—which was true. The publisher of his new book, *Think Like a Champion*, had signed him up for Twitter, and his early tweets came from its staffers or his office, not Trump's own thumbs.

These fledgling tweets are not memorable. There are little Oprah-esque, advice-flavored nuggets from his book ("Strive for wholeness and keep your sense of wonder intact"). There are tweets promoting his interviews, a commercial he made for Double Stuf Oreos, the ratings for his appearance on a *Monday Night RAW* wrestling special. There are sympathies on the death of former Trump Tower resident Michael Jackson and a thank-you to his followers for birthday wishes. His only remotely political tweet in 2009 endorsed a former *Apprentice* winner, Randal Pinkett, to be the Democratic candidate for lieutenant governor of New Jersey.

Trump tweeted, in other words, like a celebrity. Even the "real" in his Twitter handle, @realDonaldTrump, while it might seem like a ham-handed metaphor for a reality star who played himself like a fictional character, was what celebrities used to distinguish themselves from impersonators, as in the official accounts @RealHughJackman and @KevinHart4real.

In 2010, Trump began tweeting in the first person, but it was still anodyne stuff—tidbits about meeting Lady Gaga ("she was fantastic!") or seeing the musical *American Idiot* on Broadway ("An amazing theatrical experience!") or having a "fantastic dinner" at Quattro in the Trump SoHo hotel. The tone—glad-handing, inoffensive, upbeat—doesn't match his combative '80s persona or even the You're Fired Guy. It's the voice of a conventional broadcast-TV star who wants everyone to like him, a celebrity who likes to be associated with other celebrities.

When Trump became a *Fox & Friends* regular in early 2011—just as the fury of the Tea Party had been rewarded with a Republican House majority—his tweets shifted, gently at first. He mentioned a website, ShouldTrumpRun.com, that encouraged the presidential run he was teasing on Fox. But his cable-TV political persona was referenced only through vague links, and his birther crusade not at all, through his humiliation at the White House Correspondents' Dinner.

Then, on July 6, 2011, it was as if somebody flipped a switch: "Congress is back. TIME TO CUT, CAP AND BALANCE"—a reference to a Republican budget proposal—"There is no revenue problem. The Debt Limit cannot be raised until Obama spending is contained."

The attacks, the random capitalization, the CAPS LOCK: it was like Celebrity Trump had suddenly split down the middle and Politician Trump crawled out of the discarded husk.

The news site The Outline later suggested a theory for Trump's sudden social-media awakening. That same day, July 6, President Obama held the first "presidential Twitter town hall," answering questions live from his official Twitter account. Obama's had been the first presidential campaign to aggressively use social media. Now, the president who embarrassed Trump in a Washington dining room was using Twitter to send direct, unfiltered messages.

Donald Trump, a senior citizen who rarely used a personal computer, a hunt-and-peck typist accustomed to giving dictation, had never taken to e-mail. Why would he? E-mail is a medium for communicating directly to a single person, addressing them as an individual, and effectively putting them on your level. Who needed it? That's what secretaries were for.

But Twitter, as Obama's use of it suggested, was different. It was a broadcast network, a way of projecting yourself to millions.

Trump began tweeting daily, at first in spurts, then in almost a constant narration. He had stopped talking about birtherism on cable news—it was again too radioactive. But on Twitter, he found an audience who wanted to believe, and his theories became more baroque and paranoid. (He raised an eyebrow over the death in a plane crash of Hawaii's state health director, who had released Obama's birth certificate, insinuating a murder and cover-up befitting The X-Files.)

Like on Fox & Friends, he maintained a showbiz-gadfly persona— he weighed in on the breakup of the costars of the vampire romance Twilight, Kristen Stewart and Robert Pattinson ("She cheated on him like a dog")—while cheerleading Mitt Romney's 2012 campaign. On Election Night, when he briefly thought that Romney would lose the election while winning the popular vote (he didn't, though Trump would later do the reverse), Trump tweeted, "More votes equals a loss . . . revolution!"

You could overlay Trump's feed of tweets on his *Fox & Friends* appearances the way stoners would play Pink Floyd's *Dark Side of the Moon* over *The Wizard of Oz*. Twitter was the febrile, unfiltered version. There were no segment producers, no hosts to nervously redirect him, only his impulse and the immediate gratification of likes and retweets. No one could take it away from him. There was no one to ask if it sounded crazy to tweet, "Why are armed drones being released over our homeland by the Government?" There was only stimulus and response, more immediate even than the Nielsen ratings that he had become obsessed with as a TV personality.

You just poured out the sugar, and the ants swarmed. It was pure id and reflex. It was Trump's language.

* * * *

TWITTER, FOUNDED IN 2006, caught on during the early Obama era. Like many Silicon Valley products, it evangelized itself with the language of benevolence and idealism. It would be a global forum and cocktail party, forging friendships and defeating censors. The company's logo—a white-and-blue image of a bird on the wing—suggested a United Nations peacekeeping effort.

For a while, the hype seemed justified. Obama (a Twitter user since 2007) and his followers spread the campaign's "Hope" slogan online. Twitter connected protestors in Iran's pro-democracy "Green Movement" in 2009. (The protests failed, despite all the well-meaning Western supporters tinting their avatar photos green in solidarity.)

At the same time, social media became a partner to TV. It offered a "second screen" for fans to react to shows, building buzz and engagement. This drove ratings for the kind of TV that people wanted to watch live in order to chat about it in real time: reality shows like *American Idol*; dramas with constant holy-shit twists like *Scandal*; live sports and awards shows.

In July 2013, Twitter made a surprise hit out of *Sharknado*, a low-budget Syfy channel creature feature about, yes, sharks in a tornado. Its scenes included star Ian Ziering, former costar of *Beverly Hills, 90210*, being swallowed whole by a shark, chainsawing his way out of its belly, thus freeing another character who had been eaten *by the same shark* while falling from a helicopter. (Ziering later appeared on *The Celebrity Apprentice*, and almost secured a brilliant piece of comedy stunt-casting for the 2015 sequel, *Sharknado 3: Oh Hell No!*—enticing Donald Trump to play the President of the United States. Trump backed out of the role as he weighed an actual run for president, life imitating *Sharknado*.)

Syfy did very little traditional advertising, instead letting word spread virally online, to give fans a feeling of discovery. It worked: Twitter became a *Sharknado*-nado, a raucous impromptu peanut gallery with pop-culture junkies, political pundits, and Mia Farrow throwing in wisecracks. Seeing a reference to *Sharknado* on your Twitter feed, adding your own joke, you felt part of a surging phenomenon—a storm if you will—outside the advertising machine. In fact, you were the advertising machine.

For celebrities, social platforms did everything tabloids and entertainment magazines used to—delivered the candid photos and tidbits that made you feel personally connected with your faves—without negotiations over interview access or reliance on the choices of photo editors.

They especially advantaged celebrities with a penchant for being their own press agents—celebrities like Donald J. Trump, who decades before had called up reporters pretending to be his own publicist, "John Miller" or "John Barron." Twitter rewarded outrageous stars like Kanye West who could make themselves into sharknadoes. (West would later become a Trump supporter, seemingly less out of any coherent ideology than out of iconoclasm, a hunger for attention, and, maybe, a recognition of a similar sharknadic force in the celebrity president, who West said shared his "dragon energy.")

Instagram did the same for stars with a savvy eye for presentation, like West's wife, Kim Kardashian, the star of reality hit *Keeping Up with the Kardashians*, known for her fertility-goddess curves and her business instinct for brand extensions. After the tabloids obsessed over her weight gain during her first pregnancy, Anne Helen Petersen wrote, she became an "accidental activist" during her second by Instagramming her naked body. *New York* magazine art critic Jerry Saltz compared her to Andy Warhol, an artist of fame.

Social media played into the same thirst for authenticity that reality TV did, the idea that you were seeing people unfiltered, unpremeditated. (It also allowed ordinary people to edit and set-dress their own lives like reality shows.) It literally placed celebrities among your friends and family—their e-missives plopped right alongside updates from your mom and your college roommates. It made celebrities into broadcasters. It made fans into programmers (your list of social-media "follows" was unique to you). And Twitter, in particular, shrank the unit of communication to the length of a text message, or a Bible verse.

This bite-sized format made it a partner for one more kind of TV: the news. Twitter was a kind of news medium in itself, as reporters and outlets used it to link to longer stories and to break news in the moment. But it was also the social medium most suited to the excited metabolism of cable news. It was one microburst after another, a fire hose of non sequiturs. If TV news was "Now . . . this," Twitter was *thisthisthisthisthis*.

It was the perfect expressive medium for someone with a minimal attention span who got mad a lot. It had endless potential for someone who could communicate both as a celebrity (playing yourself as a character) and as a demagogue (in emotions and ALL CAPS).

And along with Facebook, it made it all the easier to do what Fox News et al. did: create a virtual chamber in which everyone thought like you and you raised your voices, together, in the communal hymn of Getting Mad on the Internet.

* * * *

SOCIAL MEDIA, infinitely customizable and niche-ified, was the ultimate medium for the culture war. But while Twitter and Facebook may have perfected the cultural bubble, they didn't invent it.

I've described how cable TV in general divided the twentieth-century mass audience into specialized audiences and how cable news, in particular, tribalized the political audience. The divides went beyond TV. Everywhere and in every way, by the twenty-first century, American culture had become partitioned.

America began as a patchwork of regional folkways, the natural evolution of a country that spanned thousands of miles. If you spent most of your time close to home, and if most of the voices you heard over the course of a day belonged to your neighbors, then—as it had been for most of human history—you would share the customs, language, and tastes of the people closest to you. In the mid-twentieth century, this changed. Mass commerce, the Interstate Highway System, and Marshall McLuhan's "global village" of telecommunication made the country smaller and flattened out local cultures. As Daniel Boorstin put it in 1962, "In the United States, we have, in a word, witnessed the decline of the 'folk' and the rise of the 'mass.'" For decades afterward, a country of hundreds of millions had a lingua franca of brands and sitcoms. Even food become less regional and more homogenous, with supermarkets nationalizing and restaurant chains spreading like fat globules via the arterial highways.

In the late twentieth century, all this shifted again, but along different lines and for different reasons. Personal technology, cable TV, niche media, and the resulting niche tastes broke the country into smaller and smaller parts. Except this time, the dividing lines weren't geographic (you liked what your neighbors liked) but demographic and psychographic (you liked what a peer group scattered across the country liked). The "grid of 200 million," as George W. S. Trow had described the mass-media landscape, was julienned and diced into tiny squares. There were no longer central gatekeepers to impose consensus or sound a communal voice. "The fragmentation of technology made it hard for anyone to control anything," wrote historians Kevin Kruse and Julian Zelizer. "The fragmentation created a world with fewer points of commonality in terms of what people heard or saw."

This happened in culture, in commerce, in food—all the intimate transactions from which people draw identity. Audiences streamed movies at home instead of gathering in theaters. Airplanes had media screens for each passenger. Cars did too, or passengers brought their own in the form of smartphones and tablets. Music moved from mass-market radio to individual playlists. Want a beer? Megabrands like Miller and Budweiser—which had once obliterated regional brands—now competed with thousands of microbrews. Coffee, once a standardized cuppa joe, became a taste hierarchy of shade-grown beans and pour-over techniques, with rules and implicit class barriers. You used to just drink coffee. Now you had to *learn* it.

And all this cultural fragmentation happened in balletic sync with the political tribalization pushed by Fox News and its peers. One byproduct of cable TV, as the channel list grew bigger and shows catered to smaller audiences, was that conservatives and liberals were not only seeing different news but also watching different entertainments.

Liberals tended to like—well, shows that TV critics like me did. According to a study by *Entertainment Weekly* and Experian Marketing in 2014, they were drawn to *Mad Men* (a dissection of the sexism of 1960s Madison Avenue); *Glee* (a high-school musical heavy on gender-identity storylines); *The Good Wife* (a feminist legal drama with a side of Democratic Illinois politics); and political comedies like *The Colbert Report*.

Conservatives had some predictable preferences: cop shows with male leads, the religious game show *American Bible Challenge*. As a 2016 *New York Times* study found, rural areas disproportionately liked *The Walking Dead*, the AMC horror drama in which a small band of rough-hewn survivors fought off zombies, and competing groups of the living, in the American South. The show's premise—that the institutions of science and society failed against a savage horde—rhymed with the conservative refrain that you could only trust yourself, not Big Government, for your welfare. In *The Walking Dead*, guns ruled, efforts at mercy usually ended in betrayal and death, and the only way to fend off the teeming invasion (analogous to immigrants or refugees or whatever scary real-world masses you liked) was to harden your heart and stay loyal to your own kind.

They also really liked reality TV. They especially liked shows that celebrated people who worked with their hands: *Fast N' Loud*, a reality show about renovating classic cars, and *Dirty Jobs*, where Mike Rowe (a frequent Fox News guest) wrangled snakes and crawled into sewers, paying tribute to people who did those jobs every day.

These reality shows, about rugged male (and usually white) individualists with big, swinging carbon footprints, might not reflect your actual life. They might not even reflect the actual lives of their stars. But they reflected an attitude: that old ways and old divisions of labor were still valued.

A particular favorite was *Duck Dynasty*, the A&E "reality sitcom" about the Robertson family of Louisiana, who ran the Duck Commander hunting-gear company. The Robertson men wore camouflage and fulsome ZZ Top beards. The theme song, in fact, was ZZ Top's "Sharp Dressed Man," that 1980s musical corporate merger of the high life and the down-home life.

The Robertsons loved practical jokes and Jesus. (Overt religiousness, like nudity and profanity, was a no-no in mass-market TV but flourished in niche cable.) The show offered the backwoods-tycoon story of *The Beverly Hillbillies* and the country-rebel spirit of *The Dukes of Hazzard*, aimed at an audience that saw the stars as kin. Like Trump's Sun King–Rodney Dangerfield persona, the family's appeal was a fantasy of you as a rich person, enjoying but not changed by wealth. (The fantasy extended to the beards. Pre-*Dynasty* photos revealed the Robertson men to be as clean-shaven as any baby-faced *Glee* star.) It echoed the anti-globalist, anti-cosmopolitan political dream of being prosperous in your own hermetic world, without any interaction with, or corruption by, outside influences—a Bayou Brexit.

Duck Dynasty launched its own political figure, Phil Robertson, a joyous patriarch on the show ("Happy, happy, happy!" was his catchphrase), a volatile religious conservative off-camera. In 2013, A&E suspended him after an interview with *GQ* magazine where he likened gay people to terrorists and suggested that black people in the South were happier before civil rights. If you lived in one America, this was a case of liberal political correctness bringing down an icon you loved just for speaking his mind. If you lived in another America, it was a forgettable story about some backwards nutjob on a show that you never watched, if you'd even heard of it.

Later, during and after the 2016 election, some readers looking to make sense of "the Trump voter" turned to J. D. Vance's *Hillbilly Elegy*. Vance's memoir of growing up in Appalachia was first embraced by conservative media for its "tough love" approach to the white underclass, as well as its support of their preferred thesis—that social dysfunction and "economic anxiety," rather than racism, explained the kind of lashing out we saw in the Trump movement. Vance described a poor white America embittered by lack of opportunity and disintegrating communities, alienated from an overclass of successful white-collar professionals identified by their neutral "TV accents."

But what was going on was not just a regional phenomenon or a class one. There was a psychographic divide, represented by media and entertainment subcultures—one that aligned people into virtual tribes defined by taste, education, race, religion, philosophy, and shared feelings of siege. It was a Beverly Hillbilly Elegy.

* * * *

THE NOTION THAT politics flow from culture is an old one. In pre-Nazi Germany and then in the United States, the theorists of the Frankfurt School critiqued popular culture—what Theodor Adorno and Max Horkheimer called "the culture industry," as distinguished from art—as an inherently consumerist force regardless of its content. "All mass culture under monopoly is identical," Adorno and Horkheimer wrote. "Films and radio no longer need to present themselves as art. The truth that they are nothing but business is used as an ideology to legitimize the trash that they intentionally produce." Mass culture, in this Marxist view, was a tool for anesthetizing the masses.

For conservative culture warriors of the twentieth century, their pro-business, pro-market philosophy ended at the outskirts of Hollywood and Manhattan. The entertainment and media industries, as they saw it, were a malign force that used people's consumer choices to corrupt them. In *The Closing of the American Mind* in 1987, University of Chicago professor Allan Bloom bemoaned a generation of liberal arts students turning from the Great Books toward the corrupting wiles of movies and popular music. Pat Buchanan, the lungfish on the evolutionary chain of Trumpism, declared in 1992 that the country was engaged in "a cultural war, as critical to the kind of nation we shall be as the Cold War itself." William Bennett wrote *The Book of Virtues* and *The De-Valuing of America* as a corrective to what he saw as secular culture's corrosion of public morals (before admitting himself to a gambling problem). They attacked "indecency" on TV with a frenzy of telepuritanism after singer Janet Jackson's nipple was exposed for a millisecond at the 2004 Super Bowl. During the 1992 campaign, Vice President Dan Quayle got in a spat with sitcom character Murphy Brown, who had a baby out of wedlock, and President George H. W. Bush went at *The Simpsons*, whose morals he compared unfavorably with *The Waltons*. (The show's brat-in-chief Bart Simpson answered on-air: "We're just like the Waltons. We're praying for an end to the Depression too.")

In other words, to the extent that traditional American conservatives had any position on pop culture, it was that they were against it. But with Fox News's war-of-all-against-all came the idea of competing pop-culture camps, icons, and subcultures. With the fragmentation of all kinds of cultures and markets—demographics who ate *this*, watched *that*, voted *thus*—came the idea of cultural choices as ideological markers.

Sometimes, this was a political hack's shorthand. "Latte liberal" survived as a cliché for elitism long after they started serving schmancy coffee drinks at McDonald's. But the divisions were often embraced by the political camps themselves, as intimate choices that separated believer from nonbeliever the way the laws of kashrut did. The president of Chick-fil-A denounced gay marriage; suddenly a chicken sandwich with waffle fries became a religious-right deep-fried Eucharist. Political camps had their own NFL quarterbacks: Tim Tebow for Christian conservatives, Colin Kaepernick for Black Lives Matter supporters.

* * * *

THE INTERNET DIDN'T CREATE this phenomenon. But it was perfectly designed to accelerate this phenomenon. It was a transformational invention, the cotton gin of culture war. If you had an obscure interest or kink, finding a like-minded community was once a life-long pilgrimage. Now it was a matter of a few keystrokes.

Joining a subculture was once a radical, defining decision, a statement by which you separated yourself from the great mainstream, like the 1970s punks whom media theorist Dick Hebdige studied. The expressions of a subculture, Hebdige wrote, "go 'against nature,' interrupting the process of 'normalization.' As such, they are gestures, movements toward a speech which offends the 'silent majority,' which challenges the principle of unity and cohesion, which contradicts the myth of consensus."

But in the fragmented Internet/cable/niche-market era, subculture was everywhere. It wasn't simply for youth severing themselves from their parents' idea of normalcy. It was for their parents too. It was for their grandparents. It was for hobbyists and enthusiasts and the religious.

It was also for political conservatives and cultural conservatives and movements that connected the two. In 2014, an online alliance of mostly male video gamers, irate at feminist criticism of sexist imagery in games, came together under the social-media hashtag #Gamer-Gate. Ostensibly, the campaign was protesting "ethics in videogame journalism." In practice, it produced a mob that threatened women, online and off, in the belief that men were the real victims of oppression: to wit, feminists saying bad things about the games they liked.

GamerGate connected backward in time to the "manosphere," a catchall term for online "men's rights" communities that had flourished for years: from "pickup artist" forums that gamified sex to Reddit's Red Pill group, for misogynists who believed that men and not women were the true oppressed class in society—its name taken from the capsule that Neo, in *The Matrix*, takes to open his eyes to the true nature of the world. The common theme was the galvanizing belief that masculinity was under siege in Western culture.

And GamerGate connected forward to the alt-right movement, which shared with the Fox News base the belief that its members were being erased from the national story. They reacted against the tearing down of Confederate monuments and the diversified casting of the *Star Wars* sequel trilogy that premiered in 2015. They wailed over a BBC history cartoon that depicted dark-skinned Britons during Roman rule, then mobbed the classicist Mary Beard when she replied on Twitter that "there's plenty of firm evidence for genetic diversity in Roman Britain." Cultural critic Angela Nagle wrote in *Kill All Normies* that the alt-right's leaders appropriated the leftist philosophy of Antonio Gramsci, "that political change follows cultural and social change." They were chatroom Clausewitzes for whom the War on Christmas was the continuation of politics by other means.

An early GamerGate supporter, Milo Yiannopoulos, launched an attack on Twitter against Leslie Jones, a star of *Ghostbusters*—the

2016 remake that committed the offense of rewriting male characters as women—referring to her as a "black dude" while his sympathizers deluged her with racist and pornographic tweets.

Trump actually beat Yiannopoulos to the subject by over a year, ranting in a January 2015 Instagram video: "Now they're making *Ghostbusters* with only women! What's going on?" It was the kind of grievance that he would make a campaign and a presidency out of, a pop-culture complaint that was really about the political fear of erasure. It resonated with an aggrieved male online fan base: "Childhood ruined," went a popular *Ghostbusters* lament on Reddit.

Keep in mind that billions of dollars a year were still being expended on producing video games, movies, and TV shows specifically tailored to these audiences. White men, the most culturally, politically, and economically superserved group in America, were simply now receiving service that was slightly less super. They reacted as if it were a form of ethnic cleansing capable of transcending time itself, and their bellyaching became a political force.

Yiannopoulos became an alt-right celebrity, flaunting his lavish wardrobe in profiles and using his identity as a gay man as a shield for Islamophobia. He was like a bigot Oscar Wilde, wielding the tropes of celebrity to brand race politics as cheeky and rebellious. He became an editor for the alt-right magnet site Breitbart, whose founder, Andrew Breitbart, believed that politics existed "downstream from culture" and whose later leader Steve Bannon would run Trump's campaign. (To Bannon, embittered online young men and the embittered geriatric Fox News audience were a natural match, and Breitbart would be the Match.com that connected them.)

In "An Establishment Conservative's Guide to the Alt-Right," Yiannopoulos rationalized the movement's ooze of online bigotry and anti-Semitism as "satirical." (Said "satire" included tweeting out digitally manipulated pictures of Trump critics in gas chambers.) But its common thread was racism—or, as Yiannopoulos preferred to put it, reaction against a society where "any discussion of white identity, or white interests, is seen as a heretical offense."

Past subcultures—punks, hippies, goths—struck against a homogenous main culture. The Internet's alt-right raged against the disappearance of one. Their tenets included, in Yiannopoulos's words, the belief "that some degree of separation between peoples is necessary for a culture to be preserved." Their weapons were memes and totems and nostalgia. Eventually, they would find a candidate who considered the battlefield of pop culture just as important as they did: "Donald Trump, perhaps the first truly cultural candidate for president since [Pat] Buchanan."

* * * *

THERE WAS A BRIEF PERIOD of wishful thinking, after Obama's reelection in 2012, that the right would see the futility of bitter culture warring and obstructionism, and "the fever would break." But it only rose, and Trump's Twitter account became more febrile to match. It also became a bigger part of his *Fox & Friends* presence. The hosts directed viewers to it as if they were Trump's publicists. On a January 2013 show, Steve Doocy summoned up a magisterial image: "Several times today, sitting at that big desk overlooking downtown New York City, Donald Trump will be doing some tweeting."

Yes, he would. On January 30 alone Trump tweeted thirty-four times. He criticized immigration reform efforts in Congress ("don't rush to give away our country!"). He quoted, multiple times, his book *Think Big* ("Go with your gut. Take chances"). He opined that the New York Yankees should fire Alex Rodriguez. He criticized the cost of an Obama speech in Las Vegas ("More money borrowed from China") and the administration's encouragement of the "Arab Spring" revolts ("Our new allies in Egypt, the Muslim Brotherhood, just called the Holocaust a 'myth' "). He promoted the March season premiere of *The Celebrity Apprentice*. He complained about wind turbines, which he opposed near his golf courses ("monstrosities"). He quoted Napoleon Bonaparte ("Impossible is a word to be found only in the dictionary of fools"). He answered several questions from followers, among them whether he drank coffee or tea ("Tea").

Trump's Twitter became his Fox News persona dialed up to 10, with no intermediation, no network chaperones, no fact-checkers, only the instant dopamine rush of likes and retweets. When a follower urged the *New York Times* to report on "vaccine damage and its price"—referring to the myth that childhood vaccines caused autism—he answered, "They should, Kim!" After one of the terrorists who bombed the 2013 Boston Marathon was wounded during his capture, Trump asked, "Is the Boston killer eligible for Obamacare to bring him back to health?" Trump was a quick puncher, with little patience for extensive (or reasoned) arguments but a talent for finding exposed nerves and karate-chopping them. *The Apprentice* used his quick-draw, pot-stirring sensibility in the boardroom; his campaign would weaponize it later; and Twitter was the perfect sparring grounds for practicing it.

Twitter was the opposite of the old school, offend-no-one, Least Objectionable Program model of twentieth-century broadcasting that prevailed when Trump first went on the *Today* show in 1980. Here, now, it paid to be the Most Objectionable Program. Trump ordered printouts of his most popular tweets to study what got his followers to click "Like": the ones that provoked shock, insult, rage. He was a pigeon in a lab, learning which button yielded the delicious pellet, and hitting it, and hitting it again. The most productive button, a campaign adviser later told Joshua Green, was immigration: "Every time Trump tweeted against amnesty in 2013, 2014, he would get hundreds and hundreds of retweets."

With the 2014 midterms approaching, Fox News, in sync with Republican candidates, latched onto the "border security" bogeyman. Trump by now was like a tuning fork that hummed on whatever frequency Fox was putting out. The network flogged a story, later debunked, that ISIS terrorists had entered the United States from Mexico. Trump responded with a tweet advocating a new cause: "The fight against ISIS starts at our border. 'At least' 10 ISIS have been caught crossing the Mexico border. Build a wall!"

In the fall of 2014, an Ebola epidemic in West Africa raised fears of a global contagion, which Fox stoked vigorously—sickness from the dark continent penetrating our border! In a politically prescient segment, Fox invited *Celebrity Apprentice* contestant and KISS bassist Gene Simmons to weigh in on the public-health issue. "In point of fact, we are completely unprepared for things like this," said the rock star, whose public-health background was limited to having written the song "Calling Dr. Love." Trump, meanwhile, launched a prodigious Twitter panic, calling for "a full travel ban" from the continent. ("Just stop the flights dummies!")

Twitter is a medium perfectly suited to epidemics, partly because it behaves so much like one. Ideas spread "virally." The denomination of Internet currency—the meme—takes its name from Richard Dawkins's term for the basic unit of culture, coined on a biological analogy to the gene. There is a Darwinian drive: nuanced opinions die unloved, while satisfying outrage and entertaining incitement thrive and reproduce.

In West Africa, Ebola was a genuine public-health catastrophe, killing more than 11,000 people. In the United States, it was minuscule. A traveler arrived in Texas from Liberia and died, infecting two nurses, who survived. Only one other person in the United States died of the disease, a patient flown in for treatment from West Africa. In New York City, a doctor returned from Guinea, spent a day in the city bowling and eating meatballs, then went to the hospital when he showed symptoms, recovering and infecting no one—except the feverish imaginations of cable news and social media, where it became a performative disaster movie, a sharknado.

* * * *

ANOTHER IMPORTANT DISTINCTION of Twitter from broadcast media is that social media are, well, social—the communication goes both ways. You might have five followers, your favorite celebrity five million, your president fifty million—but you can tweet at them just as they can at you. Those Twitter giants might or might not hear you, but the occasional sign that they did—retweeting a follower's message to their immense audiences—was, like signing an autograph or kissing a baby at a campaign rally, a gesture that you hadn't forgotten the little people. The key to a retweet from Donald Trump was usually praise, whether for Trump's *Celebrity Apprentice* or his political acumen or his personal character: "I respect your integrity sir. Rock on," earned a retweet for Twitter user @catpenis.

In a way, these fan-mail interactions were as important to Trump's project as his political ones. Or rather, they were different parts of the same message: telling the tribe that he was a member, not a visitor.

The illusion of mutual ownership, however ludicrous and insuperable the gap between your own life and the penthouse, had long been a part of celebrity fandom. The magazine photo-shoot, the carefully revealing profile, the artfully leaked tabloid item, the signed glossy for the fan club: all this gave you a sense of intimate attachment, a unique bond that happened to be shared by millions.

Social media brought this dynamic into the twenty-first century. In a society that fetishized the "real" and authentic, it made your contact with a star feel direct and unmediated. Social media allowed you, the audience, to feel seen in a way you couldn't with TV, where you were only seeing. When you followed Kim Kardashian on Instagram, you felt directly connected to her, seeing her with her own eyes through the camera she was holding. (And to be a real fan meant following a vast metanarrative that played across several media—*Keeping Up with the Kardashians*, celebrity magazines, social media, even her smartphone game *Kim Kardashian:* Hollywood—just as Trump's performance played out in pieces on *The Apprentice*, *Fox & Friends*, and Twitter.)

Getting retweeted, for a Trump follower, was like getting called from the studio audience to play on *The Price Is Right* or getting pulled out of the crowd to dance with Bruce Springsteen: it was the promise of transitioning, even for a moment, from spectator to spectacle. Even if you simply saw someone else retweeted—well, it was somebody like you. Someday it could be you. He was listening. You were heard. "If @realDonaldTrump retweeted me . . . I'd prob cry," Trump quoted @kenzoeblair.

This was an old tactic of celebrity applied to a distinct frustration of twenty-first-century politics. Even as every other area of media and culture became niche, presidential politics remained mass-market by constitutional design: you had to win an Electoral College majority. The *discussion* around politics was as microtargeted and polarized as anything in media. The *practice* of politics was not: you still had to offer enough of something for everybody to succeed in a system in which aggregation was everything.

So as a political junkie, you had talk radio, cable news, blogs, and social-media feeds creating feedback loops in which you heard your own beliefs constantly reaffirmed. If you never left those loops—and why would you?—you'd develop an inflated sense of how universally shared your beliefs were. If all you heard was people who agreed with you, it seemed obvious that *everyone* agreed with you. Why couldn't the idiots running the party see that? Why were they equivocating and compromising and acting embarrassed of you?

Trump's use of Twitter, early on, leveraged a political divide, not between parties, but between a party's candidates and its own voters. Every retweet said: I share, *wholly*, your grievance and your undisciplined anger and your paranoia about vaccines. (It also created a new type of meta-rhetoric: you could outsource the most incendiary statements to your followers, then say you were simply quoting "what people are saying.") It said: I am not ashamed of you. I am simply *of you*.

Past American leaders used the media of their day to forge a bond with an audience: Franklin D. Roosevelt with the intimacy of the radio address, John F. Kennedy the visual cool of television, Ronald Reagan the theatrical magnification of the movie screen. Social media added another element essential to someone who wanted to create a sense of blood bond with his following, to convince them they were all part of one mighty body of which he was the head. It allowed political followers to believe that they were doing more than watching and listening to their leaders, but that they, themselves— by tweeting and retweeting and adding their digit to someone's follower count—had helped to *create* that leader, that they were invested in his project, that an offense to him was an insult to them and his victories were their vindication.

The day before Donald Trump announced his presidential campaign, one observer sensed the power of that bond. It was not a political columnist or a party leader, but rather the Twitter user @ZStr8Up, whom Trump retweeted from his account: "After the liberal 60's and 70's how did we end up with Reagan? Hollywood. The Donald may have a serious chance."

PART III

PRESIDENT TELEVISION

2015–

Episode 9

RED LIGHT

DONALD TRUMP HAD ONE FRIEND WHO STUCK BY HIM HIS entire campaign, one partner who never left his service. When he spoke, he spoke to one audience: not the moderators at the debates, not the throngs at his rallies, not the "forgotten man and woman" that his speechwriters kept referring to.

He spoke to the red light.

The red light on top of the TV camera said that the machine was on. It said that a collective intelligence, in studios and control rooms, had decided you were worthy, for the moment, of attention. The red light had been there in Tom Brokaw's *Today* show studio, on *Donahue*, on *The Fresh Prince*. It was on *The Apprentice*, when he gave it a floor of Trump Tower to live in.

Between the red light and every person watching at home ran the thinnest filament, through which they transmitted their love, hate, excitement, fear. All these filaments converged in the light and made it burn. It was bioluminescence, a glow powered by pure human emotion.

He knew what the red light wanted, because it was just like him. It didn't care what you had given it before, only what you would give it next. If you didn't have anything for it, you stopped existing until you did.

At his rallies, he once explained, he often didn't look at the people. The people were easy. If they got listless, you'd yell, "Build the wall!" and they'd snap back.

But the red light's tastes were more exotic. It wanted something new. It wanted something dangerous. If he sensed that it might blink off—meaning that he was no longer being carried live on cable news—he told the *Washington Post*, "I would say something new to keep the red light on."

If what he said got someone punched in the face—well, he didn't throw the punch, did he? If what he said was the opposite of what he said before, then that was what he believed now, until the next time.

If he kept the red light sated, it would help him. The red light put you into the unreal estate of TV, the place that was everywhere, that was better than the real world. When it turned off, you died, a little bit.

* * * *

THE RED LIGHT needed a show, always. So he started with one. The morning of June 16, 2015, he appeared at the top of the Trump Tower lobby escalator with his wife Melania—sphinxlike as always, in a white skirt and shoulderless top—in front of a sign that read "Currency Exchange." They descended toward a blue-curtained stage in the building's food court. The PA system blared Neil Young's "Rockin' in the Free World," a protest song from 1989, Trump's first heyday, against exactly the consumer society he'd become famous personifying: "We've got department stores and toilet paper / Got Styrofoam boxes for the ozone layer."

Trump glided down the escalator, in front of cheering fans crowding the glass guardrail. The crowd was packed with actors who responded to a call from Extra Mile Casting, offering "$50 CASH" to "wear T-shirts and carry signs" at an unspecified, "exciting" announcement. "We understand this is not a traditional 'background job,'" the e-mail listing read, "but we believe acting comes in all forms and this is inclusive of that school of thought."

But the staging of the event had started years before that casting call. Trump riding down an escalator was a go-to visual on *The Apprentice*: the image, with "pimp walk" music, of the master ascending from on high. The framing—at a casino, an apartment building, a hotel—maximized the backdrop of gleaming metal and gilt.

Trump Tower was a stage made for TV, with its sensory overload of marble and brass and marble reflected in brass. Riding the escalator, he was like a voluptuary prince being carried on a palanquin.

The camera craned up at him. So did the reporters crowding around the stage, raising their iPhones for a memento of the time they covered what would surely be the brief, insane run for president of that guy from TV. They were on a lark, like the spectators packing picnic lunches to the First Battle of Bull Run.

* * * *

THE PRESS IMMEDIATELY picked up on the analogy between the former *Apprentice* host's announcement and reality TV. But Trump's heavy-metal descent from his pink-marble Cloud Nine borrowed from one other kind of TV show he'd starred in: pro wrestling.

Wrestling was one of the earliest forms of TV entertainment. Starting in 1948, the first year of full prime-time schedules, the DuMont Network, ABC, and NBC each had wrestling shows, and they were mainstays through the 1950s. Little Donald Trump was a fan of Antonino Rocca, a New York favorite known more for his showmanship than his wrestling ability.

Each wrestler played a character, the more caricatured and broadstrokes the better. (P. T. Barnum was one of the first impresarios to dress up wrestlers in costumes and give them biographies.) Foreign stereotypes were reliable: Russians, Nazis, shadowy figures of the Orient like the "Sheik of Araby," played by Detroiter Ed Farhat. The first megastar of TV wrestling was Gorgeous George, a melodramatic narcissist accompanied in the ring by a valet with a silver mirror.

Like reality TV, wrestling relied on caricature. It was telegraphic: "Each sign in wrestling," wrote the French semiotician Roland Barthes, "is . . . endowed with an absolute clarity, since one must always understand everything on the spot." Each fight told a simple story: hero vs. villain (or "face" vs. "heel"), America vs. the world, the masculine vs. the effeminate.

Pro wrestling toyed with the line between real and fake. It was rooted in the concept of "kayfabe"—the insistence that the fights and rivalries were real. Early audiences bought it; by the 1980s, fans' relationship to it was more complex. You believed and didn't believe. The fights were fake but the way they made you feel was real. As Lou Thesz, one of the first wrestlers to break kayfabe, put it: "The 'winner' wasn't the wrestler whose hand was raised at the end, but the one whose performance stuck in the minds of the fans."

In the 1980s, Trump lured WrestleMania 4 and 5 to Trump Plaza in Atlantic City. In the 2000s, wrestling, like Trump, got a second life from reality TV. *WWE Smackdown* and *Monday Night Raw* became hits, driven by sex appeal, conflict, and their own antiheroes. At WrestleMania 20 in 2004, Jesse "The Body" Ventura—elected governor of Minnesota in 1998 with Ross Perot's Reform Party— interviewed the host of NBC's new hit, *The Apprentice*. Ventura asked Trump for his endorsement for president: "I think we may need a wrestler in the White House!" Ventura declared. (The announcers laughed. "Yeah. And maybe a millionaire vice-president!")

The World Wrestling Entertainment's owner, Vince McMahon, recruited Trump as a guest in 2007. McMahon was one of his league's own best heels, a muscular and veiny loudmouth who loved to preen and insulting his paying customers, who loved it right back. The script pitted Trump against him as the cocky, beneficent people's champion. On *Monday Night Raw*, Trump appeared on a massive video screen—magnified, elevated—to taunt McMahon and make money rain from the rafters on the delighted crowd.

The feud built to "The Battle of the Billionaires," a proxy fight at

WrestleMania 23 where Trump and McMahon each backed a wrestler. Their wager: the loser would get his head shaved. After a melee that included Trump tackling McMahon at ringside and taking a flying Stone Cold Stunner from wrestler Steve Austin, McMahon's guy lost. McMahon was strapped into a chair, and Trump, tag-teaming with wrestler Bobby Lashley, shaved him bald.

As in his sitcom cameos, Trump was stiff in the scripted parts of the battle. But fighting McMahon, something primal seemed to come over him. He jumped McMahon wildly, pummeling him with punches (though he'd been coached to pull them). He raised his fist and roared, surging with energy as the crowd howled for his enemy's humiliation. It was a pretend victory, but the exultation was real.

* * * *

CANDIDATE TRUMP'S DEFINING EVENTS, his campaign rallies, were pure WWE spectacle. He took the stage at his first big rally—July 11, 2015, Phoenix, Arizona—to the tune of Rick Derringer's "Real American," the theme song of 1980s wrestler Hulk Hogan. In the song's 1985 video, Hogan plays a stars-and-stripes electric guitar over an American flag backdrop, which morphs into images of Washington crossing the Delaware, Robert E. Lee's surrender at Appomattox, Sitting Bull, Martin Luther King, the Vietnam War memorial, Fourth of July fireworks, and the Hulkster taking down foes in the ring.

Like wrestling itself, you can take the "Real American" video as sincere or as camp. At the 2011 White House Correspondents' Dinner, the song played ironically over a parody of the video, featuring Barack Obama's long-form birth certificate, while Trump sat stewing in the audience.

There was not a lot of irony among the crowd in Phoenix. (The fire marshal reported capacity of the hall at just over 4,000. Trump later claimed it at 10,000, 15,000, and 20,000.) It was, as Trump's rallies would become, a rejection of coolness and detachment, the crowd—mostly old, mostly white—coming together to howl against their perceived extinction.

A Trump rally, with the candidate holding forth for an hour-plus, chasing butterflies of thought, wasn't a political speech like we'd come to know them. His language was rambling but direct: *win, hit, bomb the shit out of them*. Things were *huge* and *beautiful*. He played on existing American themes—vastness, dynamism, ambition—but stripped of the noble pretense: What was in it for *you*?

It was like a variety show, a stage revue. He gave you a little of everything. And as a spectator you were yourself a contributor to the show that was going out everywhere, through "all these cameras," which Trump gestured to repeatedly.

He began in Phoenix in Don Rickles mode, riffing on his doubters and haters and antagonists. The pundits who said he'd never run ("These are real knowledgeable people, they don't know anything"). His business partners who'd dropped him over his racist anti-Mexican remarks, like NASCAR—he got a Republican crowd to boo NASCAR!—which canceled a rental at one of his properties ("I took their deposit"). His primary opponents (he pronounced "Jeb Bush" in a mopey, turtle-like drawl). His TV rivals who imitated *The Apprentice*. ("I could give you some names, but I don't want to embarrass people. [beat] Ah, I'll give you some names.")

He was easy and familiar in these parts. You were like a business associate that he was regaling over well-done steak and shrimp cocktail at Mar-a-Lago.

The crowd laughed gamely, easing into these practice grievances. But what really riled them up: conflict, anger, death. About twenty minutes in, a protester was hustled out by security. The crowd howled, chanted "USA!" Now the good stuff was starting; Trump got red and squinted and barked out his lines. "It's OK, you can shout," he told them. They did, and he let the pitch rise, stepping back from the podium, raising his arms thumbs up, like Hulk Hogan in the ring.

Mid-speech, he brought out a guest, Jamiel Shaw, whose son had been shot to death by an undocumented immigrant. "What would you do," Shaw asked, "if somebody killed your kids?"

You were often asked to reflect upon death at a Trump rally. It was memento mori theater. China was "killing" us metaphorically, and Mexicans and ISIS were doing it literally. Even opinion polls were kill-or-be-killed. "The only thing I'm not killing," Trump said of his poll numbers, "a lot of people don't like me. I said, 'What difference does it make?'"

This was the antihero pitch. Life was not some cooperative exercise like smug, comfortable politicians told you it was. It was hand-to-hand combat. If people were out to erase your culture, to take food off your table, to kill you—*to kill your children*—who gave a shit if the president was *nice*?

"We're living in medieval times," Trump said, amid a ramble about terrorist beheadings. "You always think we're all civilized. It's a jungle. It's HAH-ribble out there!"

* * * *

THE PHOENIX CONVENTION CENTER is an enclosed space, cavernous, well lit. Though the ceiling is treated with metallic fabric kites "designed to replicate the desert sky," you do not forget that you are indoors. But every Trump rally—whether in a hall, a theater, an airplane hangar—felt like it was held in a roiling public square, or before a blazing bonfire.

Barthes anticipated this. Even when it takes place indoors, he wrote, wrestling is an open-air performance:

> What makes the circus or the arena what they are is not the sky (a romantic value suited rather to fashionable occasions), it is the drenching and vertical quality of the flood of light. Even hidden in the most squalid Parisian halls, wrestling partakes of the nature of the great solar spectacles, Greek drama and bullfights: in both, a light without shadow generates an emotion without reserve.

Trump's solar spectacle was the rally. He was the sun; the audience reflected and concentrated his heat. Like die-hard followers of a rock tour, they knew the set list. They would roar for him, and he would rhythmically clap for himself, *slap, slap, slap.* There was the pre-rally music, chosen by the candidate, including Elton John's "Rocket Man" and the Rolling Stones' "You Can't Always Get What You Want." There was the call-and-response. ("Who's going to pay for the wall?" "Mexico!" "Who?" "MEXICO!") There were the insults. (Hillary Clinton "got schlonged" in the 2008 election.) There were the protesters, who were themselves as much a part of the show as the lion's dinner in a Roman colosseum: they got attention, and the energy of the rally fed off the interruptions.

There was even poetry, of a sort. Trump would don reading glasses and recite the lyrics of a 1960s soul song, "The Snake," about a "tender hearted" woman who takes in a poisonous animal and gets bitten by it. He used it as an allegory for the dangers of foreign refugees: "'Oh, shut up, silly woman,' said the reptile with a grin / 'You knew damn well I was a snake before you took me in.'" But the little fable, with its suggestions of the animal nature of man (and the womanly weakness of sympathy), also recalled Tony Soprano waxing philosophical: "Frog and the scorpion, ya know?"

Journalists at the rallies described attendees who were civil and polite outside the venue, cheerful, chatty, like they were out for a night at a theater or a concert. Which they were; Trump's crowds often described the rallies, foremost, as entertainment, a good time. They were used to feeling left out by Hollywood liberals, whom the commentators on Fox News always said should keep their politics to themselves. But now here was a big star, a genuine TV celebrity, who was *on their side,* and they loved it. They couldn't wait for the free show.

Then they went inside and grew agitated, restless, became charged with free-floating adrenaline. Trump knew what wound them up; he would later tell his staff that the crowd would roar when he recited the names of Hispanic criminals, making up some names to prove his point. The flame would leap from listener to listener, until the whole crowd was ignited. "Trump was able to take them up to the line of good taste," wrote journalist Jared Yates Sexton, "and let them take over where he could not." The *New York Times* caught it on video: "Build the wall! Fuck those dirty beaners!" That adrenaline would surge toward the journalists, whom Trump kept in pens and called out from the stage—sometimes by name—as "lying disgusting" people.

The Trump fans were seeing, on stage, what they'd seen on reality shows and Fox News: anger as entertainment. They were seeing TV, personified.

It really was TV—Donald Trump! From *The Apprentice*!—and they were inside the show, because as Trump kept telling them, those cameras were there in the back, transmitting and recording. It was intoxicating and disorienting. And it was agitating, because Trump kept reminding them that there were also reporters with those cameras, waiting to twist everything, to lie, to show the worst parts, to go back to their offices and studios and laugh at them.

It just made them want to, it made them want to—sometimes they'd leave amped up and get in a fight, or haul off and punch a protester inside. Early in the campaign, Trump was easier on the demonstrators—"Don't hurt 'em," he'd say, as security escorted them out.

But like on a reality show, stasis wasn't interesting. The red light would get bored, blink off. Every new episode had to one-up the last. The twists had to be bigger, the stakes higher.

Like the You're Fired Guy in each season of *The Apprentice*, the Rally Guy became a bigger, nastier version of himself each month. In August, he mimed holding a rifle and shooting Bowe Bergdahl, an army sergeant who had walked off his post in Afghanistan. In November, he was asked on Fox about a black protester who was punched and kicked by a half-dozen rally attendees: "Maybe he should have been roughed up," Trump said. By February, he mocked guards from the podium in Las Vegas for going too easy on a protester: "I'd like to punch him in the face."

Historically, presidential candidates avoided being associated with chaos—at least candidates with a prayer of winning did—because it was alienating. The live TV images of the police riot in Chicago, outside the Democratic National Convention, helped doom Hubert Humphrey's campaign in 1968. Swarms of blue-helmeted officers pummeled antiwar protesters in the street, swinging clubs wildly, blanketing the street with so much tear gas that you could smell it inside the Conrad Hilton hotel. The violence yoked Humphrey to the image of an America out of control and beating its own children.

But in a niche-media era, what alienates one audience strengthens the resolve of your own. They like your programming *because* it is not for everybody, and the revulsion of another subculture or of the mainstream—"mainstream media" had long since become a conservative insult—only strengthened their attachment.

In March, every news channel went live from Chicago, where a Trump rally was canceled as protesters and Trump supporters scuffled inside the rally while thousands of marchers converged on it. It seemed that night like the city, or the whole country, might explode.

It was volatile. It was dangerous. Atavistic, wild things were being exhumed. It could go in any direction.

The red light liked things that could go in any direction. It stayed on.

* * * *

IN 1985, NEIL POSTMAN wrote that "the fundamental metaphor for political discourse is the television commercial." He was speaking figuratively—the thirty-second TV spot, which relied on emotion and image rather than reason and prose, had become the dominant model of persuasion in a TV society.

But at the time it was also true literally. Reagan had just won reelection on the strength of Hal Riney's "Morning in America" ad campaign. For decades before and decades after, candidacies were defined by their best and worst TV ads. Pundits analyzed and critiqued them like film critics dissecting a summer's blockbuster movies.

But 2016 would be different. Trump didn't make many ads per se. The ones he did release were forgettable, clumsy, or disturbing. His two-minute closing ad was a rant about the "global special interests" who "control the levers of power"—paranoid dog-whistle rhetoric that, paired with images of Jewish financiers and officials, played like a TV remake of *The Protocols of the Elders of Zion*.

Mostly, Trump was the ad. As long as he kept himself on cable news, he would be the protagonist of the election: every story would be about him or about others in relation to him. He and cable news were in a mind-meld. He knew what it wanted: celebrity, outrage, volatility, novelty. Give the twenty-four-hour news panelists something to talk about, and the red light will stay on. He didn't even need to be on camera. A tweet would do, like after a mass shooting in an Orlando nightclub, by a man who swore allegiance to ISIS in a call to 911: "Appreciate the congrats for being right on radical Islamic terrorism, I don't want congrats, I want toughness & vigilance. We must be smart!"

It didn't just work on Fox, where Trump had been a virtual costar. CNN was now run by Jeff Zucker, who'd signed up *The Apprentice* when he was the head of NBC. Zucker's programming philosophy was: if something's working, do ten times as much of it. In Zucker's era, NBC ran "supersized" gimmick episodes of hit sitcoms, added a third and fourth hour to the *Today* show, and attempted a second *Apprentice*, hosted by Martha Stewart, along with Trump's.

At CNN, he found this tactic worked with news too. If people were watching something, you covered it nonstop, be it the "Poop Cruise"—a Carnival cruise ship whose sewage systems were disabled at sea—or a Malaysian Airlines flight that vanished in 2014, never to be recovered. CNN covered it for weeks, at one point polling Americans on whether they believed the cause might be "beings from another dimension."

Well now, here was Donald Trump running for goddam president. Trump was a plane that crashed every day, a Poop Cruise in perpetuity. His Trump Tower announcement, where he slurred Mexican immigrants as "rapists," began an outrage cycle that Trump kept renewing. He was a one-man solution to the problem of what to do when there's no breaking news. The news was breaking as long as his lips kept moving—calling for a ban on Muslims entering the United States or insulting a female opponent, businesswoman Carly Fiorina, with "Look at that face!"

Where Fox News worked in lockstep with Trump, CNN confronted him. Anchor Jake Tapper grilled him on his comment that a "Mexican" judge (who was in fact born in Indiana) could not treat him fairly because of his heritage, asking, "Is that not the definition of racism?" When Trump evaded an answer, Tapper rightly pressed him, following up his question twenty-three times. Trump stopped giving CNN interviews. But even tough coverage, while well deserved, made Trump the protagonist of the election. The ratings boosts were just as real if your audience hated Trump. Love, hate—it was all currency, and it spent just the same.

Media critics of the twentieth century envisioned a political dialogue for a country of ever-shortening attention spans—we would ultimately end up with something like the one-second-long "blipverts" of the dystopian TV show *Max Headroom*.

The Trump campaign was something different. It was made for an audience that either had an intense attention span or none at all. If you were in the niche, a Trump diehard, you could immerse yourself in endless fan content—those rallies, reposted online, could last for hours, and forums like The_Donald on Reddit were endless rabbit holes of Trumpiana. The algorithms of social media amplified the message; once you'd shown an interest in Donald Trump videos, YouTube would suggest more and more, hours and hours, a virtual Trump Channel.

And if you had no interest, there was just the ambient noise of the campaign everywhere—the cable news playing in your gym, the comics on late-night, Trump Trump Trump.

* * * *

TV COULDN'T RESIST IT. The idea that Trump might say something wild at any moment meant, to producers, that he was inherently newsworthy. That he might say the opposite thing tomorrow didn't matter—that just meant more material. "Newsworthy" and "entertaining" had long since become synonyms.

Cable news carried his rallies beginning to end. Sometimes the channels would show his empty lectern, waiting for him to take the stage. The ratings went up, and Trump took his cut of the profits: $5.6 billion in free media over the election, more than every competitor, in both parties, combined. "It may not be good for America," CBS chairman Les Moonves said of Trump's campaign, "but it's damn good for CBS."

A few media outlets resisted, like the *Huffington Post*, which relegated Trump coverage to its entertainment section. (My *Times* colleague Amy Chozick, in her memoir *Chasing Hillary*, writes that when Trump announced his run, an editor initially told her that political reporters would not be writing about him: "Let the TV writers do it.") More of them succumbed, like the news programs that bent their usual rules and let Trump phone in for interviews rather than turn up in-studio—which allowed him to cram in more appearances and refer to notes to answer questions.

Either Trump was dismissed as a celebrity, or he was deferred to as a celebrity. Sometimes it was both, to his benefit, like on a September 2016 NBC forum on military issues. Matt Lauer, who for years had done promotional interviews with Trump about NBC's *The Apprentice* on NBC's *Today* show, grilled Hillary Clinton for specifics, while telling Trump that "nobody would expect you" to have read deeply into foreign policy. Meanwhile, NBC's Jimmy Fallon invited him on the *Tonight* show, where he tousled Trump's cotton-candy hair and performed a skit with the candidate, playing his reflection in a dressing-room mirror—Trump seeing himself in the magic mirror the way he saw himself in the magic mirror of TV.

He played by celebrity rules. He was the only candidate to host *Saturday Night Live* during the campaign (which he'd done in 2004 as host of *The Apprentice*). The show had guest Larry David yell, "Trump's a racist!" because a group had offered a $5,000 bounty to any audience member who disrupted the broadcast, letting *SNL* flagellate itself all the way to the bank while making an in-kind contribution to Trump's campaign.

In another sketch, Trump played himself as president, three years in the future, having easily defeated ISIS and made Mexico pay for a border wall, just as he'd airily promised. The sketch's premise was also the justification for letting him host—and for the rest of the media's gorging at the Trump trough: everybody knew he was never actually going to *win*, so why not have a little fun and make a dollar?

It was just so crazy! *Donald Trump* was running for president! It was like we were living in a movie—*President Billionaire*, a raunchy '80s comedy about a crass tycoon who upsets Washington high society by buying his way into the Oval Office. He gave his opponents insulting nicknames, the way Muhammad Ali did to Sonny Liston and Joe Frazier ("Big Ugly Bear" and "The Gorilla"). Lyin' Ted Cruz, Low-Energy Jeb Bush, Crooked Hillary Clinton. It was outrageous, it was surreal—who *does* that?—so the press repeated the names and with them, the message: Ted Cruz is a liar, Jeb Bush is low-energy, Hillary Clinton is crooked.

When you ran as an entertainer, you could claim an entertainer's prerogative—especially the prerogative of "joking." It was a joke, Trump said, when he wished aloud at a press conference that Russia would hack Hillary Clinton's e-mails; and when he mocked a *New York Times* reporter's physical disability; and when he said that climate change was a "hoax" invented by the Chinese; and when he called Barack Obama "the founder of ISIS."

Jokes! If you made a big deal of them, you were too sensitive, a "snowflake." A lie, a mistake, a bigoted insult could be dismissed because the real point was how the other side reacted to them—Trump was just "triggering the libs" again.

There was a whole school of punditry that enabled this, by insisting that critics take him "seriously but not literally." Of course, if you *liked* what he said and wanted to take it literally, he wasn't going to stop you. That's what he'd been doing since his first appearance on *Fox & Friends* in 2010, demanding that Al Gore be stripped of his Nobel Prize: "Yes, I was kidding . . . But when I get down to it, was I really kidding?"

He was like the WWE: he didn't care if you thought the kayfabe was fake or real as long as you bought the pay-per-view.

Jason, a young Cuban American man in Florida, told a reporter for *Politico* that he believed "Trump is fucking crazy," as well as racist against Hispanics like himself. But he planned to vote for him anyway. "The whole system is fucked, so why not vote for the craziest guy, so we can see the craziest shit happen? . . . At least Trump is fun to watch."

* * * *

AT LEAST TRUMP IS FUN TO WATCH is a horrifying statement on a civic level. But give Jason credit for seeing Trump for what he was: the number-one TV show in America.

The Trump Show played out across multiple platforms: it was the news programs, and the debates, and the interviews, and the late-night talk shows, and the jokes on sitcoms like Netflix's *Fuller House*, and the Twitter meltdowns. In a time of a thousand channels, he was the one program that everyone was watching.

Trump used his years of on-camera experience like Caesar used his military skill to take Rome. In news studios, he would request specific camera angles and "gold gel" lighting-filter sheets to bathe him in a honeyed glow. (The camera would literally sheathe him in gold, like one of his high-rises.) After TV interviews, he would ask for a playback and watch his entire appearance with the sound off, just to see how he looked.

Politicians had gone on TV for generations to ingratiate themselves with the public. Nixon said "Sock it to me" on *Laugh-In*, Bill

Clinton put on shades and blew the saxophone on *The Arsenio Hall Show*. Barack Obama filled out his NCAA brackets on ESPN. But the pilgrimage always went in one direction: the politician went to the show, which allowed the politician into its space.

With Trump, the dynamic was reversed. TV came to him. He was a master narrative, allowing one program or another to have a part of him. He badgered CNBC into shortening a Republican debate to two hours, then bragged about the coup at another debate, the way a past candidate might have cited negotiating a peace treaty.

Donald Trump didn't really guest-host *Saturday Night Live* for a night. He let *Saturday Night Live* guest-host him for a night.

As Trump's campaign defied predictions that it would flame out—by fall, by the new year, by the primaries—analysts reached for a familiar comparison: Ronald Reagan, the former actor and *General Electric Theater* host. But the differences between Reagan and Trump were as important as their similarities.

Reagan was an actor; Trump was a reality-TV star. Reagan came from the world of fiction; Trump came from nonfiction-based entertainment. Reagan played characters; Trump played an amplified version of himself. Reagan's job was acting; Trump's job was acting out.

Reagan's preparation for being president, in other words, was years of imagining himself in the heads of other people. "Reagan's experience as an actor," wrote film scholar Leo Braudy, "far from trivializing his performance as president, allowed him to project a much more complicated character than he may have actually possessed." Reagan's own assessment, to his biographer Lou Cannon after leaving office, was that "being an actor had taught him to understand the feelings and motivations of others."

Reality TV did not require you to do that. You needed to understand other people as obstacles, or as creatures who would react to stimuli, but not necessarily as full human beings with the same complexities as you. If anything, too much empathy was a liability. It was noise that kept you from expressing your fullest *you*. (In the words of Omarosa, who became the most famous *Apprentice* contestant by styling herself as a "mirror" of Trump: "My objective was to methodically eliminate each contestant, one by one, so why would I want an emotional attachment to any of them?")

Reagan had trouble separating movies from reality. He often recounted a heroic scene from the WWII film *A Wing and a Prayer* as if it had actually happened. Trump did not have the problem of losing himself in character. Just the opposite: he did not seem to recognize that other people were fully real, that they continued to exist when they were not interacting with him.

Some observers suggested that he had never completely achieved "theory of mind": the cognizance, which most people develop at age two or three, that other people have consciousness and emotional states. Instead, like the crowds at his rallies, they were objects that yielded outputs (anger, approval, love) in response to inputs (*Lock her up, build the wall, we're going to say Merry Christmas again*).

This is a frightening attribute for a person who has power and responsibility for others. But on live TV, it is damn near perfect. It is the mentality of the red light: no memory, no empathy, just on-state and off-state and the reaction in the moment.

It's the difference between being on television and *being television*.

* * * *

LATER, JOURNALIST MICHAEL WOLFF would describe President Trump, who did not like to read one-page documents, much less books, as "postliterate—total television." But he was also *pre*literate, or at least pretextual. He was an electronic-era phenomenon, and his rallies were like something out of ancient, tribal oral tradition. His effect was to erase everything between Gutenberg and the cathode-ray tube.

The Trump campaign did, however, produce one memorable text. It was a hat.

A wide-brimmed rope hat, usually red and white, sometimes white and navy, that said MAKE AMERICA GREAT AGAIN, a phrase Trump trademarked two weeks after the 2012 election. He didn't invent the slogan. Ronald Reagan, for one, campaigned on it in 1980. But, Trump told the *Washington Post*, "He didn't trademark it."

The four words announced that the Trump campaign was a nostalgia act. The phrase was, like many successful branding slogans, *consistent with the product*: a white senior citizen who was as associated with the 1980s as Pac-Man and shoulder pads. It was strategically vague. Maybe America was last great in the 1980s, or the 1950s, or before. Maybe it was when you were young and happy and healthy; maybe it was a time your grandparents told you about; or maybe—best of all—it existed only in your imagination. You could bring to it whatever you liked.

What Trump liked about the old days was the violence. The violence was *first-class* in the old days.

In the old days, football players didn't get penalized for violent hits. "You used to see these tackles and it was incredible to watch," he told a crowd in Iowa. "Now they tackle, 'Oh, head-on-head collision, 15 yards' . . . Football has become soft like our country has become soft."

"In the old days, spies used to be executed," he said about Edward Snowden, who'd leaked classified secrets about government surveillance. Likewise the fugitive soldier Bowe Bergdahl: "In the old days, when we were strong and wise, we'd shoot a guy like that."

"In the old days, when we were strong and respected," he told another rally, General Pershing would have Muslim insurgents in the Philippines shot using bullets dipped in pig's blood. (This never happened in real life, but it did in the crowd's shared dream of the old days.)

"In the good old days, they'd rip him out of that seat so fast," he said about a protester in Oklahoma. "In the good old days, this doesn't happen, because they used to treat them very, very rough," he said of another protester in North Carolina. "Nobody wants to hurt each other anymore," he complained at a rally in St. Louis.

"I love the old days," he told a crowd at a Las Vegas rally disrupted by a protester. "You know what they used to do to guys like that when they were in a place like this? They'd be carried out on a stretcher, folks."

I love the old days. Guys like that. A place like this. You could interpret it any way you wanted.

At a Trump rally in March, a seventy-eight-year-old white man interpreted it by sucker-punching a young black protester being walked out of the Crown Coliseum in Fayetteville, North Carolina. The angry white past was smacking down the young brown future. The crowd cheered. It had no illusions about what "Make America Great Again" meant, or whom America was to be made great again for.

Trump brought his nostalgia act to places like my home state, Michigan. (In Warren, he promised that if anyone hurt a protester, "I'll defend you in court.") To have grown up in southeast Michigan was to have grown up in a culture soaked in nostalgia. It was to hear, generation after generation, about how life was better before you were born, when the car factories were pumping out Fords and Chevys and paychecks. It was to see the skyline of Detroit, whose dominant feature, the Renaissance Center, has been named after a promise to bring back better days since it opened in 1977. It was to hear about the 1967 Detroit riots and suburban white flight. It was to see, in a state that sent soldiers to die for the Union, Confederate flags on Lynyrd Skynyrd T-shirts and baseball caps and pickup trucks. It was to hear wistful nostalgia in the young-old-man songs of Bob Seger, who sang about "Old Time Rock 'n' Roll" and reminisced about "the back seat of my '60 Chevy" in "Night Moves"—an elegy for lost youth he released when he was thirty-one years old. And it was to see nostalgia gone ugly and curdled in Ted Nugent— the deer-hunting used-to-be rock star who once called Barack Obama a "subhuman mongrel"—and to know the dog-whistle tune Nugent was playing when he opened an election-eve Trump rally in Sterling Heights, insulting black former Detroit mayors, longing for the "*real* Michigan . . . the old, real Michigan" from when he was born in 1948, and asking, "Are there enough working-hard, playing-hard, American Michigan shitkickers left to take this state back and vote Trump for president?" (There were, barely; Trump would win the state by 10,704 votes, his narrowest margin in America.)

The old days had their own old days. Archie Bunker, Trump's sitcom John the Baptist, opened *All in the Family* in 1971 singing "Those Were the Days," whose verses pined for the early twentieth century. The early twentieth century had *Birth of a Nation*, the D. W. Griffith film that lionized the emergence of the Ku Klux Klan after the Civil War, which President Woodrow Wilson screened at the White House in 1915. And the Civil War was in one sense a nostalgia product itself. The battle to preserve slavery and a racist slaveholding society was bound up with the self-valorizing self-conception of white Southerners, which had been fed by a craze for the idyllic romances of Sir Walter Scott. In the faded medieval English nobility of *Ivanhoe*, the slaveholding South saw itself, self-aggrandizingly then self-pityingly. "It was Sir Walter that made every gentleman in the South a major or a colonel. . . . He is in great measure responsible for the war," wrote Mark Twain, who later painted Scott's name on the wreckage of a steamboat in *The Adventures of Huckleberry Finn*.

There's a whole popular culture trope about how the past is white-man territory. Science-fiction franchises from *Men in Black* to *Hot Tub Time Machine* include minority characters who can't be as carefree with time machines as their white peers. The black engineer Rufus in the 2016 NBC time-travel series *Timeless* protests, "There is literally no place in American history that will be awesome for me." Whereas for white characters, everywhere and everywhen is awesome. (At least as long as they're traveling backward, unlike Charlton Heston's white astronaut in 1968's *Planet of the Apes*, who lands on a future Earth and ends up among the enslaved humans in a racial allegory.) In *Back to the Future*, 1985 white boy Marty McFly

(Michael J. Fox) travels to 1955 and "invents" rock and roll by teaching a black band Chuck Berry's "Johnny B. Goode."

So you don't have to come out and say who "Make America Great Again" is for. You just set the dial on the time machine and see who climbs in.

* * * *

THE HAT ITSELF was a text. Donald Trump wearing the hat was a text. A red trucker-style hat on top of a business suit. This was a Trump motif—high and low visual-status markers, paired together, over and over. A photograph of Trump, in his calfskin leather seat on the private jet with his name painted on it, eating a bucket of KFC chicken with a knife and fork. A tweeted picture of the candidate in his Trump Tower office, eating that most Anglofied of Mexican foods, a taco salad. ("I love Hispanics!")

That was *Duck Dynasty*. That was *The Beverly Hillbillies*. It was the fantasy of being prosperous and triumphant and respected, without making any concession to the tastes and language and social mores of an alien group. It was Trump as, in a phrase Fox News took to repeating, the "blue-collar billionaire."

That was a ludicrous idea: Trump grew up in a mansion; had a chauffeur to take him on his paper route when it rained; had once told *Playboy*, "If I had been the son of a miner, I would have left the damn mines."

But that didn't matter as long as you wanted to believe. You made yourself believe because you were on the team, you *belonged* to something, and every time you made yourself believe, it cemented your commitment. You were invested; you couldn't back out, no matter what he said, no matter what evidence anyone produced, without loss of face. This enabled Trump, at a rally in Charleston, West Virginia, to don a miner's helmet and mime shoveling coal—*Donald Trump*, whose closest experience to mining was breathing the recirculated air in Trump Tower—and not be received as an absurdity like Michael Dukakis riding a tank in 1988.

The Republican party was used to running *against* pop culture. George H. W. Bush went to war with *The Simpsons*, Bob Dole with Hollywood and rap music. In 2008, John McCain ran an ad that disparaged Barack Obama, with his massive, rock-star crowds, as a "celebrity."

Donald Trump was an *actual* celebrity. It was his job. Without pop culture, he would be one more New York rich kid who inherited his dad's business. This allowed him to forego the Clinton campaign approach of surrounding the candidate with stars—guest-starring on Comedy Central's *Broad City*, holding an election-eve rally with Beyoncé and Jay-Z—in the hope that their fans' enthusiasm would transfer to her, a hoary TV-era strategy that dated back to Eisenhower and his "Ike Day" CBS special.

But Trump's argument was that he was of *your* pop culture—not like Obama, palling around with rappers and poets and the cast of *Hamilton*—and he would defend your culture, your totems, from the enemy.

Because Trump saw life in terms of fighting, he understood pop culture as a political war, which it had become, and which he gladly exacerbated. A 2014 poll found a thirty-eight-point gap between the parties on whether *Twelve Years a Slave* should win an Oscar (Democrats pro, Republicans con). Neither party had taken a position on the film; partisans simply intuited where their tribe would line up. To white-male pop conservatives, as described earlier, the female remake of *Ghostbusters* was an attempt by feminist Hollywood to climb into the *Back to the Future* DeLorean time machine and erase them from history, like Marty McFly fading out of his family photos. Trump's rallying cry was that they—that polymorphous, alien *them*—were taking away your status, your dignity, your pride of place, even your childhood memories, and he would give them back to you, starring a white man.

In 2014, during the Super Bowl (the most American TV show

there is), an ad for Coca-Cola (the most American beverage there is) was set to the music of "America the Beautiful"—with the lyrics sung in English, Spanish, Keres, Hindi, Tagalog, Senegalese French, and Hebrew. Coca-Cola had long sold itself as an American beachhead in every inhabited square inch of the Earth. But it had been about projecting America outward—"I'd like to buy the world a Coke"— whereas this ad, with its panoply of faces in cowboy hats and hijabs, was about bringing the world in to America.

The culture-right did not care for it. To Coca-Cola, said a columnist on Breitbart, America was no longer "a nation governed in the Anglo-American tradition of liberty. It is instead a nation governed by some all-inclusive multi-cultural synthesis of the various forms of government in the world." This was the atmosphere of carbonated nationalism in which Trump ran his campaign. He understood the power of nostalgia as a political force. But as a pop figure, he could express it culturally, where it comes across on a gut, nonliteral level.

During the campaign, and especially after Trump won, there was a long debate about what really motivated his voters. Were they dispossessed workers? Status-anxious bourgeois? Nationalists? Xenophobes? Racists?

But to argue about whether Trump's appeal was economic *or* racial *or* religious *or* xenophobic misunderstands how figurative language works. "Make America Great Again" is a branding slogan, an appeal to nostalgia—and the political power of nostalgia is that it can be all of those things at once without having to say that it is any of them. "Have a Coke and a smile" doesn't mean one thing. It's a palimpsest of nonliteral messages: Coke tastes good; you feel good drinking Coke; you drink Coke *when* you feel good; you, drinking Coke, *are* good. Whatever makes you smile—that's Coke.

Just so, "Make America Great Again" translates into: Make America like it used to be, when people like me had it better, when we got respect, when we didn't have to press goddam one for English, when we were *the main thing* in America.

This halcyon past does not need to ever have actually existed to be appealing, any more than the medieval Britain in a Sir Walter Scott novel. It doesn't have to make logical sense to say, as a Trump voter would tell Oprah Winfrey after the election, that she felt "safer" because "I can say Merry Christmas to anyone I want wherever I want." It makes *advertising* sense; it operates on that narcotic dream-level of emotion and image where safety is Christmas is freedom is a red hat and a bucket of KFC.

* * * *

AT SEVENTEEN CANDIDATES, the 2016 Republican primary was almost precisely the size of a cast of *The Apprentice*. Donald Trump, having presided over fourteen seasons of that show, recognized intuitively what the televised debates were: an elimination-based reality show.

Traditionally, a candidate's biggest fear in a TV debate was making a memorable mistake: cosmetic, like Nixon sweating opposite JFK, or rhetorical, like Gerald Ford implying that Poland was not under Soviet domination. But in a reality-TV debate, the biggest sin was being forgettable. You'd get a bad edit, become part of the wallpaper. In 2016, that had cascading practical effects. There were so many candidates that the hosting networks exiled the lowest-polling ones to "undercard" debates before the prime-time main events. These were the cannon fodder, the contestants doomed to be eliminated in the early rounds.

You stood out, like Omarosa, by getting in fights. That was what got you a meaty edit, in the form of heavy rotation on the news clips the next day. The substance of the fight didn't matter. Trump's pugilism could be petty and indiscriminate. He'd tell Senator Rand Paul, whose polling numbers were barely a rounding error, that he "shouldn't even be on this stage." You fought even if you didn't need to; you fought *because* you didn't need to. The point of the fight was to prove that you were a fighter.

It was like the adage that a new prisoner should punch out

another inmate on the first day. Better to be the instigator than the instigated-upon: this allowed you to set the agenda, get in people's heads, change the narrative. For the partisan audience cultivated by Fox News, politics wasn't ideological but attitudinal. Its ultimate goal wasn't policy so much as the lamentations of one's enemies, and every petty debate attack was a promise to deal more satisfying pain in the future.

As *The Real World* taught, the highest value was to "stop being polite." Trump got stronger every time he committed a foul that would have disqualified a past candidate. At a debate in August, Fox News's Megyn Kelly questioned his temperament: "You've called women you don't like 'fat pigs,' 'dogs,' 'slobs,' and 'disgusting animals.' " Later, he complained on CNN about her questioning: "There was blood coming out of her eyes, blood coming out of her—wherever."

If you supported Trump, maybe you believed him when he denied what seemed obvious—that he was saying Kelly was on her period and therefore irrational. Maybe you didn't believe him, but thought it was one more case of people being oversensitive. Maybe you heard it as a man being unapologetic about being a man. Maybe you just liked how Trump talked: that blunt Northeast alpha-male *get outta heah* of Archie Bunker, of Tony Soprano, of reality stars like "Boston Rob" Mariano of *Survivor*, which TV had taught us registered as authenticity.

Trump's behavior was reality-TV provocation, a *Survivor* "rat and snake" speech, a Real Housewife of New Jersey flipping over a restaurant table. Every fight provided enough material for another episode.

His poll numbers went up. Pundits were sure it couldn't last. Trump was too offensive. He had no traditional qualifications. What they didn't see was the audience for whom smacking down people on TV *was the qualification*. Argument and insult and dominance weren't simply indicators that someone might be tough enough to govern. To an audience that was used to seeing politics exercised in the form of arguments on Fox News, they were *the act of governance*.

Of course it was shocking. The shock was the point. Demagogues and would-be tyrants in other times and in other countries came to power through stunning acts of rule-breaking and dominance. Mussolini's Italian Fascists in the 1920s assaulted government officials and beat men in the streets, which not only terrified their opponents but made the opposition look weak in the eyes of its own supporters. All this sent a message: the old rules are gone, the old proprieties can't protect you, best to get on the side of this terrifying and virile force creating its own rules. Trump's followers didn't practice organized mass violence, though there were some incidents, like two men who assaulted a Hispanic man in Boston in August 2015, one of them telling police, "Donald Trump was right, all these illegals need to be deported." Trump dismissed the incident at a news conference, saying, "People who are following me are very passionate."

But Trump's campaign was a twenty-first-century version of dominance politics, a reality-TV version, where unprovoked attacks—retweeting a meme that insulted the looks of Ted Cruz's wife, say—argued that your leader was strong, that his opponents could not adequately protect themselves or their loved ones, and therefore, how could you expect them to protect *you*? If Trump didn't (for the most part) have thugs carrying out beatdowns in the streets, there were swarms of them online. They enlisted once-harmless cartoon frog Pepe as an alt-right mascot. They harassed liberals and Jewish Twitter users and insufficiently Trumpist conservatives. (They called the latter "cucks," short for "cuckservative," derived from "cuckold"—implying that their targets were emasculated and adding a bonus layer of racism by referencing interracial cuckoldry porn.) They spread violent cartoons and altered images, which Trump would sometimes retweet: such as a hurtling "Trump Train," like an image out of Italian Futurism, crushing a person with a CNN logo for a head. The assault was virtual, but the message was plain: The old order is being overturned, this election is about the strong vs. the weak, and you want to be on the side of strength.

Trump's campaign ran on reality-TV morality, which deflected conventional attacks of dishonesty (*It makes me smart!*) and impropriety (*I know the crooked system!*) and flip-flopping (*I did what I had to do!*). When he was called out for hypocrisy—such as giving money to the politicians he now disdained—he owned it as shrewdness. This argument was Richard Hatch in the first *Survivor* finale: *Like me or not, you've got to admire how I played the game.* It substituted brazenness for truthfulness.

So it didn't hurt Trump either that he lied. A lot. Blatantly and obviously. When the fact-checking outfit PolitiFact named his campaign statements, collectively, 2015's "Lie of the Year," it was as damaging as a marshmallow gun. "He says what he means," his supporters said, which did not mean, "He tells the truth." It meant he did not consider whether his words were kind or responsible or pleasing—or true—but simply whether he wanted to say them. That was *being real*, which was better than being honest, more liberating than being tethered to fact.

When he said he saw thousands of Muslims cheering the destruction of the World Trade Center in Jersey City (it never happened) or tweeted a claim that 81 percent of white murder victims were killed by blacks (it was 15 percent)—well, he was right about their *feeling*, that a chaotic brown tide was washing over the world. When he connected Ted Cruz's father to the JFK assassination, it said that he would not be squeamish in attacking his enemies. When he embraced the right-wing base's darkest hoaxes and conspiracy theories—like the big one, birtherism—it said he wanted what they wanted, that he supped from the same table they did, that he truly got them.

Trump was building on twenty years of groundwork by Fox News, whose audience Roger Ailes severed from the rest of the media. "Fair and Balanced" implied that no one else was balanced, and thus any contradictory information could be dismissed. Forget newspapers, scientists, egghead fact-checkers. There was only Fox.

This was a powerful tactic for Fox against CNN, but it left it vulnerable to someone like Trump, who would channel it so purely that its audience would imprint on him, transferring their allegiance. When Trump challenged Fox in the primaries, first with Megyn

Kelly, later by skipping a Fox debate in January, he was asking the base to choose: him or Fox. They chose him. Fox, through the gradual Trumpification of its commentators, sued for peace. Fox would have to access its viewers through Trump, on his terms. When Trump showed that he could delegitimize Fox to his followers, there was no countervailing authority left. Now there was only Trump.

* * * *

THE LAST REAL Republican challenge to Trump came in early March. Mitt Romney, the previous Republican nominee for president, gave a televised speech against Trump—"a phony, a fraud," running on "bullying" and "misogyny" and "third-grade theatrics." If Trump were to become president, Romney said, "his personal qualities would mean that America would cease to be a shining city on a hill."

For Trump, who preferred shining casinos on the boardwalk, Romney's disdain was perhaps the most important endorsement of the campaign. Romney made himself into a stuffed-suit sitcom neighbor— Milburn Drysdale, the snooty banker on *The Beverly Hillbillies*, Ned Flanders on *The Simpsons*—and the Fox News Republican subculture knew whom they were supposed to root for in that showdown. Romney was a "loser," Trump answered that day, who by the way wasn't too morally repulsed to ask for Trump's support in 2012: "I could have said, 'Mitt, drop to your knees.' He would have dropped to his knees."

Trump didn't so much win the argument as prove the argument no longer existed. Its terms were moot. Romney might as well have donned a powdered periwig and slapped Trump with a white glove.

That night, at a Fox News debate in Detroit, Trump turned against Marco Rubio, one of Romney's preferred candidates, who had tried to tweak Trump in kind by reviving a *Spy* magazine insult about his small hands. It was an awkward attack for Rubio, a programmable android of a politician whose gift for glib soundbites made him a 2016 frontrunner until Trump rendered it instantly antiquated. Trump seized on the insinuation—that his penis must be small—and spelled it out: "I guarantee you there's no problem."

Come at Donald Trump with Marquess of Queensberry rules and he would go below the belt, possibly his own. Bring coy, prime-time broadcast-TV insults, and he would go late-night cable. It was a deliberate redrawing of cultural terms. He reverse-polarized the Republican argument from decency to indecency.

Trump won the next Tuesday's primaries in Michigan and Mississippi. He celebrated with a speech, live on cable, at his golf club in Jupiter, Florida, flanked on one side by American flags and on the other by a table of Trump-branded products, among them a heap of raw "Trump Steaks," though that brand had gone out of business years before and the label on the packaging said "Bush Brothers," a local Florida meat company.

But like in the soundstage boardroom of *The Apprentice*, the symbolism—bloody red meat, *abbondanza*—spoke louder than the reality. A Trump Steak was a Trump Steak because you wished it to be a Trump Steak. These were the terms of the arrangement: Trump would win, would cause woe to the enemy, and you would agree to take his word over the evidence of your senses. You had gone this far. You were invested. You were in too deep to back out.

* * * *

TRUMP'S REPUBLICAN NATIONAL CONVENTION in July was a disaster. Everybody knew it. His wife Melania's speech plagiarized, of all people, Michelle Obama. The schedule was undisciplined, leaving the night's climactic speeches to end well after prime time. The energy was angry and ugly. Video monitors went on the fritz. The endorsements by Republican politicians were tepid. The celebrity appearances were the likes of Scott Baio and Antonio Sabato Jr., each of whom had starred on separate VH1 dating shows. This was the nominating convention of a network TV star?

The convention was a disaster, in other words, by the established standards of political TV, which made running a four-night miniseries a synecdoche for running the country. Chaos was bad; a smooth, choreographed build to an uplifting speech and balloon drop was good. It signified competence and management skill. The parties had gotten so good at this competency that the broadcast networks, in recent elections, had cut back on their coverage of the slick, boring infomercials.

By this measure, the Democratic National Convention the following week was orders of magnitude better. It ran on time. It looked good. Big stars offered musical tributes. It was coherent, showcasing speeches on the upbeat themes of inclusion and tolerance as a small-d democratic virtue.

There was some disorder—protests in the stands from disappointed delegates for Bernie Sanders—but the most attention-getting theatrics were targeted at the opponent. (In particular, an emotional speech by Khizr Khan, the father of a Muslim American soldier killed in action, baited Trump into a public feud over his Islamophobia.) The DNC promised a Hillary Clinton presidency not as reality-TV chaos but professionally scripted drama: a reliable, top-shelf sequel from the producers of *Obama!*

Maybe the starkest example of how America's political camps were speaking different cultural languages came when Vice President Joe Biden turned Trump's most famous phrase against him: "No matter where you were raised, how can there be pleasure in saying, 'You're fired'?" To one audience, it was a devastating moral takedown. But to another—one that enjoyed *The Apprentice*, that chanted "Lock her up!" at rallies—it was a free ad for Trump, a sign that Biden was an old pearl-clutcher who didn't get the joke.

The only TV world in which Trump's convention made any kind of sense was the TV world he'd thrived in. Fox News, where life was assumed to be a continual zero-sum struggle. Reality TV, where unpredictability signified authenticity. Conservative pop culture, where the scorn of hoity-toity sophisticates bound the audience in fraternal resentment.*

And pro wrestling, in the form of a WWE-style showdown with Ted Cruz. Cruz, Trump's bitter primary rival, had not backed Trump but was given a prime-time speaking slot anyway. It was the sort of "dramatic showdown" decision moment that reality TV thrived on: Would he endorse? Cruz—the sort of politician who seems to draw sustenance from the animus of his fellow man—maintained the suspense for eighteen minutes before urging the audience to "vote your conscience." The crowd, knowing that "conscience" was the opposite of "Donald Trump," bayed and howled. Cruz held a tight little coin purse of a smile on his lips.

Suddenly, the boos became mixed with cheers—angry, lusty cheers. Trump had walked into the hall, on an upper level, scowling but clapping, *slap, slap, slap,* and waving to the delegates. The red light took interest. CNN quickly put him picture-in-picture with Cruz, Trump's image larger and higher on the screen, dominant—just like when he'd appeared on a WWE Jumbotron and insulted the supercilious Vince McMahon before making dollar bills rain from the sky.

It was the opposite of the thing TV conventions usually strove so hard to broadcast, unity. It was the promise of *disunity*, because that was the state of man. The fight would go on and on, against enemies and insufficiently zealous friends, and it would be good, because fighting is productive and enriching and sustaining—and you would be *winning that fight, forever,* perched on the high ground like Trump against McMahon, punching down, over and over, against your enemies and into their stupid, shit-eating, "Vote your conscience" grins.

That promise, the forever fight, would be ratified the next night

---

* Willie Robertson of *Duck Dynasty*, in a stars-and-stripes bandana, addressed the RNC with a prayer—the same way every episode of the show ended—and mocked the "media experts" who "don't hang out with regular folks like us, who like to hunt and fish and pray and actually work for a living."

in Trump's acceptance speech. The house lights cut out, and the PA played Queen's "We Are the Champions"—"We'll keep on fighting 'til the end"—as Trump walked out, backlit and silhouetted, from a rectangle of blinding light. It was the mirror image of the opening credits of *The Apprentice*, in which a shadowed figure walks to the camera from a golden-lit rectangular doorway.

Unlike at his rallies, he stuck to a script: upholding "law and order" in a world of "death, destruction, terrorism, and weakness." It was not an optimistic speech, or rather, it was the optimism that, very soon, you would beat someone instead of them beating you. Only when he mentioned his campaign's naysayers did he allow himself a brief, improvised aside: "We love defeating those people, don't we?"

It was the one moment in the speech when he sounded truly happy.

A PARTY PRIMARY is to a general election as cable TV is to broadcast TV. There are many options, as opposed to two or three. The audience—in this case, voters—is divided into more, smaller niche groups.

In TV, as we've seen, different environments reward different kinds of programming. The move from three major networks to hundreds of cable channels meant a move away from the Least Objectionable Program and toward programming designed to stand out and attract a smaller but passionate following.

Winning a primary, especially one the size of 2016, is nichecasting. You develop a strong brand, you make sure you don't blend into the background, and as one competitor after another goes off the air, you absorb their followers until you have a plurality.

Candidate Donald Trump, in other words, was a successful niche product. But a general election for president is, by constitutional mandate, a mass-market enterprise. You need a majority of the Electoral College. Two candidates, in this system, have a realistic chance of winning. Its incentive structure is much more like broadcast TV in the mid-twentieth century.

How does a niche-media product win in a broadcast environment? Trump's campaign aimed to do what network reality TV did: sell the figure of the antihero to a mass audience.

This meant making the Vic Mackey argument, that if you're in a struggle against extinction, no one cares if the president is a scoundrel so long as he's *your* scoundrel. It meant making the *Survivor* argument, repositioning the villain as a rogue who played the game well. ("Nobody knows the system better than me," he said at the convention, "which is why I alone can fix it.") It meant doing what *Breaking Bad* did with Walter White—keeping the audience on the side of the antihero by convincing them that his enemies were even worse. It meant casting Trump as the wrestling figure that Barthes called "the bastard": "Someone unstable, who accepts the rules only when they are useful to him and transgresses the formal continuity of attitudes."

But also, specifically, Donald Trump was running against a woman. He framed Hillary Clinton the way antihero stories so often framed their female characters—or, at least, the way male fans of the shows often saw those female characters: as the killjoy, the tryhard, the scold, the ice bitch, the phony, the hypocrite, the wet blanket who holds men back from being awesome.

Ta-Nehisi Coates would later call Trump, with his bald appeals to racism, "the first white president"—the first not only to be white but to put the preservation of white privilege at the center of his agenda. Likewise, running against the first female major-party nominee for president, he made himself the first male candidate for president.

There was a long history of presidential candidates campaigning on virility and their physical exploits—Andrew Jackson, Theodore Roosevelt—and attacking political opponents as unmanly or effeminate. Bill Clinton's expressions of empathy ("I feel your pain") were so widely mocked as feminizing that sketch comic Dana

Carvey once portrayed him exposing a breast and nursing a baby. At the 2004 Republican National Convention, California governor, action-movie star, and future *Celebrity Apprentice* replacement host Arnold Schwarzenegger dismissed Democratic nominees John Kerry and John Edwards as "girly men," quoting one of Carvey's old *Saturday Night Live* sketches. Modern Republicans routinely positioned themselves as the "daddy party" vs. the Democrats' "mommy party."

But implicitly and sometimes explicitly, Trump ran on masculinity as an idea, a Strangelovian value, a vital essence to be preserved.

From his first days in the tabloids, the character of Donald Trump was a performance of hyperbolic maleness. He cultivated gossip columnists to describe him as an alpha ladies' man. He echoed Hugh Hefner, the fantasy of a sultan-letch who can indulge his every carnal desire. *The Apprentice* styled him as a "pimp," the WWE as a wild man. He underlined his harem-keeper image by buying Miss Universe, a pageant which distinguished itself from Miss America by dispensing with the pretense of a talent competition and focusing on T&A. "If you're looking for a rocket scientist, don't tune in tonight," he told Howard Stern about the pageant in 2005. Stern's show was basically an Animal Planet mating display for Trump, who would list the celebrity women he wanted to have sex with, critiqued their plastic surgery, and rated them on a scale of 1 to 10.

If Trump seemed to represent an antiquated, Rat Pack, ring-a-ding-ding sexuality—well, that too was the point. *I love the old days*.

He emphasized his physicality. He had "stamina" and Clinton did not, he repeated over and over, which made no literal sense—he was a creature of conveyances, taking the escalator and riding in golf carts. But it implied a message: Man strong, woman weak. He highlighted his testosterone level in a medical report that he brought on daytime TV's *The Dr. Oz Show*. He marketed himself as a political Viagra pill for a following anxious about its potency. (Quite literally: psychological researchers found that Trump's 2016 support correlated to regions of the country with a high rate of Google searches for terms like "erectile dysfuction," "penis enlargement," and "how to get girls.")

And his attacks on Clinton relied on a dynamic of antihero fiction: the audience will punish women for qualities—ambition, aggression, self-assuredness—that they reward in men. For Trump, having worked the system meant he alone could fix it; for Clinton, it meant she was corrupt. For him, greed meant he would be greedy on behalf of the country; for her, it meant she was in it for herself. If she knew her material, it meant she was "overprepared," dull, and inauthentic, whereas he was an improviser who went with his gut. If she was sarcastic, she was a "nasty woman," whereas he was a rogue. If she was angry, she should learn to smile more, whereas he was a fighter.

As journalist Rebecca Traister wrote, "There is an Indiana Jones–style, 'It had to be snakes' inevitability about the fact that Donald Trump is Clinton's Republican rival." Everything that defined Clinton as a woman defined Trump as a man, the Man-in-Chief, the defender of men's glory days. This too was a mark of the cable-TV antihero: Tony Soprano, Don Draper, Nucky Thompson of *Boardwalk Empire* were all men raging against a dying era, against the feeling, as Tony put it, of coming in "at the end" of something.

Trump showed up to their debates in Tony Soprano mode, hulking and heavy breathing, stalking Clinton like a mob goon around the stage. (He had taken on Fox News's Roger Ailes as a debate consigliere, Ailes's ouster from Fox over sexual harassment no apparent liability in the Trump campaign.) Like James Gandolfini's, Trump's bearing emphasized his size. Clutching the sides of his debate lectern, he became Tony Soprano squeezed into the chair of his therapist's office, as if the constraints of a civilized setting strained to contain him. Their first debate often played like a therapy session, with Clinton as the Dr. Melfi, prodding for psychological pressure points (she rattled him with a story of a Miss Universe contestant whom he ridiculed for her weight by calling her "Miss Piggy") while he snapped at her in punchy sentences: "Typical politician. All talk, no action. Sounds good, doesn't work."

Which one of them won depended on which version of the show you wanted to be watching.

* * * *

ONE MONTH BEFORE election day, the campaign was interrupted by a very special episode of *The Apprentice.*

On Friday, October 7, 2016, the *Washington Post* unearthed a video from 2005 of Trump having what it tactfully called an "extremely lewd conversation about women." It originated in a trifecta of corporate synergy: Trump, whose *Apprentice* was then near its peak on NBC, rode on a bus with Billy Bush, host of NBC's entertainment-news show *Access Hollywood*, to tape a cameo on the NBC soap opera *Days of Our Lives.*

As the *Access* camera crew rolled audio, Trump regaled the giggling Bush with a story of trying to seduce Bush's cohost Nancy O'Dell ("I moved on her like a bitch"). After Bush pointed out the *Days* star Arianne Zucker waiting for the bus—"Your girl's hot as shit!"—Trump said,

> I better use some Tic-Tacs just in case I start kissing her. You
> know, I'm automatically attracted to beautiful—I just start kiss-
> ing them. It's like a magnet. Just kiss. I don't even wait. And
> when you're a star, they let you do it. You can do anything. Grab
> 'em by the pussy. You can do anything.

It's not just what Trump and Bush say but how they say it: chuckling about life as an endless dim sum buffet of pussy, Bush griping when another woman briefly disturbs his line of sight to Zucker's legs. It's what we see: Trump stepping off the bus, politely greeting Zucker, who has no idea that the two men whom she's profession-ally obligated to be nice to were just discussing her like an item on the à la carte menu. "How about a little hug for the Donald?" Bush asks, and Zucker acquiesces. This is showbiz. You've got to keep the talent happy.

The tape was a disaster. Everybody knew it. The video played on repeat in the news, and more women came out in the press with stories of having been groped and attacked by Trump—a passenger on an airplane, a contestant on *The Apprentice*, a reporter for *People*. It would be the end for any candidate, but for Trump especially, it cemented his image as a pig, a lecherous boor, a toxic, selfish caveman. TV had made Donald Trump, and now TV would end him.

*   *   *   *

IN SEPTEMBER 1952, vice presidential candidate Richard Nixon was facing his political death over reports of a "secret fund" set up by supporters for his political travel. His running mate Dwight Eisenhower, who never much liked him, let him twist while Republicans called on him to drop Nixon from the ticket.

Nixon's one chance was to throw himself at the mercy of the red light. Television sets were then in only about 15 million households, many of them well-to-do Republican ones like Fred Trump's. (Intellectual Adlai Stevenson liberals, Rick Perlstein wrote in *Nixonland*, "were the types who took pride in themselves, already, for *not* owning them.") He bought a half hour on NBC after *Texaco Star Theater*, the network's biggest lead-in. He built suspense by not addressing rumors that he might quit the campaign on-air.

Nixon began solicitously: "The best and only answer to a smear or to an honest misunderstanding of the facts is to tell the truth." His version of the truth was a story of humility with a subtext of resentment. Sitting at a desk on a suburban-den-like stage set—his wife Pat gazing lovingly at him from a floral-print chair in the corner, hands clasped on the lap of her sensible skirt—he laid out his assets and debts (a 1950 Oldsmobile, two mortgages, and $3,500 owed to his parents) and reminded the audience that "I don't happen to be a rich man." His script was plain dollars-and-cents talk, George Bailey explaining how the old building-and-loan worked in *It's a Wonderful Life*. Finally, in the moment that would give the "Checkers speech" its name, he confessed one gift from a supporter that he would not return: "a little cocker spaniel dog" that his daughter Tricia named Checkers.

Viewers sent two million telegrams to the Republican National Committee, nearly all in Nixon's support. That little cocker spaniel gave America another twenty-two years—that's 154 in dog years—of Richard Nixon in public life.

The night of October 7, 2016, Trump released what you might consider the anti-Checkers speech to Facebook, Twitter, and cable news. He shot it at home—Trump Tower—sitting not in a bourgeois den but against a night-lit sea of Manhattan skyscrapers. His face was red, his voice crabbed and defiant. He read his lines as if submitting to an uncomfortable medical exam. (Few sights convey unhappiness as much as Donald Trump having to read something.)

"I've never said I'm a perfect person nor pretended to be someone that I'm not," he said. "I said it, I was wrong, and I apologize." The apology portion of the video took precisely twenty seconds. The remaining minute and change pivoted back to his sales pitch: "We're living in the real world. This is nothing more than a distraction from the important issues we are facing today." Then he counterpivoted to an all-out attack: "Bill Clinton has actually abused women, and Hillary has bullied, attacked, shamed, and intimidated his victims. We will discuss this more in the coming days. See you at the debate on Sunday."

Nixon, who like his audience grew up with pre-televisual ideas of rhetoric and argument, took thirty minutes to lay out a case. Trump, whose motor idled at the speed of 2016 media, went from contrition to intimidation in ninety seconds.

Did any person with eyes and ears believe the guy in the video was sorry for anything? The guy in the video sure as hell didn't. "If anything," political reporter Maggie Haberman wrote in the *New York*

Times, "Mr. Trump's videotaped statement was a truncated version of a speech that he had given countless times."

The recording was the illustration of the Most Objectionable Program principle of polarizing the audience. Whatever you thought of Donald Trump before it, you believed twice as much now. It changed nothing.

But.

* * * *

ON NOVEMBER 8, what everyone knew was going to happen, didn't. The evening's election coverage began telling the story of how Donald Trump lost before the returns even came in. The news anchors reported the results of exit polls that suggested that Americans didn't respond to his fearmongering. Trump's campaign manager Kellyanne Conway blamed the Republican establishment for insufficient support. It was over. Everybody knew it. And then, as Wolf Blitzer and John King stood before CNN's "magic wall" touch screen going over the returns from Florida early in prime time, the margin between the candidates started wobbling—Clinton was ahead, then Trump, then Clinton, then Trump—as Blitzer excitedly pointed to the flip-flopping graphic like a child watching fireworks. At the *New York Times* website, the "needle"—the data-driven prediction meter that began the night at a high confidence of Clinton winning, slammed toward Trump's side like the altimeter on a crashing airplane.

Donald Trump lost the popular vote by almost three million. He won the presidency by a margin of fewer than 80,000 votes in the decisive states of Michigan, Pennsylvania, and Wisconsin. He was a TV program that lost the total audience but won in the key advertising demo.

In an election that close, any number of things could be the deciding factor. The proffered explanations have included: FBI director James Comey's reviving, days before the election, the issue of Clinton's use of a private e-mail server; computer hacking and online propaganda by the Russian government; the release of stolen Democratic National Committee and Clinton campaign e-mails and their blanket coverage in the media; "economic anxiety"; "identity politics"; third-party candidates; the strategy of the Clinton and Trump campaigns; sexism; racism; nationalism; populism; fake news; mainstream news; Fox News; the collective assumption by everyone—the media, protest voters, the Obama administration, the Trump campaign itself—that Clinton was going to win, so nothing that they did would really matter.

Someone else can sort that out. But to get into the position where it was even possible, where the election of the guy from *The Apprentice* as leader of the world's singular superpower was more than a premise for an *SNL* skit, a large enough portion of America had to accept the idea of cheering for the antihero, for the Tony Sopranos and Richard Hatches of the world. They had to accept the sales pitch that the president did not need to be morally admirable, or trustworthy, or empathetic, or self-sacrificing, or curious, or self-reflective, or capable of acting as though other people's interests were as important as his own—as long as they believed he could do the job they wanted done. That was the real argument of his *Access Hollywood* "apology": *We're living in the real world.*

Even Richard Nixon felt the obligation to go on TV and tell Americans that he was not a crook. Donald Trump only had to promise his voters that he'd give them their cut—conservative judges, or tax cuts, or the punishment of immigrants, or the pain of the liberals.

It's not as simple as saying that TV "made" people vote for Donald Trump (though it surely helped him) or that people were misled by reality TV into seeing him as other than he was (though surely some were). One psychological study found that *Apprentice* fans developed a "parasocial bond" with Trump—the kind of empathic connection TV viewers feel with characters they visit every week, because our brains didn't evolve to distinguish mediated relationships from real ones. But what little polling there was on the preferences of *Apprentice* viewers in 2016 was wildly inconsistent; one poll found Trump with a twenty-plus lead among fans of the show, another found a nearly identical margin for Clinton among the same group.

But once a set of ideas and archetypes enter the culture, they become part of the common language that a politician can build a story from. Trump made that sale—*You knew damn well I was a snake before you took me in*—and having done it, anything he did in the campaign or could be shown to have done in the past simply solidified his support by solidifying his opposition.

Sometimes he boggled at it himself. He had a way of stepping out of his body and commenting on his own campaign like an analyst, as if he were a show that he was watching on TV. At a rally in Iowa he said, "I could stand in the middle of Fifth Avenue and shoot somebody"—he made a little finger gun, dead at the camera—"and I wouldn't lose any voters." Why would he lose any for shooting his mouth off on the NBC lot?

When you're a star, they let you do it. You can do anything.

*   *   *   *

IN THE BLUE-CURTAINED BALLROOM of the New York Hilton Midtown—"Manhattan's largest self-contained function space"—Donald Trump walked onstage election night with his family, to the theme "The Parachutes," from *Air Force One*, a 1997 Harrison Ford action movie about a president who kills terrorists. He passed a "Bikers for Trump" sign. He clapped rhythmically, *slap, slap, slap*. He smiled tightly, almost a grimace, and gripped the podium.

It was 2:49 in the morning. Before he started his victory speech, he searched one more time, over the heads of the crowd, for the red light of the TV-news camera, the one thing on Earth that was most like him. It never slept. It was always hungry. It ate and ate and ate, and when it had eaten the entire world, it was still empty.

THE GORILLA
CHANNEL

DONALD TRUMP AND TELEVISION HAD BEEN WORKING TOWARD this moment for seventy years, since he emerged squalling into the world and it burst forth in a spray of static and radiation. From his youngest days in Queens, he sunbathed in it, let it soak into his skin, the shootouts and the breakneck football tackles and the barrel-chested macho men grappling each other in the ring. TV, for its part, had spent decades preparing America for the kind of campaign that Trump would run, for the idea that seizing attention was an act of leadership, for a kind of rhetoric that depended not on logic or narrative but a nonstop, channel-flipping series of excitements. He watched TV, and then he courted TV, and then he starred on TV, and then he became TV. He achieved a psychic bond with the creature, and it lowered its head, let him climb on its back, and carried him to the White House.

Now he was the master of it, or so he thought. Days after winning the election, he summoned to Trump Tower the heads and anchors of the major news networks—without whose attentions he might now be trying to launch his own cable-news channel, or maybe weighing a reality-TV comeback, rather than selecting a cabinet—and yelled at them. They had got it wrong. They had bet against him, belittled him, made him look bad. Unfair! "It was like a fucking firing squad," said one news staffer, Trump sitting in a Trump Tower boardroom and blasting people around the table, the way he would an *Apprentice* team for having blown the Sotheby's charity-auction task.

Things would be different from here on. He'd won. There was one show in America and it had one star and he was it now. And everyone knew you had to keep the star happy. Trump thought it would be with TV news the way it had been with every other partner that he'd taken on and gotten invested in building up his image—the gossip-column reporters, his branding partners, his creditors, the WWE, Mark Burnett. TV would get its cut: the ratings had skyrocketed during the campaign and would continue to grow as he issued a geyser of outrages and provocations. But he would get the sweetest part of the deal, the double scoop of ice cream; he would feed first. TV had been the perfect medium for his sensibility, for picking fights, for whipping up people's hatred and fear and resentment, for taking the express lane around logic. It had gotten him where he wanted to go, and it had benefited from him. But ultimately, he was the boss.

TV had other plans. Like the new president, it had also been putting its brand on the American consciousness for decades. It had become the national language, framing history and forging emotional bonds and teaching people to think in microbursts of image and impulse. It suckled Donald Trump and taught him to think the way it thought. He took to the lesson hungrily and became its best pupil. "Trump is an avid television viewer," said former CNN host Larry King, who had covered and socialized with him since the 1980s. "He's a product of television. He loves television." TV was in him, and now he was in the White House. Donald Trump thought that TV was his tool. TV realized that Trump was, in fact, its vessel.

As a candidate, Trump controlled TV, feeding the red light drama, monopolizing its attention. As president, he would be controlled by TV. TV—the news shows that he inhaled hour after hour—motivated him and enraged him; it moved him to action and paralyzed him in self-surveillance. It was, though he had access to the intelligence apparatus of the US government, his chief source of information. He was no different as president from when, as candidate, he told Chuck Todd of *Meet the Press* how he got his military advice: "I watch the shows" (that is, TV news programs like the one he was currently on). He was like Chance the Gardener in the novel and film *Being There*, the tabula rasa, educated by non-stop TV watching, who was mistaken for a philosopher ("Chauncey Gardiner") and eventually became the favorite to become the next president. Except that unlike with Trump, we never got to see Chance actually become president.

Trump had always been obsessed with the media. He craved the approbation of gatekeepers like the *New York Times* and *Time* magazine; he scoured his clippings and sent reporters copies of articles about him marked up in angry Sharpie. But as much as he coveted print coverage, TV—oh, *that* was the stuff. In the 1980s, his executive assistant kept a trove of videotapes of his TV appearances for him to rewatch: "a form of ego sustenance," according to his biographer.

So imagine it. You have been consumed by fame all your life. You grew up with TV. You wanted to get on TV, so you did. You prefer TV to reading. And you prefer TV *about you* to anything else. You absolutely burn to know what is being said about you at all times.

Now you live in a time when TV is more readily available than tap water. No need for a shelf of videotapes, just punch up a menu on the TiVo. Oh, and you're the most powerful man in the world, which makes you the protagonist of the news. The news is a TV show, twenty-four hours a day on multiple channels, in which the president is always the star. You have always thought that you were the most important person in any room, and now *you actually are*, and there are talking rectangles affixed to every surface in sight to remind you of it.

You are on the show, or the people who work for you are on it, or other people, talking about you, you, you. Whether you are winning or losing. How big are your crowds. Who is enthralled with you and afraid of you. It excites you and it enrages you, and you pull out your phone and you tweet your thought, and your thought floats away from you and crosses the barrier and becomes part of the show. People talk about your thought, they wonder what it means, the markets react and people protest and applaud.

When do mortal humans have the experience of seeing a story that is entirely about them, and thinking a thought, and then seeing that thought materialize itself before their eyes? Only when they dream. But you are the one lucky boy in all of history whose real life is that dream, who gets to live out the impulse of every toddler smushing a chubby hand against a glass screen: *To go inside the TV.*

Why would you ever do anything else?

* * * *

AS LONG AS TV HAS EXISTED, science fiction has imagined it as a handmaid for dystopia. George Orwell's *1984* imagined the "telescreen," a two-way device for surveillance and propaganda. Aldous Huxley, in *Brave New World*, envisioned a cowlike population narcotized by "feelies" (movies with "amazing tactual effects" that were "far more real than reality"), "scent organs," and, of course, television.

In Ray Bradbury's *Fahrenheit 451*, a totalitarian state banned books and celebrated television. In Suzanne Collins's *Hunger Games* novels the poor fought to the death on reality TV. On "The Waldo Moment," an episode of *Black Mirror*, a foul-mouthed cartoon character, controlled by malign producers, ran for office and was elected as a politically incorrect truth-teller.

All these stories differed on *how* the state would use the media. Neil Postman believed that Huxley was more correct than Orwell: visual media would not be a lash, to subjugate people, but a honeytrap, to distract them. "In the Huxleyan prophecy," he wrote, "Big Brother does not watch us, by his choice. We watch him, by ours."

But what these many warnings agreed on was that the state would *use* the media, rather than be used by it. The entertainments were for the unwashed, the chumps. The leaders would have better things to do. They would have more sophisticated, potent sources of intelligence. Media was the opiate of the masses. Big Brother did not get high on his own supply.

Donald Trump did. He employed TV, but he was also addicted to it. That was arguably how he used it so instinctually: it was in his veins. The rich history of dystopian warnings about media—many of them praised as prophetic after 2016—did not anticipate this situation. They foresaw leaders who would wield media as a weapon. They did not foresee a media that might select for a certain kind of leader who shared and would propagate its psychology. (Author Douglas Rushkoff described Trump as a human "media virus," his term for a cultural sensation that spreads irresistibly, carrying encoded ideas with it.)

If there's a better fantastical analogy for Trump, it might be neither *1984* nor *Brave New World* but *The Lord of the Rings*, in which the One Ring gave power to grasping, vain creatures like Gollum but also warped and tormented them, enslaving them to the red light of Sauron's dark tower. TV was Donald Trump's Precious. Fusing himself with the culture's most powerful force, he became possessed by it.

Trump got elected. But TV became president.

* * * *

REPUBLICAN ESTABLISHMENT POLITICIANS, who were skeptical of Trump before happily accepting the spoils of his win, hoped that he would be the Mark Burnett of his administration, the maestro running a smooth production. This was the Ronald Reagan analog, a template they could at least understand. The "master showman" would razzle-dazzle the nation, while advancing the party's agenda behind the scenes like a real honest-to-God president. The presidency had been a TV production for decades, so what the hell;

maybe it wouldn't hurt to have the guy from NBC running it. "Donald J. Trump is going to be the executive producer of a thing called the American government," said Newt Gingrich. "He's going to have this huge TV show called leading the world."

The hitch was that, on *The Apprentice*, Trump had a team of producers to impose coherence on his actions. His presidency would be more like a live raw feed, chaotic, non sequitur, unedited.

Shortly after Trump's election, C-SPAN set up a daily live-cam in the lobby of Trump Tower. Hour after hour, it was trained on the mirror-finished golden doors of the lobby elevators. It was mesmerizingly boring, a gilded human aquarium. Holiday shoppers would drift into the frame, set down their bags and gossip with cameramen. Occasionally, someone would emerge from the elevator or approach it—a Trump child, or a potential cabinet secretary, or Kanye West, or The Naked Cowboy, a New York street busker known for performing in Times Square in his underwear.

Then the golden doors would slide shut, and the waiting would begin again. It was a surreal metaphor for the coming fake-gilded age. America was about to get, *Let's Make a Deal*–style, what was behind door number 2.

What presidents-elect usually kept hidden—the parade of supplicants and prospects—Trump put on display. It was public, yet not transparent. The flow of boldface names paying obeisance kept the press in a state of whispering excitement. Who was in? Who was being toyed with? When you have a surplus of visuals and a paucity of actual information, then rumor becomes the default mode of news.

Those elevator doors recalled the elimination segments on *The Apprentice*, where ejectees would wheel their sad little suitcases into the lobby and onto the street. Trump allowed himself to be courted openly. He was photographed at a candlelit dinner of frogs' legs and diver scallops with Mitt Romney, once his harshest critic, now a simpering hopeful for secretary of state. It was a dominance display, the royal court reimagined as reality TV. Romney grinned for a humiliating photo, then was asked to pack his things and go, a first-episode rejectee whom no one would remember by the finale.

* * * *

TRUMP'S TV INSTINCTS were most apparent in his attention to symbolism. One of his first military actions, eighty-three days into his presidency, was to order the dropping of the most powerful conventional explosive in the US arsenal on an ISIS cave network in Afghanistan. The MOAB—which stood for Massive Ordnance Air Blast, or, informally, "Mother of All Bombs"—was Donald Trump in munitions form, a hypertrophic object that represented the exaggerated Looney Tunes conception of itself. Thirty feet long and more than ten tons, with grid-shaped fins and a gleaming nose cone, it looked like something that Wile E. Coyote would mail-order from Acme to drop on the Road Runner. Presidents Bush and Obama had it at their disposal and never used it. In her post–White House memoir, Omarosa recalled Trump being "obsessed" with the bomb, telling visitors with delight how "I was sitting there with my chocolate cake" when his "generals" gave word the bomb would drop. "He kept repeating it, almost like he was reliving it with whomever was in his company," she wrote. " 'Did you see that "mother of all bombs" drop?' " He loved the branding and the imagery. It would look *great* on TV. *Fox & Friends* replayed aerial footage of the MOAB exploding, to the tune of "Courtesy of the Red, White, and Blue (The Angry American)" by country singer Toby Keith. "That is what freedom looks like," said cohost Ainsley Earhardt.

At a press conference, Trump insisted that he had separated himself from his private businesses by pointing to a table stacked with manila folders and papers, not unlike the "Trump steaks" at his campaign press conference. Staffers blocked reporters from examining them. They may or may not have had printing on them. But like the props on a reality show, they conveyed a visual concept: "Documentation."

He handled hiring like a casting director. Appearances mattered. He did not care for mustaches. He wanted the gender roles to be visually clear: the men should look good in a suit, women should wear skirts, like they did on *The Apprentice*, like they did on Fox News.

The thing was to "look the part." His first secretary of defense, for instance, was General James "Mad Dog" Mattis. The choice upended a long tradition of civilian control of the Pentagon. But of course he picked a general. In Trump's mind, one glance at a person needs to be enough to tell you the character they play. He built his celebrity by playing a broader cartoon of "rich guy" than *The Simpsons'* Charles Montgomery Burns. The symbol, Trump learned, is more important than the reality; it creates the reality.

So what does Donald Trump picture when he hears the words "Secretary of Defense"? Probably the same thing that you do, if you've never thought much about the job. Do you think of some pencil-pusher in a suit? No. You think of a general, a barking Patton type out of an editorial cartoon. He's square-jawed—he's a *he*, of course—and he has epaulets and one of those grids of badges on his chest and a nickname, like, I don't know, "Mad Dog." If Mattis had not come equipped with that nickname, Trump surely would have had to assign it to him. "This is central casting," he told Mattis at a luncheon after his inauguration. "If I was doing a movie, I pick you, general."

* * * *

OCCASIONALLY, TRUMP WOULD executive-produce an event, TV style, like his 2018 summit with North Korean dictator Kim Jong Un. Kim was the quintessential adversary for the Trump era: a terrifying clown, like a Batman villain, a starstruck, mass-murdering despot who had befriended former NBA star and *Celebrity Apprentice* contestant Dennis Rodman. (Pop-culture obsession ran in the family. Kim's father, Kim Jong Il, was so fixated on the movies that he had a South Korean director and actress kidnapped.) One could argue, as some of Trump's supporters did, that it would take a volatile celebrity figure—someone who brought his own spotlight and made Kim feel like he was feeding off the energy of a costar/enemy—to really engage the attention-seeking dictator. The way that sober leaders of the past seemed to be cast for each other (Churchill and Stalin, say), Trump and Kim were picture-perfect antagonists for an era of postmodern nightmare-farce.

Trump's feud with Kim was like a reality-TV Cuban Missile Crisis. First, Trump escalated tensions over North Korea's nuclear weapons programs in trash-talking tweets and speeches, threatening to "totally destroy" the nation with "fire and fury," boasting that *his* "nuclear button" was bigger than Kim's. Kim eagerly played the heel, escalating tensions until he got what North Korean dictators had craved for decades: a one-on-one meeting, in Singapore, with the president of the United States. (Rodman also showed up, his visit sponsored by PotCoin, a cryptocurrency for the cannabis industry.)

Trump came prepared with a bizarre, movie-trailer-style video—complete with horses romantically galloping through foamy surf—promising Kim prosperity and glory if he cooperated. The two leaders took a dating-show stroll through a garden for the cable-news channels, they smiled and shook hands, and suddenly, lo and behold, "Little Rocket Man" was now a "very smart negotiator," enviable for his "tough" guards and his fawning state media. One obsequious North Korean anchor, Trump marveled, was even nicer to Kim than Fox News was to him.

And just like that, we were never at war with Eastasia. There was no actual diplomatic breakthrough. But as in the *Apprentice* board-room, there were all the visual signifiers of a "deal"—Handshakes! Men signing things! That little had happened to reduce the actual nuclear threat was irrelevant for TV purposes. If anything, it was better, because it held open the promise of a sequel: See what happens in the next exciting installment of *The Celebrity Apocalypse*!

* * * *

BUT TRUMP WAS more often mastered by TV than he was the master of it, as became clear with his administration's pilot episode, his inauguration.

Trump's inaugural address was an antihero's monologue. Inaugural speeches almost universally involve a call to conscience and morality. Kennedy said that "a good conscience [is] our only sure reward." George H. W. Bush declared that "America is never wholly herself unless she is engaged in high moral principle." Trump's speech was about strength, winning, resentment: "You will never be ignored again." Unique among modern inaugurals—even Nixon's— it did not make so much as an obligatory gesture toward ethics. In the Trump era, if you wanted to be good, for whatever stupid reason, you would be good to your own kind and on your own time. (Trump later gave Paul Ryan, the Speaker of the House, the nickname "Boy Scout." He did not mean it as a compliment.)

This was a niche argument—a powerful one in enough parts of the country to take the Electoral College, but niche nonetheless. And the images of Inauguration Day made this graphically clear. Where Barack Obama had been sworn in before a crowd estimated at 1.8 million, aerial photographs of Trump's inauguration showed vast empty swaths on the National Mall. (Crowd scientists assessed the turnout at one-third Obama's.) The next day's Women's March protests were the largest demonstrations in US history. The humiliating comparisons were all over TV: against him, streets swollen with pink; on his side, a gaping void.

Trump had always fudged his stats. He got the tabloids to call him a "billionaire" when he wasn't one; he added ten phantom stories to Trump Tower and his buyers were glad to agree on the fiction. He called the practice "truthful hyperbole." TV, with its overnight Nielsens, only fed and intensified this scorekeeping fixation: you got a number, *immediately*, quantifying your success.

Donald Trump, president, was, like Donald Trump, reality star, a niche success. This is a valuable thing to be if you leverage it the right way: in TV, by delivering a select audience to advertisers; in an election, by adding just enough voters in key states to take the Electoral College while you lose the popular vote.

But Trump's ego needed to win the total audience, not just the key demo.

Reporters who covered the TV business in the *Apprentice* years were used to Trump lying about his ratings. Back then, delusion-maintenance duty would fall to his publicist, Jim Dowd, who recalled Trump demanding that he phone up TV reporters and boast, " 'Number-one show on television, won its time slot,' and I'm looking at the numbers and at that point, say season five, for example, we were number 72."

Now, his press secretary, Sean Spicer, was the publicist who had to keep the talent happy. The day after the inauguration, he assailed journalists for believing their lying eyes. "This was the largest audience to ever witness an inauguration, period, both in person and around the globe," Spicer insisted. Trump echoed this the same day at a speech to CIA staff: "It looked like a million, a million and a half people." (He also improved on the day's weather—"God looked down and he said, 'We're not going to let it rain on your speech' "—though live TV images of the rain demonstrated that the Almighty had thought otherwise.)

White House spokeswoman Kellyanne Conway coined a defining phrase; Spicer, she said, had offered "alternative facts." Facts now had teams. This was an extension of the project of Fox News, which had turned its news audience into a sports audience, driven by rooting interests, convinced that every call should go their team's way no matter what the instant replay said.

On the one hand, you had a few pictures, a mere testimony of photographic reality waved around by the smug media who wanted to make your president seem small. On the other, you had *your team*, which, whatever the pictures said, had done something amazing, something nobody thought was possible, by electing him. Those were the sides. *Pick one.*

The trick of con artistry (or salesmanship, to use the polite term) is not to fool your audience. It's to get them to fool themselves. Once they've bought in, they'll ignore an uncompleted border wall the way heavily invested tenants, wanting to believe they made a smart purchase, will ignore the bad fit on a kitchen fixture. Both are minor details next to the grander construction—elegance, strength, Making America Great Again—that they've signed on to. In a speech to the VFW, Trump told his audience to disregard any negative news about him: "Just remember, what you're seeing and what you're reading is not what's happening." Anyone can believe something that's merely *true*. It takes loyalty to look past truth and believe what the team needs to be *right*.

Politics was full of ordinary lies, the purpose of which was merely to get the listener to believe them. This was a different kind, identified by Orwell in *1984*; its aim wasn't deception but solidarity. "The Party told you to reject the evidence of your eyes and ears," he wrote. "It was their final, most essential command." In the aftermath of World War II, the German political philosopher Hannah Arendt wrote about how, in the dictatorships of the mid-twentieth century, lying was a demonstration of power more than a means of persuasion: "Not Stalin's and Hitler's skill in the art of lying but the fact that they were able to organize the masses into a collective unit to back up their lies with impressive magnificence, exerted the fascination." The leader placed himself above reality itself, and the crowd committed to the ideal of a people with one body, with the leader serving as their eyes, ears, and mouth. "Ideological thinking," Arendt wrote, "becomes emancipated from the reality that we perceive with our five senses, and insists on a 'truer' reality concealed behind all perceptible things." (Half a century later, the American political philosopher Stephen Colbert expressed a version of Arendt's idea on *The Colbert Report* when he defined "truthiness," a term for the bastardized reality we end up with when feeling becomes more important than thinking: "We are divided between those who *think* with their *head* and those who *know* with their *heart*.")

Trump also positioned himself as the People's Mouth—"I am your voice," he said at the Republican convention—but of course, he was not a midcentury dictator with the coercive power of a totalitarian state behind him. His power was in the winking, postmodern arena of twenty-first-century media, which had groomed its audience toward a kind of cynicism that, paradoxically, made it possible to believe anything. The kayfabe of pro wrestling told you that everything was a show while allowing you to invest in the fight as if it were real. Reality TV's adherents believed more strongly than anyone that "there's no reality in it," but they immersed themselves in the stories anyway. Fox News and Internet trollery convinced people that everyone was working an angle, anything could be faked, so what really mattered was not what was technically true but what rang true with your preconceptions. An overwhelming flood of information and provocations from social media, as communications scholar Zeynep Tufekci has argued, can control a population more effectively than a state clampdown on media.

Arendt identified this dynamic long before cable news or Facebook: "In an ever-changing, incomprehensible world the masses had reached the point where they would, at the same time, believe everything and nothing, think that everything was possible and that nothing was true."

This was the strategy of the propagandists in Vladimir Putin's Russia, whose hackers and social-media trolls had supported the Trump campaign in the 2016 election. They controlled the Russian population less through iron-fisted clampdowns than through an overwhelming flood of disinformation and reality-TV-style spectacle. This philosophy told the audience: You're no fool. *You get it.* You know that everybody lies, that there are a million different versions of every story, that everyone's trying to put one over on someone else. So be smart and stick with the team. Thus it now worked in America. Did you see the pictures of Obama's inauguration? Yes. Did you see the pictures of Trump's? Yes. So why do you believe Trump's was bigger? Because fuck you, that's why.

This became the Trump administration's guiding principle, articulated by his surrogate, lawyer, and chief postmodern relativist Rudy Giuliani when he told Chuck Todd on *Meet the Press* that the president should not have to testify to special counsel Robert Mueller and risk perjury according to "somebody's version of the truth."

"Truth is truth," Todd said.

"No, it isn't truth," Giuliani insisted. "Truth isn't truth."

* * * *

TRUMP TOLD HIS STAFF, the *New York Times* reported, to think of every day as an episode of a reality show in which he defeated his enemies. Sean Spicer's briefings became the daily arena. He insisted, straight-faced, that the travel ban against majority-Muslim countries—which Trump had called a "ban"—was not a ban. He repeated a false story that President Obama had tapped a Fox News reporter's phone. His briefings were not informative in the sense of disseminating facts. But as a live demonstration of the contortions required to maintain Trump's reality, they were a revelation.

There was another character in Spicer's daily drama: Trump, a giant flaming eye just off camera. He watched constantly, and like an overinvolved network executive scrutinizing the dailies, had continual notes. Spicer never defended Trump strongly enough for his liking. Sometimes, he would be passed slips of paper scribbled with a red Sharpie—Trump's writing instrument of choice—and would reverse himself on the spot.

Spicer's look was all wrong too, shifty and doughy, squinched into an ill-fitting suit, a harried Applebee's manager in a losing battle with the customers. When *Saturday Night Live* parodied him—with Melissa McCarthy in male drag as a ball-buster who was more commanding than the real thing—Trump was infuriated. For his guy to be mocked, *and by a woman*, was emasculating. As spring 2017 dragged on, Spicer carried himself like a man sent out to take a daily beating, with the expectation of a second one for how poorly he took the first.

But Spicer had one saving grace: his cringe comedy was drawing four million viewers every afternoon. "I'm not firing Sean Spicer," Trump said in April. "That guy gets great ratings."

Spicer lasted until July, getting a sixteenth minute of fame at that fall's Emmy Awards by imitating McCarthy's imitation of him. (His successor, Sarah Huckabee Sanders, survived longer by playing the martyr rather than the sad sack. When she was booted from a Virginia restaurant whose staff were appalled at the administration's treatment of transgender people and immigrants, she became one more Joan of Arc for the culture war.) Like a reality show, the administration recast every few months, preferring staffers who had auditioned on cable. Frequent cable-news guest Anthony Scaramucci, during his brief tenure as communications director, proposed an online lottery for a golf game with Trump and "video content that constructively operates as 'The President Donald J. Trump' Show" [sic]. From Fox News, Trump brought in the former executive Bill Shine, whose ignominious record in handling Roger Ailes's sexual harassment scandal bothered Trump not at all. Shine had the president record cranky little op-ed videos from the Rose Garden, modeled on the online-video "Trumpvlogs" in which Trump had once bemoaned the female remake of *Ghostbusters*. John Bolton and Larry Kudlow became senior advisers because Trump loved how they talked about him on his programs. No matter your job title in the Trump White House, TV was job one. (Of Sebastian Gorka, a bombastic defender on cable, Trump "told colleagues he had no idea what Gorka actually did but loved him on TV.")

Trump also hired Omarosa Manigault Newman, the villainess of multiple *Apprentice* seasons, as communications director of the office of public liaison. No one in or outside the White House seemed to know what she did. But she was visible cheering Trump on at press appearances, and she got married in the spring, at the Trump International Hotel in Washington, in a bridal gown she got free for appearing on TLC's *Say Yes to the Dress*.

After Omarosa was pushed out of the White House late in 2017, she rebranded as a Trump Resistance celebrity. Her change of heart seemed, like her latching on to Trump's coattails in the first place, transparently opportunistic. But transparent opportunism was part of what made her the most Trump-like of all the personalities associated with him. She too had a sixth sense for taking advantage of strife, knew the utility of a public fight, and was keenly aware of how others perceived her and how to use that.

This would be a pattern in the Trump administration. His most effective adversaries were not his high-minded critics, like the ramrod-stiff FBI chief, James Comey, whom Trump fired in angst over the Russian election-interference investigation. They were people with savvy TV and social-media skills and no encumbering sense of shame, like Stormy Daniels, the porn star who charged that Trump had sex with her in 2006—when he was newly married, with a baby son at home—then paid her off illicitly during the election to keep quiet.

Omarosa's 2018 tell-all, *Unhinged*, got publicity for an unproven charge that Trump had used "the n-word" on the set of *The Apprentice*; nothing is more Trumpian than seizing attention with a provocative claim. But—just like Rona Barrett, the gossip columnist who saw a president in Trump in 1980, when no one else did—Omarosa could also be more insightful about his character than traditional pundits, who strained to cram him into the templates they'd used to understand other presidencies. She was especially sharp in seeing how he ran his reality-TV boardroom the way he would run a country: "Whenever there was a disagreement or an argument, his eyes lit up," she recalled. "He loved seeing people argue or fight."

It was a tabloid presidency; maybe Trump needed tabloid historians and reality-TV rebuttals. When Omarosa denounced the administration during her run on CBS's *Celebrity Big Brother*, Deputy White House Press Secretary Raj Shah assailed her from the podium. "Omarosa was fired three times on *The Apprentice*," he said, "and this was the fourth time we've let her go."

We. The Trump administration, Shah was as good as saying, was a continuation of *The Apprentice* on a global scale.

* * * *

TVS WERE RAISED on the walls of Trump's White House like the flags of a conquering army. In May 2017, Trump took reporters from *Time* magazine on a tour of the White House, bypassing the renovated moldings and new crystal chandelier to show his interviewers "something amazing": a massive flat-screen TV, hanging opposite the fireplace in the dining room, and equipped with a capacious DVR. (He boasted to advisers about having "the world's best TiVo," as if it were a perk of office superior to Air Force One.) In an accompanying photo, Trump stands next to Vice President Mike Pence, staring grimly forward, clutching a remote control in both hands. He's a king posing with the ceremonial instrument of his rule, the orb and scepter replaced with a DVR clicker.

TV became the language of his administration. His daily briefings were turned into television, figuratively and literally: "Trump likes to pore over visuals—maps, charts, pictures, and videos," the *Washington Post* reported. He became alarmed during a national security meeting when a TV playing Fox News showed video of North Korean missiles blasting off; he had to be reassured that it was old footage and not a live missile launch. He made no apparent distinction between seeing something on a screen and seeing it in person, except maybe that the screen version seemed more authentic. After a massive hurricane hit Texas, he posted an assurance on Instagram that he had been "witnessing first-hand the horror & devastation." The picture showed Trump looking at a map of Texas on an enormous flat-screen monitor.

Barack Obama had disdained TV news. "Not watching political television," he told *The New Yorker,* "is part of how you stay focused on the task, as opposed to worrying about the noise." Trump craved the noise. As CNN carried his first photo op on Air Force One live, the clicks of the cameras were drowned out by the "800 588-2300, *Em-piiiire!*" commercial jingle for Empire Today carpet and flooring, playing on a speaker in the background. His eyes would wander to the muted cable channels during meetings. Reportedly, there were three televisions in his bedroom, where he would repair early in the evening with a cheeseburger. If he felt he'd had a good day, he looked forward to TV as his dessert. "Tonight, I'm going to enjoy watching television," he would tell Melania, "because I did great."

But often, the stories would not be the story he thought he was watching all day. They would be about the bills not passed through Congress, the critics who called him a racist, the investigation into his campaign and Russia. The stories called him a liar, if not in so many words, then by pointing out the gap between his words and the truth. Without Mark Burnett and his teams of *Apprentice* editors on the case, there was no one to edit out his flubs, no one to keep unflattering images from leaking—a gust of wind, say, hoisting his comb-over and exposing his bare pink skull as he boarded Air Force One. After 9/11, news channels had invented the "zipper" graphic to deal with the deluge of news; now they developed a new graphic—the fact-checking chyron—to deal with the deluge of disinformation. "PENCE DENIES TRUMP SAID THINGS HE SAID," ran one on CNN; on MSNBC, "TRUMP CLAIMS 'WE WON IN A LAND-SLIDE'/CLINTON WINNING POPULAR VOTE BY OVER 2.5 MILLION."

Pointing out Trump's lies, however, had the side effect of spreading them, and Trump, building on the work of Fox News, was conditioning his audience to dismiss any source but him. Simply pointing out common-sense reality made you an "Enemy of the People," in Trump's words, which happened also to have been the words of Lenin, Stalin, and Mao Zedong. Trump, not a reader, may or may not have known the origins of the phrase, just as he may or may not have known his phrase "America First" was used by fascist sympathizers before World War II. As with many things about Trump, figuring out his intention was less important than his action, which was to put his followers at war with information and define an injury to him as an injury to all.

"Enemy of the People" put the press in a double bind. On the one hand, it framed them as on the opposing team from Trump, which invited his supporters to disregard any bad news accordingly. On the other hand, it pressured them, subtly or overtly, to calibrate their coverage so as not to be *perceived* as if they were the opposition party. This led to such Trump-era clichés as the umpteen million interviews with elderly conservative diner customers in the Rust Belt—attempts to prove that the media hadn't "forgotten" this exhaustively covered demographic—and to the worry that, if news outlets pointed out every lie or ill-informed statement Trump made, in so many words, they would look biased simply for representing reality. There's a term in political philosophy, the "Overton window," which describes the range of acceptable public discourse, which can be shifted by persistent enough extreme speech. Trump's effect was to fling open the Overton window and shove the truth, arms flailing, straight out of it.

Trump made a similar acquisition of "fake news," another term he rebranded to suit his marketing purposes. During the campaign, it had been a term for online news hoaxes—many of them in support of Trump, like a phony report that the Pope had endorsed him. As with "Make America Great Again," he co-opted the phrase, secured the cultural copyright. Like "Make America Great Again," "fake news" meant whatever you needed it to. At first it was a literal denial—"This news is untrue"—but it quickly entered the half-literal, pro-wrestling kayfabe-osphere of so many Trumpisms. Maybe it meant the news was true but unfair. Or it was true but disrespectful. Or it was true but it made the wrong people happy, and you were not going to give them the goddam satisfaction of admitting it. It was tribal signaling. It meant, "I give you permission to ignore this fact that is not good for our team." Trump blurted as much in a tweet complaining about TV coverage: "91% of the Network News about me is negative (Fake)."

Still, he watched. He couldn't help himself. He attacked CNN regularly, tweeting a doctored video of him downing Vince McMahon at WrestleMania, with the CNN logo imposed on McMahon's head. When Mika Brzezinski of *Morning Joe* mocked Trump for hanging fake *Time* magazine covers with his picture in his golf clubs, he tweeted the claim that she had once shown up at Mar-a-Lago "bleeding badly from a facelift." (Trump claimed never to watch CNN or *Morning Joe*, like an actor who "never reads the reviews.") White House aides fretted that the *Morning Joe* feud "overtook the president's fight with CNN, which seemed in their eyes to have clearer villains and heroes."

These fights themselves would become the news. On CNBC, a "BREAKING NEWS: TRUMP TWEET" graphic would spin out onto the screen shortly after the president hit "Send." For decades, Trump had essentially been a cable-news channel in human form: loud, short of attention span, and addicted to conflict. Now he and cable had achieved the singularity, a meshing of man and machine into a symbiotic consciousness, the perturbation of each amplifying the other.

He would get angry watching people badmouth him on TV. He would lash out, and TV would get excited and cover it, and then he would get angry watching himself be angry. A White House staffer said that his fury at his first attorney general, Jeff Sessions, for recusing himself in the Russia investigation got worse because "Trump watches TV coverage of him criticizing Sessions and gets madder." In January 2018, the federal government shut down amid a budget fight in Congress. Trump "spent much of his day watching old TV clips of him berating President Barack Obama for a lack of leadership during the 2013 government shutdown."

During the campaign, Trump used to watch the Golf Channel to relax. Now he watched nothing to relax. He was like a man in a Finnish sauna, blasting the heat, flogging himself with birch branches, believing that it stimulated the circulation.

But above all, he wanted his love. That, he got from Fox, which he could count on to tell him what a good day he had when nobody else would. Best of all was *Fox & Friends*, which would tell him what a good day he had before the day even began.

* * * *

WHEN DONNY TRUMP WAS a little boy in Queens, a childhood friend of his recalls, he used to watch *Andy's Gang*, a Saturday kids' show hosted by Andy Devine. Once a popular comic-relief actor in cowboy movies, Devine was a gentle giant with a big lopsided smile. Every episode, his naughty puppet sidekick Froggy the Gremlin would work the studio audience into wild-edged peals of hysteria with his pranks. But at the end Devine would calm things down and speak straight to the kids at home: "Yes, sir, we're pals. Pals stick together. Now gang, don't forget church or Sunday school!"

This was the promise of the show: you would be swept up into a communal frenzy until you could barely control yourself, but in the end you would be accepted, loved, reassured that you were good.

Fox & Friends in the Trump era morphed into a morning children's show for the president of the United States. Kids' programs often hold the attention of their distractible audience by addressing them through the fourth wall. Dora the Explorer asked kids to help her chase off Swiper the Fox: "Say, 'Swiper, no swiping!'" Elmo became the most popular Muppet on *Sesame Street* by talking to toddlers directly. The local hosts of *Romper Room* would pretend to look through a "magic mirror" and see the children in the home audience, calling them out by name.

Fox & Friends applied that formula to an audience of one. Its hosts offered Trump encouragement, flattery, and advice. When he tweeted, his tweets—many mornings, in perfect sync with the show's topics—would materialize on a giant video wall. One morning in January 2017, the show put a video feed of the White House on screen and asked Trump to flash the lights on and off if he was watching. The producers added an effect of the lights flickering, a "TV trick" the hosts later acknowledged.

But for Trump, the childhood illusion—that your favorite show is as aware of you as you are of it—became real. *Fox & Friends* was Donald Trump's magic mirror.

The president was the show's audience, its subject, its publicist, and its virtual fourth host. His morning tweets set the focus of the show, which often scrambled to keep up. After the failure of a Republican healthcare plan, his ragetweets careered from "REPEAL failing ObamaCare now" to "As I have always said, let ObamaCare fail" to advocating "full repeal" again. The *Fox & Friends* caption tried to impose order on the morning's whiplash: "As Congress Spars, President Focuses on Jobs." Spurred by a Trump tweet complaining that Senate Democrats were holding up his judicial nominees, Kilmeade called the Democrats' resistance "anti-American."

"Well, it's anti-Trump, ultimately," Doocy said.

"Which is anti-American," Kilmeade answered.

But just as often, the show drove Trump's agenda, and thus the nation's. When it aired an incorrect report that former FBI director James Comey had leaked "top secret" information about a meeting with the president, Trump repeated the charge on Twitter: "So illegal!" (Swiper, no swiping!) Easter morning 2018, *Fox & Friends Weekend* reported an "army" of Central Americans—in truth, a ragtag group of refugees from Honduras—traveling to the United States through Mexico. Trump's tweets that morning, after some benign Easter wishes, became increasingly agitated about the "caravan" of invaders. ("NEED WALL!") By the end of the week, he'd deployed the National Guard to the border. (Thereafter, an immigrant "caravan" managed to appear whenever Fox News and Trump needed it—before the 2018 midterm elections, in the midst of a government shutdown Trump precipitated to pressure Congress to fund his wall.)

Media critics took to calling this obsequious iteration of Fox "state TV," but that term implied that the state was controlling the media. More often in this case, the media was controlling the state.

In July 2017, I wrote a column in the *New York Times* about the feedback loop between Trump and *Fox & Friends* that ended up as part of that loop. The show's hypnotic influence on Trump, I wrote, made it "the most powerful TV show in America." Fox, seeing an opportunity to tweak the *Times*, took out a full-page ad in the paper highlighting that quote; the hosts of *Fox & Friends* showed off the ad on the air (not mentioning, of course, *why* I'd said the show was so powerful).

Minutes later, Trump tweeted out the quote from my column. Magic mirror time had begun for the day.

* * * *

THERE WAS A TRAGIC DIMENSION to Trump's TV dependence. TV was the true love that he could never confess. To a gaggle of reporters on a trip to Asia, he griped, "People that don't know me, they say I like to watch television. . . . But I don't get to watch much television, primarily because of documents. I'm reading documents a lot." On that same trip, he had tweeted that he was "forced to watch @CNN" because Fox News was unavailable in the Philippines.

His denials of his TV-watching were jarring for being so obviously, needlessly false. Trump clearly loved TV and loved being on it. His administration boasted about *The Apprentice*. His aide Stephen Miller defended the president to CNN's Jake Tapper as "a self-made billionaire who revolutionized reality TV." Sometimes, Trump would slip and refer to the Cabinet Room as "the boardroom." At a particularly low point in summer 2017, he held a live-TV cabinet meeting in which members around the long table competed to praise him—chief of staff Reince Priebus thanked Trump for "the opportunity and blessing" of working for him—exactly like *Apprentice* contestants kissing up before an elimination.

TV was mother's milk to Trump; it was the focus of one of the few memories he shares of his actual mother in *The Art of the Deal*, watching Elizabeth's coronation when he was a boy in Queens. But on some level—maybe it was that voice of Fred Trump telling Mary, *For Christ's sake, turn it off*—he also seemed to find TV-watching shameful, weak, infantile. When he saw a *New York Times* report that his campaign manager Paul Manafort would try to send him messages by going on TV, he erupted: "Am I like a baby to you? I sit there like a little baby and watch TV and you talk to me? Am I a fucking baby, Paul?"

"Baby" was one of Trump's most common, seemingly deep-rooted, insults. Fred Trump raised Donald to admire the strong and the active; to sit and watch was weak and passive; to be weak and passive was to be a baby; and he was not a baby. "I am not a baby," he said—twice—to Lesley Stahl of *60 Minutes* during a combative interview in October 2018. To give a weak interview on TV: that was also being a baby, as he told Rudy Giuliani after what Trump considered an insufficiently zealous defense following the *Access Hollywood* tape, a time when Giuliani was one of the only people willing to speak up for him in public at all. "Rudy, you're a baby!" Bob Woodward recounted him saying. "They took your diaper off right there. You're like a little baby that needed to be changed." Trump saw all this, of course, because he'd been watching TV, like a—but *he was not a baby*.

He was like a binge-eater self-soothing with tubs of ice cream: he would indulge, then spiral, then deny it all, chocolate sauce still staining the corner of his lips. "I have very little time for watching T.V.," he tweeted one morning. The three days before that, he had retweeted six different videos from *Fox & Friends*.

* * * *

DENIALS OR NO, magic mirror time began to run longer and longer. The president's daily schedule included "Executive Time"—unstructured blocks available for TV and ragetweeting—until 11 a.m., with further such breaks in the afternoon, until the work day wrapped at 6 p.m. Weekdays, he was reportedly watching four to eight hours a day. Some weekends, he might not do much else besides eat and play golf.

You could say that the president was hardly working. Or you

could say that he was doing the only job he was truly elected to do: monitoring, stoking, and embodying the cultural anger machine.

Political coalitions are complicated things. Some of Trump's voters were mainline Republicans who wanted tax cuts or conservative Supreme Court justices or rollbacks of regulations. If Trump was the monster they had to ride to get to the land of small government, so be it.

But for the true believers—the rallygoers, the meme-sharers, the retweet-seekers—the tantrums and grievance and spite weren't the means, they were the end. Shocking the system. Making liberal heads explode. Putting on a show.

Even more than winning, the faithful enjoyed seeing the enemy losing, the wounded bayoneted. They couldn't get enough of Hillary Clinton–bashing, long after she lost. On Fox News and in Trump's tweets, she became a perpetual bogeywoman, the equivalent of "Emmanuel Goldstein, the Enemy of the People" from the daily "Two Minutes Hate" in *1984*. Trump's diehards bought collectible mugs, after the election, labeled "LIBERAL TEARS." Trump's job was to fill 'em up.

Tears, in Trump's America, were for losers. Trump mocked Senator Charles Schumer as "Cryin' Chuck," for choking up when, while criticizing Trump's Muslim ban, he remembered his relatives killed by the Nazis. Trump himself once told a Christian-TV reporter that he had never cried. (Babies cry. *I am not a baby.*) The Trump administration made an ethos of reality TV—that empathy is weakness, whereas meanness equals strength and authenticity—into a principle of governing. You have to harden your heart to win. It's a jungle out there.

So thorough was the administration's conviction that in June 2018, when it started separating undocumented families at the border and imprisoning the children, it was surprised that anyone objected. On Fox News, Trump's former campaign manager Corey Lewandowski mocked a Democratic strategist for bringing up the story of a girl with Down Syndrome separated from her mother, making a "sad trombone" noise: "Womp womp."

"Womp womp" was the Trump National Anthem. Trumpism, beyond any policy, was the attempt to redefine cruelty as virtue. (Arendt had seen this same tendency in the intellectuals of Europe between the wars: "their brilliant and witty praise of violence, power, and cruelty.") "Virtue," meanwhile, became a vice—specifically "virtue signaling," the successor catchphrase to "bleeding heart," but with a twist. Nixon-era conservatives at least acknowledged that "bleeding-heart liberals" were moved by genuine feelings. "Virtue signaling" added the implication that no one was *really* virtuous, that people simply faked it to make themselves look good—just like the "'respectable' guys who make careers out of boasting about their uncompromising integrity" whom Trump, in *The Art of the Deal*, compared unfavorably with his role model, Roy Cohn.

* * * *

TRUMP STARTED HOLDING his rallies again, as his pick-me-up when the job got him down. He went back to Phoenix following the deadly August 2017 racist riots in Charlottesville, Virginia, by white nationalists chanting "You will not replace us" (some substituting "Jews" for "you"), after which he'd crabbily insisted that there were "very fine people" on both sides. In September 2017—with the Russia investigation dragging on, his polls flagging, his various Obamacare-repeal attempts failed—he held a rally for a Senate candidate in Alabama, during which he decided to talk about football and TV.

"The NFL ratings are down massively, massively," he said. Part of the problem, he added, was his old bugbear: not enough violence. "If you hit too hard—15 yards! Throw him out of the game!" But this time he had a new gripe, the players who were kneeling during the National Anthem to protest police brutality against African Americans. "Wouldn't you love to see one of these NFL owners, when somebody disrespects our flag, to say, 'Get that son of a bitch off the field right now. Out. He's fired. He's fired!'"

It was textbook Trump culture warring. The between-the-lines racism. The obsession with ratings. The "You're fired!" callback. The way his stream-of-consciousness rant tossed together a combo of resentments—America had gotten soft, liberals hated the flag, these black sons of bitches didn't know their place—into a kind of freeform hate salad.

This (and not Trump's endorsement of the Republican candidate, who lost) took over TV for days. And it recurred over weeks, as every football Sunday became a cycle of players kneeling in defiance of Trump, and Trump—aggravated by what he was seeing on TV—inflaming both the protest and the rage against it. By the next fall, when Nike prodded Trump (and boosted its sales) by making an ad with protest leader Colin Kaepernick, the football proxy war had become a new national fall tradition.

Nearly any other president would have sought to calm the matter (or at least have someone else fight the battle, like Spiro Agnew did for Nixon). But because Trump thought like a cable-news network, he couldn't resist a conflict. And because he thought like the cable-news audience, he couldn't resist making it worse—or, from the standpoint of his base and the red light, better.

The fight might be about policy—his draconian immigration measures, a Supreme Court appointment, restricting rights for transgender Americans. But just as often, it would be over symbols and slights: comedian Michelle Wolf lambasting his press secretary, Sarah Huckabee Sanders, at the White House Correspondents' Dinner; ABC's firing his supporter Roseanne Barr over a racist tweet. Like Breitbart and Bannon, Yiannopoulos and the GamerGaters, Trump saw culture—sports, TV, Christmas—as another part of politics, maybe the main part. More than policy, people see culture as an extension of themselves, their ancestors, and the people they love. No one dances to a budget agreement, gathers with their family to watch healthcare legislation, or wakes their excited kids on Tax Day morning.

To ask why Trump would pursue an unnecessary fight is to forget that, in reality TV, *every fight is necessary*. Fighting is the end, not the means. So too in Trump's politics. When you lose (though you never admit losing), your bloodied team cleaves closer to you, aggrieved and craving revenge. If you win, and you win in the ugliest possible way (narrowly, with no concessions or graciousness, the losers' suffering taunted and enflamed), you ensure that the tears of your enemy will be flavored with the sweetest sorrow and pain and that the next fight, when it comes, will be even uglier, charged with recriminations that will draw your partisans tighter to your hip. It will make better TV.

* * * *

IN EARLY 2018, Michael Wolff, a journalist who specialized in Manhattan media and power circles, published *Fire and Fury*, an account from inside the Trump White House. It depicted an administration in chaos. At the center of the chaos, invariably, was TV.

The president, Wolff wrote, would refer to himself in third person, like a character in a story. (This rang true if you'd watched *The Apprentice*—"You see why Trump is Trump"—or followed him on Twitter.) He would watch an interview on Fox and then post a misspelled, false ragetweet claiming that President Obama had ordered intelligence agencies to "tapp my phones" during the campaigns. He would replay slights to him on his DVR, fuming, his mood worsening, like Nixon with upgraded technology. He would refuse to watch MSNBC's *Morning Joe* out of pique, then have his twenty-eight-year-old assistant Hope Hicks—formerly a PR aide to Ivanka—tremulously recap the show for him every morning. (Wolff got White House access in the first place because Trump had seen him say nice things about him on CNN's *Reliable Sources*.)

Shortly after *Fire and Fury* came out, the cartoonist Ben Ward posted what looked like an excerpt on Twitter, with the comment, "Wow, this extract from Wolff's book is a shocking insight into Trump's mind":

On his first night in the White House, President Trump complained that the TV in his bedroom was broken, because it didn't have "the gorilla channel." Trump seemed to be under the impression that a TV channel existed that screened nothing but gorilla-based content, 24 hours a day.

To appease Trump, White House staff compiled a number of gorilla documentaries into a makeshift gorilla channel, broadcast into Trump's bedroom from a hastily-constructed transmission tower on the South Lawn. However, Trump was unhappy with the channel they had created, moaning that it was "boring" because "the gorillas aren't fighting."

Staff edited out all the parts of the documentaries where gorillas weren't hitting each other, and at last the president was satisfied. "On some days he'll watch the gorilla channel for 17 hours straight," an insider told me.

The parody so perfectly comported with the stories about Trump—the endless TV watching, the lust for conflict, the tantrums—and so deliciously satisfied his critics' desire to see him exposed as an addled child, that Ward's joke was widely shared as true. Ward finally had to go on Twitter to clarify that the gorilla channel wasn't real.

But also, the gorilla channel was real.

It was real that the president's staff tried, fruitlessly, to manage him by managing what TV he saw and limiting his "screen time." (Bannon, seeing that his boss was mainlining up to eight hours of tube a day, asked, "Think what your brain would be like if you did that?")

It was real that TV personalities—who cast his world in terms of exciting victories and wicked antagonists—were more persuasive to Trump than his own staff. He directed his secretary of state to "closely study" a white-nationalist conspiracy theory that white South African farmers were targeted for "large-scale killing," because Fox's Tucker Carlson had promoted it. Sean Hannity, who fulminated about conspiracies against Trump nightly on Fox, was the most influential White House counselor. "He basically has a desk in the place," a Trump adviser said. Trump ordered the release of classified intelligence on the Russia investigation at the behest of his favorite TV hosts: "the great Lou Dobbs, the great Sean Hannity, the wonderful great Jeanine Pirro." He disastrously shut down the government for five weeks, in a failed attempt to pressure Congress into funding his border wall, after *Fox & Friends* said he would "look like a loser" if he didn't. He was as impressionable as a 1950s kid eating Cheerios because the Lone Ranger said to. Sometimes he would hire people who talked about him on his programs, like Scaramucci, then fire them when the flesh version disappointed.

It was real that political reporters would get thousands of dollars' worth of dental work, to look more telegenic when the president saw them on his programs, the better to get their calls returned from the White House.

It was real that critics, lobbyists, and corporations trying to persuade or curry favor with the administration started reaching out to the president, not by booking meetings, but by buying commercial time on the TV news shows he binge-watched.

It was real that Trump's own staff created TV events to placate, control, and persuade him. Things were more real to Trump if he saw them on TV. *People* were more real if he saw them on TV—even people he saw, in person, every day. White House officials would go on TV "to emphasize points to their boss, who was likely to be watching just steps away in his residence." When that didn't work, they booked outside experts onto his shows. When Trump took a shine to Fox's Pirro, a former prosecutor who offered him on-air advice on his legal troubles, someone from the White House had to go on her show every week to get the staff's voice into his head.

The president was like Jim Carrey's character in *The Truman Show* (1998), except in reverse. In the film, Truman Burbank, an ordinary man, is raised from infancy on an island that serves as a vast, hermetically constructed reality-TV set, which he takes to be the real world. In fact, he's being surveilled for a long-running, voyeuristic TV series, which he finally discovers one day when he sails off for the horizon and his boat punctures the skin of a sky-colored dome. On *The Trump Show*, the president was the star of the TV series that he lived inside, but he was also its sole audience; it was the rest of the world that needed to be conscripted as stage set and players, to perform the required story.

Others quickly got the idea, crawling inside the magic mirror to ask Trump to bomb Syria, to fire Robert Mueller, not to fire Robert Mueller. Ann Coulter, conservative TV's perpetual font of spite, went on Fox amid news coverage of children being imprisoned at the Mexican border—"I get very nervous about the president getting his news from TV"—and told Trump, directly to the camera, that the suffering kids were "child actors": "Do not fall for it, Mr. President." "One of the ways to influence the president," a high-profile white nationalist told the *Boston Globe*, "is to make sure there's things on Fox that interest him." Maryland representative Elijah Cummings, seeking a meeting with Trump about opioid abuse, said on *Morning Joe*: "To the president: I know you're watching, so I'm looking forward to meeting with you." That morning, Trump called him.

At times, the president would attempt to program the gorilla channel himself. An associate of his reported getting a call in April 2018 from Trump, who asked the source to go on TV and tell Trump to fire the special counsel investigating him. It is possible, of course, to see this as the act of the president as canny media manipulator, attempting to engineer a "Will no one rid us of this turbulent priest?" chorus to excuse putting himself above the law (although he ended up taking no action). But you could also see it as a frustrated couch potato, unhappy with his programs, fiddling with the antenna, smacking the sides of the box, demanding that it tell him a better story.

The performances for the audience of one could take on the high drama of a reality-show season finale, as when Trump's second Supreme Court nominee, Brett Kavanaugh, was accused by research psychologist Dr. Christine Blasey Ford of sexually assaulting her when they were high school students in the 1980s. Dr. Ford was called to testify to the Senate Judiciary Committee, a live-TV spectacle that recalled the wrenching 1991 hearings where Anita Hill accused Supreme Court nominee Clarence Thomas of sexual harassment. But this time, with the Senate entrenched along partisan lines, Kavanaugh's fate would largely depend on the continued support of the News-Junkie-in-Chief.

Ford spoke the morning of September 27, 2018, her tremulous account moving some spectators in the hearing room to tears. Trump, the TV native, knew how persuasive she came across; even Fox News was calling her testimony a "disaster" for Republicans. Trump had been upset for days, since Kavanaugh had given a numb, robotic interview to Fox, stumbling over canned lines like "I've always treated women with dignity and respect." What bothered Trump was his meekness. Why wasn't Kavanaugh hitting back? Jesus! He'd fired people for that on *The Apprentice*.

When Kavanaugh took the stand that afternoon, he delivered what the president wanted to see: an imitation of himself. The judge showed up hot and angry, roaring that the hearing was a "national disgrace," his features twisting and reddening, his plosives smacking against the microphone. His rage was discomfiting and divisive. But he knew that there was one show, and there was one viewer, who required one performance—who wanted to see his guy stop being polite and start getting real. Almost the second the closing gavel struck, Trump tweeted his review: "Judge Kavanaugh showed America exactly why I nominated him."

Trump's choleric face was mirrored in the face of the next associate justice of the Supreme Court; it was reflected in the legislators who learned to ape his blown-gasket affect to win over his followers and avoid his displeased tweets; it was reflected in the campaign ad for the winning gubernatorial candidate in Georgia, who threatened to "round up criminal illegals" in his big ol' pickup truck; it was reflected in the conservative news pundits spinning uglier conspiracy theories and sharper vitriol to enflame his imagination; it was reflected in the Montana congressional candidate who won his election, and Trump's enthusiastic endorsement, after body-slamming a reporter for asking him a question; it was reflected in the school bullies yelling, "Build the wall!" at their Hispanic classmates.

The world had become a closed-circuit TV network dedicated to the cultivation, appeasement, emulation, and management of one excitable viewer. Every character on the channel mattered only in relation to him, for how they could affect him or be affected by him. It was tacitly understood that American civic life had become a show, and that there were expectations when one was called to perform in it. The president would be satisfied only once the gorillas were fighting.

THE IDEA
OF A PRESIDENT

DURING PRESIDENT TRUMP'S FIRST SUMMER IN OFFICE, THE mainland United States experienced its first total solar eclipse since 1979. From Oregon's Pacific coast to Charleston, South Carolina, the sun hid from America. News coverage for days coached Americans on what kind of protective eyewear to use, how to make a pinhole projector, and above all, why you should never look at the eclipse with your naked eyes.

At the White House, the president and first lady stood on a balcony for a ceremonial viewing. Below them an aide shouted to Trump, who had not put his eclipse glasses on yet, "Don't look!"

He looked.

This was not a healthy way to behave. One of the most consistent themes of Trump's public life was modeling unhealthy behavior. He didn't smoke or drink, but he ate voluminously: well-done steaks and meatloaf and cheeseburgers, shovelsful of potatoes au gratin, buckets of fried chicken, double scoops of ice cream, chocolate cake, Vienna Fingers, Filet-o-Fish sandwiches, potato chips, bags of candy. (The Trump White House cut back on events in Michelle Obama's kitchen garden, a symbol of her healthy-diet advocacy as well as her husband's green environmental policy.) He resisted exercise, preferring to drive a cart for his golf games. ("He gets out, walks two feet, hits, and gets back in the cart," an associate told sportswriter Rick Reilly.) The porn star and the *Playboy* Playmate who said that Trump had extramarital affairs with them while he starred in *The Apprentice* each alleged that he had not used condoms. It was as if Trump wanted to stick it to "the so-called experts"—they say everything's bad for you!—by consuming and consuming, without denying himself a pleasurable sensation through moderation or prophylactic measures.

His media diet—hours upon hours of rage-making cable—was of a piece with his other appetites. The kind of nonstop exposure that made viewers sour and moody, that painted the world as a hellhole of enemies and threats, was his sustenance.

Trump had a way of Trumpifying everyone around him. Cable-news ratings, which usually fall after an election year, rocketed on the updrafts of national anger—most of all at MSNBC, home of TV's most anti-Trump audience, which tantalized its viewers with breathless reports of Trump's scandals that made it seem like he might be marched out of the Oval Office in manacles any day now. Even cable shows that were tough on Trump had an interest in inflating every tweet, every insult, every rally. News alerts pinged on smartphones constantly. To live in America post-2016 was to live inside the rattled mind of a septuagenarian insomniac cable-news junkie.

Often it was the Americans most appalled by Trump's presidency who ended up most closely matching his media appetites, communing with like-minded TV hosts like MSNBC's Rachel Maddow, pouring political podcasts into their ears—*Trumpcast*, *Pod Save America*, *Trump, Inc.*—constantly refreshing their Twitter feeds and checking their news notifications, dreading the next stab of spite and insult but unable to look away. The only cure for this creature that came from the media, they decided, was more media, like a homeopathic cure.

Or tapes. Maybe there were tapes! There grew an obsession with the idea that, somewhere in Trump's decades of electronic monitoring, there was a video or audio recording that would undo him.

Maybe it would be the supposed "N-word" tapes that Omarosa wrote about. Maybe it would be the "pee tape": the rumored Russian state-security blackmail video that, according to an intelligence dossier on Russian election interference leaked to the press after the 2016 election, allegedly caught Trump, on a visit to Moscow in 2013 for the Miss Universe pageant, having two prostitutes urinate on a Ritz-Carlton hotel bed that the Obamas once slept in. The speculation was endless: maybe there was a tape from Trump Tower, or a beauty pageant, maybe it captured violence or lechery or bigotry. Tom Arnold, the D-list actor, got cameras to follow him as he searched for these legendary totems; he found no silver bullet, but he did get an eight-episode TV series, *The Hunt for the Trump Tapes*. There was something mythic about this conviction that only video, the black magic that had forged Trump, could unmake him. It was as if Donald Trump were a basilisk, and the only way to destroy him was to hold up a mirror and turn his maleficent force back on himself.

You could try not to live this way; you could try to tune it all out. "Social-media fasts" became a mini-trend, a Trump-era equivalent of the macrobiotic small-planet diets of the '70s. The artist Jonathan Sun created a Twitter account, @tinycarebot, to remind its followers to look away from Twitter: "don't forget to just breathe please! be kind to urself!" A nationwide gym chain banned cable news at its 130 locations. The *New York Times* found a fifty-three-year-old-man living on a pig farm in Ohio who had quit the news—entirely—after Trump's election, staying off the Internet, turning off the TV, swearing the baristas at his local coffeehouse to silence.

But short of taking a monastic vow, you couldn't really avoid the media that Trump consumed, because you now lived in a reality whose metabolism and tone were set by that media. The ideology of cable—to make sure that the gorillas were always fighting—was now state policy. It was like secondhand smoke; you inhaled even if you didn't light up. The news was a feedback cycle of Trump being inflammatory, the news becoming inflamed, Trump growing inflamed by the coverage. The numbing round of feuds and outrages, shock after shock, felt like it had been programmed by a ratings-mad TV executive, because in a way, it was.

It was totalizing. It was personal. It was exhausting. It was in Facebook arguments and family dinners and in the way you looked at strangers. The eclipse was everywhere, even inside your eyelids.

* * * *

YOU CAN'T SAY we weren't warned. In *The Making of the President 1960*, Theodore H. White wrote that the first televised presidential debates permanently changed the currency of discussion: "Television had won the nation away from sound to images, and that was that." Neil Postman worried that politics would become a contest of entertainment values. George W. S. Trow anticipated Trump's relativistic arguments—that any claim is valid if "many people are saying it"—when he analyzed the surreal logic of the game show *Family Feud*, where contestants won by guessing not which answer to a poll question was objectively correct (like the average height of the American woman) but which answer most *other people* thought was correct.

The movie *Network* (1976) depicted a viewing public entranced by a raving madman who ratified their anger. Mike Judge's *Idiocracy* (2006) was set in a dumbed-down future America ruled by wrestler Dwayne Elizondo Mountain Dew Herbert Camacho, "five-time Ultimate Smackdown champion, porn superstar, and president of the United States," who punctuated a presidential address by firing a machine gun into the air. Now the actual president was a WWE Hall of Fame member and *Playboy* video star who said that his frequently misspelled and ALL-CAPS tweets were "not Presidential" but "MODERN DAY PRESIDENTIAL."

Trump was the human avatar of TV and the prognostications about it. But Trump was ultimately just one mortal person, subject to term limits (though he joked, or "joked," about doing away with them), the ballot box, and the Constitution. TV is not. There's a bigger question here, finally, than one presidency. Is TV our permanent God Emperor? Is the weltanschauung of cable news and reality TV—life as a constant, frenzied highlight reel of smackdowns and table-flipping—now hardwired into democracy? Is this simply our life now?

Yes and no. Yes, you can't undo the screen-centeredness of our society, the technology that divides us into sub-sub-subcultures. The idea that people will simply wake up, cast aside their devices, and return to a more contemplative, more elevated way of life (if one ever existed) is itself a kind of palliative nostalgic fantasy: not MAGA but MAMA, Make America Meditative Again.

But no, there's no reason that American life has to forever run at the Speed of Trump, that the only way to power is through acrimony and the culture war of all against all. The television culture that Donald Trump grew up with, thrived in, and embodies is not the only kind of television. His story is not the only kind of story it can tell.

* * * *

TRUMP'S ENTIRE PUBLIC EXISTENCE has been in nonfiction or nonfiction-based media. He developed a character in the 1970s and 1980s. He caught the curiosity of Rona Barrett and Tom Brokaw, rose as a celebrity in talk and lifestyle shows and on reality TV—formats that are all about ego and the projection of the self. As a performer, he played himself in the *Apprentice* boardroom and the WWE ring, reality-based entertainments about aggression and the defeat of enemies in a world of absolute winners and losers. As a viewer, he preferred first sports, then political news—real-life programming about conflict and competition, in which the only way to succeed is through someone else's defeat. As a longtime media star and epicurean cable-news consumer, he knew exactly how the meal was cooked and how the customers wanted it to taste.

But there's an entire realm of television that has been mostly out-

side the scope of this book because it is mostly outside the scope
of Trump's life. This is the TV that, like novels, film, and theater,
explores the lives of other people, on the premise that there is a value
in understanding people other than you besides learning how to
beat them.

While Trump was creating his celebrity persona in the 1970s and
the 1980s, this sort of TV was bringing women into the working
world in *The Mary Tyler Moore Show* and *Murphy Brown*. While he
presided over the boardroom free-for-alls on *The Apprentice*, NBC
was also airing *Friday Night Lights*, a drama about high school football in small-town Texas that emphasized the importance of community and defied easy red-state-blue-state clichés—it had stories
about abortion and characters who played in Christian speed-metal
bands. It aired *Parks and Recreation*, an oddball, optimistic comedy
about a small-city bureaucracy in Indiana. Each of these argued for
a definition of "team" that was inclusionary instead of tribal. They
argued for the idea that you could accomplish more working with
people than against them, that another person's gain did not mean
your loss.

In many ways, Trumpism has been a reaction against exactly
these sorts of stories—against the expansion of the American story,
in general. Trumpism was the warning that his followers were being
rewritten into supporting characters, and the promise that he would
restore them to their rightful place as the leads.

In 2014, while Trump was gearing up for his eventual run, he tweeted
a complaint about a new sitcom about an African American family
that dealt with what it meant to be black in the Obama era. "How is
ABC Television allowed to have a show entitled 'Blackish'? Can you
imagine the furor of a show, 'Whiteish'! Racism at highest level?"

Donald Trump ran for president as an antihero, on the concept,
borrowed from pop culture, that it takes a rough guy to get a job
done in this ugly world. But the very genre that that archetype came
from contains its own critique. However much fun Tony Soprano
was to watch, he was also a toxic, destructive monster devoid of

empathy, a hulking, selfish child who ruined nearly everyone close to him and toddled on his way. However charming and brilliant *Mad Men*'s Don Draper was, he was also a bred-in-the-bone liar, a coward whose instinctive reaction to problems was to cut bait and run.

Trump, not himself a fan of any of these dramas, ran on a willful misunderstanding of the ideas behind them that had permeated the larger culture. But the president before him, the president he defined himself against, was, in fact, also a storyteller.

Barack Obama—not just a reader and author but a fan of *The Wire*, *M*A*S*H*, and *Game of Thrones*—understood the power of figurative language and metaphor. Like Trump, he extrapolated a story about himself—in Obama's case, the son of a black father and a white mother, the "skinny kid with a funny name"—into a metastory about his voters: in Obama's case, that expanding the idea of America can mean more for everybody. As president, he engaged with American pop culture. He hosted musicians like Kendrick Lamar and James Taylor. It was at his White House that Lin-Manuel Miranda previewed a rap from *Hamilton*, the hip-hop musical that embodied the idea that diversity was America's strength, by spotlighting the poor Caribbean immigrant—dismissed as "a creole bastard," the "son of a whore and a Scotsman"—who laid the foundations for America's government and economic system. In its casting (mostly actors of color), its voice, its story, its musical pluralism, *Hamilton* both memorialized the white colonists who created America as it was and celebrated the varied multitudes who make America what it is. (Pointedly, Trump's vice president, Mike Pence, attended the musical after the election, and after cast members appealed to him from the stage in the name of "the diverse America who are alarmed and anxious that your new administration will not protect us," Trump broke off meetings with potential cabinet members to tweet, "Apologize!")

In the very same popular culture that Trump scrutinized for flaws and breaking points, fissures from whence this group could be separated from that, Obama found narratives of optimism and commonality. (He didn't nearly achieve that commonality as president—Trump's campaign was proof of that—but stories are ideals.) And the same country that elected Trump elected him.

You could argue that the division in American politics isn't so much between parties or even ideologies but between narratives. One sees diverse groups as adding to the country's strength and talent; another sees them as competitors for limited resources. One sees cultural pluralism as enriching the country, another as diluting it. One sees life like *Friday Night Lights*, where the team can only be as strong as the larger community; another sees it as *The Walking Dead*, where you hang tight with your own kind against teeming hordes of the Other.

The #MeToo movement that rose during Trump's Rat Pack presidency was on one level a cultural fight over stories and who gets to tell them. Many of the men disgraced for sexually preying on women dominated the media and entertainment industries. They created ideas and disseminated archetypes. Harvey Weinstein's movies won Academy Awards. Les Moonves ran the country's most-watched TV network, CBS, whose prime-time cop dramas were a parade of middle-aged male authority figures hunched over the corpses of beautiful women. Roger Ailes was the prime mover of conservatism, which he packaged through a tableau of blond women in skirts whom he victimized off-camera. Bill Cosby and Louis C.K. defined TV-comedy fatherhood. Journalists like Charlie Rose, Matt Lauer, and Mark Halperin were the paternalistic shapers of the national story. (And many of the media men exposed as letches happened to be among the most dismissive of Hillary Clinton as a candidate.)

Our culture, like any culture, has its set of myths and archetypes that our leaders borrow material from and that the rest of us use to frame and make sense of our lives. *All in the Family* and *Breaking Bad* are as much a part of that corpus now as Shakespeare and the Bible. Speaking the language of metaphor and story shouldn't be considered a frivolity beneath serious civic discussion. Just the opposite. Unless we engage with it to find the narratives that appeal to the best in people, someone else will gladly use it to appeal to the worst.

On one level, the level of gut and story and memory, politics is an ongoing battle of cultural criticism. Beyond policies and laws, it's an argument over what our canon is and how to read it.

But that argument always has to be made and remade, regardless of who wins or loses any given election. There's no permanent victory that simply makes people see the light forever. History can't be erased. There's no imaginable do-over in which we can tell ourselves, like Don Draper told Peggy Olson, advising her to give up her baby and move on after an unwanted pregnancy: "It will shock you how much it never happened."

* * * *

DONALD TRUMP WILL ALWAYS have happened. We will never not be the country that elected him. He will be in portrait galleries and TV reruns and children's history books. There will presumably be a Donald J. Trump Presidential Library, even if it's just a giant TiVo.

And he is already ensconced in democracy and entertainment's holiest shrine: the Hall of Presidents at Walt Disney World.

The hall, with its "Audio-Animatronic" semblables of every US president, was the descendant of Walt Disney's 1950s attempt at creating a talking Confucius for a "Chinatown" section of Disneyland. After it failed (the philosopher, reportedly, could not speak without his rubber skin horribly tearing) Disney redirected his Imagineers to create a speaking, moving Abraham Lincoln for the 1964 World's Fair. They implored Disney to use human actors, but he answered that only a robot could look exactly like Lincoln, and besides, "You can't have human beings working three or four shifts; we can't afford to pay 'em, or they'll make mistakes, or somebody won't show up." The Hall of Presidents opened in 1971, five years after Disney's death, the star-spangled expression of his lifelong drive to create imitations of life that improved on the real thing.

Today, the show begins with a park staffer in colonial garb welcoming the audience to a "reverent celebration of America's leaders, past and present." Though the mechanical presidents on stage are the main attraction, most of the program consists of a short film: *The Idea of a President*, added in 2017 to accompany the hall's new occupant. The previous film, retired when Obama left office, emphasized the personal qualities of individual presidents: Andrew Jackson's brashness, Abraham Lincoln's righteous torment. The new one sets all that aside to focus on the office of the presidency instead.

It starts with the writing of the Constitution and the establishment of an elected chief executive, continuing through civil war (here, robo-Lincoln gets his showcase, standing stiffly and reciting the Gettysburg Address), depression, space exploration, and civic upheaval. It runs through a presidential greatest-hits list, bringing us to the present with a clip reel of the post–World War II leaders. The steady narration and serene string music tell us: America has been through hard times—*Brother, can you spare a dime?*—and it will again. But everything will be OK. We have a president, and our system, whatever you think of anyone who once held the office or the guy who holds it now, is stable.

Then the screen rises, revealing every president in what appears to be a massive nineteenth-century drawing room. (Ulysses S. Grant, fittingly, appears to have a snifter of something strong on the table next to him.) In the middle of them all is the new Donald Trump machine, gazing about, great bags of flesh hanging from its jowls. Its hair is tamed, and it wears an expression unfamiliar from the face of the actual Trump: reverent, emotive, humble. It looks awed by the moment, as if it might be moved to tears. It does not scowl. It does not smirk. It does not clench its fists or stab at the air when it speaks, the way the actual Trump does, although it gestures courteously to Lincoln when the hall's star is mentioned.

The narrator introduces every president, in order, through Barack Obama. "And now," she continues, over an orchestral swell, "we come to the present. Once again, we place our trust in the *idea* of a president [her emphasis], as we have from the beginning." The robo-George Washington says a few words on the terrifying honor of being chosen to lead the country. Then he throws the spotlight to the former host of *The Celebrity Apprentice.*

The AnimaTrump's voice is Trump's own, recorded by him at the White House. Yet it sounds nothing like him. It's reassuring, anodyne, reciting boilerplate about "the achievements of the American spirit" and "the blessings of liberty." (The one Trumpian flourish is the superlative "great" thrown into "our great Constitution.")

But more than that, it doesn't *act* like him. The robot's bearing is placid and unassertive. Its gestures are smooth and calming— hands patting downward in an *easy, easy* motion. This is not Donald Trump. This is a Generic American President.

Which of course is the point of the performance: to try to force Trump into the traditions of the American presidency.

Think again of the way Umberto Eco described Disneyland's animatronic crocodile in *Travels in Hyperreality.* The crocodile, Eco wrote, is more believable because it behaves the way you *imagine* a crocodile should, roaring open its mouth and showing its teeth, rather than how a crocodile in the wild actually would. You know that it is not a crocodile. You know that, if you were to fall off the boat into the water, it would not swim over and eat you. But that too is part of the pleasure: "The public is meant to admire the perfection of the fake and its obedience to the program."

The AnimaTrump is constructed in the same spirit. But it takes the reproduction one fateful leap too far. It isn't trying to conform to our expectations of what Donald Trump is like. It's trying to conform to our expectations of *what a president should be like* ("the *idea* of a president").

Once Trump won the election, Disney had a challenge. It had built an exhibit premised on the assumption that all presidents recognized a tradition and a responsibility greater than themselves. (A line from the previous show's narration, conspicuously missing from the new one, expressed this idea: "All of liberty's leaders have one thing in common, one trust they have all accepted.") Trump had never shown any sign of this. He governed according to pique and self-interest.

He appealed to prejudice and fear and anger. If there was a fight, he stoked it; if there was a division, he sought to exploit it. He goaded Americans to embrace hate and their pettiest instincts. He wanted what the red light wanted—conflict and drama—and he presided as the leader of the Americans who voted for him, engaged in eternal payback against the ones who didn't.

But the exhibit had a choice: either admit that its premise was now fractured, or pretend that Trump, whatever his nature, was a president like in stature and temperament to every one who preceded him.

Disney was not alone in its need to fictionalize Trump. There were the TV pundits who, desperate for signs of normalcy, seized on any remotely conventional behavior—sticking to the TelePrompTer for a speech, say—as "the moment Donald Trump finally became president." There were the religious conservatives who—needing to find a way to support the amoral man who made their political dreams come true, yet still think of themselves as good people—shared kitsch artworks on social media that painted Trump as a godly, empathetic man. In one, he signs papers in the Oval Office guided by the figure of Jesus Christ. In another, he sits down with a despondent young man (led astray by a stack of books labeled "SOCIALISM" and "JUSTICE WARRIOR") and kindly teaches him how to fish.

In order for Trump to be installed in the Hall of Presidents, he needed to be made presentable to children. He needed not to agitate paying customers who would later go on the Pirates of the Caribbean ride together. He needed not to upset the premise of the spectacle. He needed to be the continuation of a tradition. Respectable. Predictable. Normal.

As a result, the machine seems false, uncanny, monstrous.

This misshapen thing pretending to be Donald Trump ended up here because of the actual Donald Trump's skill at creating facsimiles. He built a skyscraper that looked like wealth. He sat in a TV-stage boardroom that looked like power. He played a character, "Donald Trump," that looked like strength and success.

The robot is the copy of a copy, but it's a corrupted one, because

Disney is trying to fuse it with a historical idea greater than a single person. The AnimaTrump strains under the contradiction. It rejects the transplant.

It's a simulacrum that finally proves the limits of simulacra. The robot George Washington might be real enough to you, since you have no videotape or recordings of George Washington to compare it with. You have no evidence to the contrary. With Trump, you have nothing but evidence: on TV, on the Internet, in the air you breathe and the conversations you hear on the street.

As a reproduction, the AnimaTrump is a failure. But perversely, precisely because of that failure, it is also the most fitting and educational monument one could ever build for President Donald J. Trump, better than a marble statue or a portico on the National Mall. You see it, you hear it, and it triggers a voice inside you that says: This is not right, this is weird, this is not how I remember it at all.

That voice you're hearing? It's called reality.

ACKNOWLEDGMENTS

I want to thank TV first, because this book isn't always kind to it. I blame society: my subject matter requires me to focus here on some of the more corrosive aspects of a medium that I write about because I love it. I'll get to the good stuff, I promise.

I started writing this book years before I realized it; it ties together threads in television, culture, and politics that I didn't realize were connected when I first wrote about them. So I want to thank my earliest editors at Salon, particularly Susan Lehman, who took my first submission over the transom and shortly thereafter assigned me to review *The Art of the Comeback*, by one Donald Trump.

Thank you to my former editors at *Time* magazine, where I did sixteen years of writing on HBO dramas, reality TV, news media, politics, and sundry other topics that ended up in corners of this book: among them Walter Isaacson, Jim Kelly, Richard Stengel, Nancy Gibbs, Jan Simpson, Belinda Luscombe, Tim Morrison, Josh Tyrangiel, Radhika Jones, Jessica Winter, Isaac Guzman, and Gilbert Cruz. Thank you to my colleagues and editors at the *New York Times*, who encouraged me to do the work in the 2016 election and after that planted the seeds for this book, including Dean Baquet, Danielle Mattoon, Gilbert Cruz (again!), Mary Suh, Lorne Manly, Sia Michel, Patrick Healy, Jeremy Egner, and Aisha Harris—not to mention every coworker I annoyed or disappointed while working on this book, or before, or after.

Thank you to friends and colleagues who read drafts or chapters, let me bounce ideas off them, or answered my newbie questions about the publication process, among them Emily Nussbaum, Alan Sepinwall, Matt Zoller Seitz, Joy Press, Dana Stevens, Laura Miller, Liz Stein, Mark Harris, Anne Helen Petersen, Virginia Heffernan, Jennifer Senior, and Alyssa Rosenberg. Thanks as well to the readers, in the *Times* and on Twitter, on whom I tested/inflicted many of the ramblings that ended up in these pages.

Thank you to my agent, Chris Calhoun, who waited patiently for many years for me to finally write a damn book, then suggested after the 2016 election that this might be my subject. Thank you to my brilliant editor, Robert Weil, who believed that I could finish said book; motivated me to make it more ambitious, substantive, and rigorous; and helped me look past the firehose blast of current events toward the broad sweep of history. Few writers get to work with an editor this polymathic and attentive, but every writer should. Thanks as well to the heroic staff at Liveright, including Marie Pantojan and Gabriel Kachuck, who handled my many, many first-time-author questions with thoroughness and grace; to William Avery Hudson for a sharp-eyed copyedit; and to Pete Garceau and Brian Mulligan for the big-league cover and interior design.

I can thank, but cannot name, the anonymous archivers who have squirreled away hard-to-find videos in the corners of the Internet; you are the medieval monks of the reality-TV era. Thanks also to the Paley Center for Media, that temple of video rarities.

Thank you, finally, to my mom and dad, who let me watch more television as a child than may have been strictly advisable; to my sons, Milo and André, who watched TV with me (research!), understood when I locked myself up in my office, and entertained me when I let myself out; and above all, to my wife, Beth, my best reader, my best editor, and my best friend, without whom this book would not be possible and, honestly, neither would I.

NOTES

INTRODUCTION

xi   **"I've always felt that money, power, and sex"**: Rona Barrett, interview by Robert Samuels, https://www.washingtonpost.com/wp-stat/graphics/politics/trump-archive/docs/rona-barrett-interview-by-robert-samuels.pdf.

xii   **The *Washington Post's* Tom Shales**: Tom Shales, "Rona to Riches," *Washington Post*, July 24, 1981.

xii   **Thirty-five years later**: Interview with Donald J. Trump, *Fox & Friends*, Fox News Channel, June 15, 2015.

xiii   **"The choice of this theme"**: Neil Postman, "Amusing Ourselves to Death," *Et cetera* 42, no. 1 (Spring 1985): 13–18.

xiv   **Postman expanded on this argument**: Neil Postman, *Amusing Ourselves to Death* (New York: Penguin, 1985).

xiv   **Cable TV was not yet in half**: Nielsen Company, "Television Audience 2008," 2, https://tvbtn.files.wordpress.com/2009/07/tva_2008_071709.pdf.

xv   **Richard Hofstadter warned that electronic media**: "The Pseudo-Conservative Revolt," *The American Scholar* 24, no. 1 (Winter 1954–55): 9–27.

xv   **George W. S. Trow argued**: George W. S. Trow, *Within the Context of No Context* (Boston: Little, Brown, 1981).

xvi   **"the massive collection"**: Postman, *Amusing*, 161.

xvi   **"The whole age of computer"**: "Trump: Computers Complicate Lives," CNN.com, Dec. 30, 2016.

xviii **The *Crain's* article actually repeated a claim:** Timothy O'Brien, *TrumpNation* (New York: Open Road, 2015), Kindle edition.

xviii **"What Trump does not like is losing":** James Poniewozik, "BREAK-ING: Donald Trump Begins Not Running for President," Time.com, Feb. 11, 2011.

  xix **"For television purposes, he looked the part":** James Poniewozik, "What *The Apprentice* Taught Donald Trump About Campaigning," *New York Times*, Oct. 9, 2015.

  xxi **"Like so much about Trump":** Tony Schwartz, "I Wrote 'The Art of the Deal' with Trump. His Self-Sabotage Is Rooted in His Past," *Washington Post*, May 16, 2017.

  xxi **"No good has come of it":** Trow, *Within the Context*, 45.

  xxi **Postman lumped in:** Postman, *Amusing*, 160.

Episode 1: UNREAL ESTATE

  3 **More than 140,000 people:** James A. Von Schilling, *The Magic Window: American Television, 1939–1953* (Binghamton: Haworth, 2003), 73.

  3 **According to a "Talk of the Town" item:** "At the Knife & Fork," *The New Yorker*, June 29, 1946, 16.

  4 **"I still remember my mother":** Donald J. Trump, with Tony Schwartz, *Trump: The Art of the Deal* (New York: Random, 1987), 80.

  5 **"information-action ratio":** Postman, *Amusing*, 69.

  6 **"For most people there are only two places":** Don DeLillo, *White Noise* (New York: Penguin, 1985), 66.

  6 **the guitar-strumming preacher:** Michael Pollak, "Rex Humbard, 88, Dies, Pioneer of TV Evangelism," *New York Times*, Sept. 23, 2007.

  6 **Trump later recalled watching Billy Graham's televised Crusades:** *Fox & Friends*, Fox News Network, 25 Apr. 2011.

  6 **"as if it were a theatrical performance":** Robert Lacey, *Monarch: The Life and Reign of Elizabeth II* (New York: Simon & Schuster, 2008), 183.

  7 **The monarchy ultimately granted access:** Mark Easton, "Coronation 1953: Magic Moment the TV Cameras Missed," BBC.com, June 4, 2013.

  7 **NBC and CBS raced to get footage:** Anton Reminih, "Crowning Joke of Coronation: Costly TV Race," *Chicago Tribune*, June 6, 1953, sec. F, 1.

  7 **"a symbolic marker of the beginning":** John Finch, Michael Cox, and

Marjorie Giles, eds., *Granada Television: The First Generation* (Manchester: Manchester University Press), 2.

7 **derived from a song:** David Haven Blake, *Liking Ike: Eisenhower, Advertising, and the Rise of Celebrity Politics* (New York: Oxford University Press, 2016), 57.

7 **In October 1956, Dwight Eisenhower capped off:** Blake, *Liking Ike*, 16–20.

9 **"Tomorrow's children, through the great new medium":** Cecilia Tichi, *The Electronic Hearth: Creating an American Television Culture* (New York: Oxford University Press, 1991), 191.

9 **"Television can be the window to the whole world":** "Tomorrow Television," *Army-Navy Screen Magazine*, 1945.

9 **A 1954 study cited "television addiction":** Joost A. M. Meerloo, "Television Addiction and Reactive Apathy," *The Journal of Nervous and Mental Disease* 120, nos. 3–4 (Sept.–Oct. 1954): 290–91.

9 **His family owned a color TV set:** Paul Schwartzman and Michael E. Miller, "Confident. Incorrigible. Bully: Little Donny Was a Lot Like Candidate Donald Trump," *Washington Post*, June 22, 2016.

9 **A neighbor later recalled:** Jason Horowitz, "Trump's Queens Neighborhood Contrasts with the Diverse Area Around It," *New York Times*, Sept. 23, 2015, A15.

9 **Fred Trump had applied a rudimentary form:** Michael D'Antonio, *The Truth About Trump* (New York: Thomas Dunne, 2016), 30, 38, 62.

11 **In a 1994 interview:** Nancy Collins, "Donald Trump Talks Family, Women in Unearthed Transcript: 'When I Come Home and Dinner's Not Ready, I Go Through the Roof,'" *Hollywood Reporter*, Oct. 13, 2016.

11 **Jack Webb's *Dragnet*:** Alyssa Rosenberg, "How Police Censorship Shaped Hollywood," *Washington Post*, Oct. 24, 2016.

12 **after Fred Trump discovered his son's collection of switchblades:** Michael Kranish and Marc Fisher, *Trump Revealed: An American Journey of Ambition, Ego, Money, and Power* (New York: Scribner, 2016), 37–38.

13 **"a young, healthy, simple girl":** Oriana Fallaci, "Hugh Hefner: 'I Am in the Center of the World,'" *Look*, Jan. 10, 1967.

13 **"a Midwestern Methodist's vision of sin":** "Think Clean," *Time*, Mar. 3, 1967.

13 **"That's how we learned about women":** *The Choice 2016*, PBS, Sept. 27, 2016.

13 **"I was attracted to the glamour":** Trump, *Art of the Deal*, 77.

14 **In a 1997 profile:** Mark Singer, "Trump Solo," *The New Yorker*, May 19, 1997, 56.

14 **In a 2002 interview:** Errol Morris, interview by Anthony Audi, *Literary Hub*, Oct. 27, 2016.

14 **At age twenty-three:** Michael Paulson, "For a Young Donald J. Trump, Broadway Held Sway." *New York Times,* March 7, 2016, C1.

15 **In Clive Barnes's eventual *New York Times* review:** Clive Barnes, "Theater: 'Paris Is Out!' " *New York Times,* Feb. 3, 1970, 35.

15 **including a plan to coproduce W.C.:** *Playbill* for *Paris Is Out!*, Jan. 1970.

15 **"It's a crummy business":** Graydon Carter, "Donald Trump Gets What He Wants," *GQ*, May 1984.

15 **"I am going to go into real estate":** Timothy O'Brien, *TrumpNation* (New York: Open Road, 2015), Kindle edition.

15 **Trump was eventually able:** Robert E. Tomasson, "Deal Negotiated for Commodore," *New York Times*, May 4, 1975, 41.

16 **"I'm not Walt Disney":** "Walt Disney (Part 1)," *American Experience*, PBS, Sept. 14, 2015.

17 **"Girls of Trump":** Wayne Barrett, *Trump, The Greatest Show on Earth: The Deals, the Downfall, the Reinvention* (New York: Regan Arts, 2016), 421.

17 **Years later, Trump recognized the connection:** Surya Yalamanchili, "My Night at the Playboy Mansion with Donald Trump," *Politico*, Apr. 15, 2016.

17 **Rupert Murdoch, the Australian tabloid mogul:** Jonathan Mahler, *Ladies and Gentlemen, the Bronx Is Burning: 1977, Baseball, Politics, and the Battle for the Soul of a City* (New York: Picador, 2005), 33–43.

18 **Former *Newsday* gossip columnist A. J. Benza:** *The Confidence Man*, dir. Fisher Stevens, Netflix, Jan. 26, 2018.

18 **"Like an elephant in your bathtub":** Susan Mulcahy, *My Lips Are Sealed: Confessions of a Gossip Columnist* (New York: Doubleday, 1988), 226.

18 **"Donald would always gather me up":** Liz Smith, "I Think I Invented the Trumps: Part I," *New York Social Diary*, Aug. 24, 2015.

18 **Trump's big early coup:** Judy Klemesrud, "Donald Trump, Real Estate Promoter, Builds Image as He Buys Buildings," *New York Times*, Nov. 1, 1976, 41.

18 **It was actually leased by his father:** David Barstow, Susanne Craig, and Russ Buettner, "Trump Took Part in Suspect Schemes to Avoid Tax Bills," *New York Times*, Oct. 3, 2018, A1.

18 **The school's newspaper later debunked this:** Alex Rabin and Rebecca

Tan, "Was Trump Really a Top Student at Wharton? His Classmates Say Not So Much," *Daily Pennsylvanian*, Feb. 15, 2017.

19 **"By surrounding the consumer with images":** Christopher Lasch, *The Culture of Narcissism: American Life in an Age of Diminishing Expectations* (New York: Norton, 1978), 180–81.

Episode 2: THE LEAST OBJECTIONABLE PROGRAM

22 **"I just wasn't prepared":** Trump, *Art of the Deal*, 174.

23 **The science writer Sharon Begley:** "Trump Wasn't Always So Linguistically Challenged. What Could Explain the Change?" *Stat*, May 23, 2017.

25 **The ideal TV show of the time:** Paul Klein, "Why You Watch What You Watch When You Watch," *TV Guide*, July 24, 1971, 6–10.

26 **Political analysts disagree:** Lydia Saad, "Presidential Debates Rarely Game-Changers," Gallup.com, Sept. 25, 2008; Gary Langer, "The Impact of Debates? It's Debatable," abcnews.com, Sept. 26, 2016.

27 **whom cultural critic Kurt Andersen:** Kurt Andersen, "Entertainer-in-Chief," *The New Yorker*, Feb. 16, 1998, 34.

27 **"how they looked, fixed their gaze":** Postman, *Amusing*, 97.

29 **CBS executive Michael Dann:** William Grimes, "Michael Dann, TV Programmer, Dies at 94; Scheduled Horowitz and Hillbillies," *New York Times*, May 31, 2016, A16.

30 **By the mid-'70s, the networks wanted optimistic:** Josh Ozersky, *Archie Bunker's America: TV in an Era of Change, 1968–1978* (Carbondale: Southern Illinois University Press, 2003), 104–21.

31 **As *Time* magazine put it in 1985:** Richard Corliss, "Video: Coming Up from Nowhere," *Time*, Sept. 16, 1985.

31 **In 1980, according to Nielsen:** Nielsen Company, "Television Audience 2008," 3.

32 **One of Trump's biographers:** Emily Yoffe, "Is Donald Trump a TV Addict?" *Politico*, July 7, 2017.

32 **The Nielsen top ten in the 1970s:** Tim Brooks and Earle F. Marsh, *The Complete Directory to Prime Time Network and Cable TV Shows: 1946–Present* (New York: Ballantine, 2007).

34 **"Maybe it wasn't completely coincidental":** David Bianculli, *Dictionary of Teleliteracy: Television's 500 Biggest Hits, Misses, and Events* (New York: Continuum, 1996), 78.

34 **Later, in a 1990 interview with *Playboy*:** Glenn Plaskin, interview with Donald Trump, *Playboy*, March 1990.

35 **It was a modest success and tepidly reviewed:** Chris Nashawaty, *Caddyshack: The Making of a Hollywood Cinderella Story* (New York: Flatiron, 2018), 7.

36 **told Ramis to rewrite the script:** Nashawaty, *Caddyshack*, 160.

Episode 3: MONOPOLY

38 **The French philosopher Jean Baudrillard:** Jean Baudrillard, *Selected Writings*, Mark Poster, ed., second ed. (Palo Alto: Stanford University Press, 2002), 60.

39 **So is the lettering on the nameplate:** Wayne Barrett, *Trump: The Greatest Show on Earth* (New York: Regan, 2016), 179.

40 **He encouraged the rumor:** Harry Hurt III, *Lost Tycoon: The Many Lives of Donald Trump* (Brattleboro, VT: Echo Point, 2016), Kindle edition.

41 **Leach had squabbled with a producer:** Robin Leach, interview by Oprah Winfrey, *Oprah: Where Are They Now?* Nov. 30, 2014.

41 **In People magazine, he said:** Lee Wohlfert-Wihlborg, "In the Manhattan Real Estate Game, Billionaire Donald Trump Holds the Winning Cards," *People*, Nov. 16, 1981.

42 **Culture journalist Anne Helen Petersen has written:** "The Key to Trump Is Reading Him Like a Celebrity," *BuzzFeed*, Dec. 12, 2016.

42 **Trump chatted up Haskell:** *The Nikki Haskell Show*, season 1, episode 11.

43 **"Don't you need fresh air?":** *Donald Trump All American*, BBC2, Nov. 28, 2010.

46 **As the sociologist Juliet B. Schor:** Juliet B. Schor, *The Overspent American: Why We Want What We Don't Need* (New York: Basic, 1998).

47 **Thorstein Veblen identified the idea:** Thorstein Veblen, *Theory of the Leisure Class* (1899; Mineola, NY: Dover, 2012), Kindle edition.

47 **In her close read of 1980s MTV:** E. Ann Kaplan, *Rocking Around the Clock: Music Television, Postmodernism, and Consumer Culture.* (New York: Routledge, 1987), 30.

48 **"We'll be doing for TV":** Mark Goodman, MTV, Aug. 1, 1981.

48 **Unlike many previous pop-music phenomena:** Rob Tannenbaum and Craig Marks, *I Want My MTV: The Uncensored Story of the Music Video Revolution* (New York: Plume, 2011), e-book edition.

48 **"pop open an MTV":** "Pop Open an MTV," posted on YouTube, Jan. 23, 2013, https://www.youtube.com/watch?v=v5t_fVX7zdY.

49 The 1980 best seller: Lisa Birnbach, Jonathan Roberts, Carol McD. Wallace, and Mason Wiley, *The Official Preppy Handbook* (New York: Workman, 1980).

51 he'd proudly wear blue jeans: "Carter Says He'll Wear Jeans," Associated Press, Dec. 14, 1976.

51 In Washington, the Reagans transformed: Lou Cannon, *President Reagan: The Role of a Lifetime* (New York: Public Affairs, 1991), 5, 446.

52 The number-one nonfiction book: Lee Iacocca, with William Novak, *Iacocca: An Autobiography* (New York: Bantam, 1984).

54 "The most successful celebrities are products": Trow, *Within the Context*, 48.

54 But Trump kept a fond opinion: Grace Marston, "Andy Warhol Talks About Donald Trump Throughout the Mid-1980s," *Warhol Blog*, Jan. 21, 2016.

55 He boasted to GQ in 1984: Carter, "Donald Trump Gets What He Wants."

55 He tried to sell NBC: Eliot Brown, "Remember Trump City?" *New York Observer*, Aug. 5, 2008.

56 Jimmy Breslin, the Newsday columnist, described it: "The Art of the Trump: Call It Corum's Law," *Newsday*, June 7, 1990.

56 *Playgirl* magazine named him to its 1986 list: Wayne King and Warren Weaver Jr., "Washington Talk: Briefing; More Sex," *New York Times*, Aug. 5, 1986.

57 According to Jeffrey Breslow: Kranish and Fisher, *Trump Revealed*, 110.

58 Monopoly, the most direct inspiration: Mary Pilon, *The Monopolists: Obsession, Fury, and the Scandal Behind the World's Favorite Board Game* (New York: Bloomsbury, 2015).

Episode 4: AS HIMSELF

61 When *Home Alone 2* came out: "Company News; Trump's Plaza Hotel Bankruptcy Plan Approved," *New York Times*, Dec. 12, 1992.

61 There was an almost impossible neatness: Barrett, *Trump: The Greatest Show on Earth*, 417.

61 Trump was "astonished": Barrett, *Trump: The Greatest Show on Earth*, 427.

62 But he was put on a $450,000-a-month budget: Kranish and Fisher, *Trump Revealed*, 195.

62 **Frank Rich christened "mediathons":** Frank Rich, "The Age of the Mediathon," *New York Times Magazine*, Oct. 29, 2000.

62 **The real-life drama played:** Mary H. J. Farrell, "The Trumps Head for Divorce Court," *People,* Feb. 26, 1990.

62 **fed to the paper by Trump himself:** Jill Brooke, "The Real Story Behind Donald Trump's Infamous 'Best Sex I've Ever Had' Headline," *Hollywood Reporter*, Apr. 12, 2018.

63 **The New York satire magazine *Spy*:** *Spy*, Sept. 1990, Oct. 1986, and July 1990.

64 **You can understand the Trump of this period:** Aaron Hanlon, "Postmodernism Didn't Cause Trump. It Explains Him," *Washington Post*, Aug. 31, 2018.

64 **copy or representation:** Fredric Jameson, *Postmodernism, or, The Cultural Logic of Late Capitalism* (Durham, NC: Duke University Press, 1991).

64 **"The image can no longer imagine the real":** Jean Baudrillard, *The Perfect Crime* (New York: Verso, 1996), 4.

64 **Increasingly his business ventures:** D'Antonio, *The Truth about Trump*, 233.

64 **"It's Donald J. Trump. All 52 stories of him":** Robin Pogrebin, "52-Story Comeback Is So Very Trump; Columbus Circle Tower Proclaims That Modesty Is an Overrated Virtue," *New York Times,* Apr. 25, 1996.

65 **In 1877, the Quaker Oats company registered a trademark:** "Our Oat Origins," The Quaker Oat Company, 2019, http://www.quakeroats.com/about-quaker-oats/content/quaker-history.aspx.

65 **In 1890, a grain-milling company hired a former slave:** Maurice M. Manring, *Slave in a Box: The Strange Career of Aunt Jemima* (Charlottesville: University of Virginia Press, 1998).

65 **In 1964, when Colonel Harland Sanders sold his company:** William Whitworth, "Kentucky-Fried," *The New Yorker*, Feb. 14, 1970.

68 **In the sitcom business at the time:** Kranish and Fisher, *Trump Revealed*, 264.

69 **By 1991, its cover featured a bicycle:** Janice Castro, "The Simple Life," *Time*, Apr. 8, 1991.

70 **"one step removed from animals":** Donald J. Trump, with Charles Leerhsen, *Trump: Surviving at the Top* (New York: Random, 1990), 225.

72 **He de-emphasized traditional TV ads:** Elizabeth Kolbert, "Perot's 30-Minute TV Ads Defy the Experts, Again," *New York Times*, Oct. 27, 1992.

73 **In Dallas, the *Los Angeles Times* reported:** Tom Furlong, "Perot as

Hometown Hero: Just Don't Get in His Way," *Los Angeles Times*, June 10, 1992.

74 It was, to borrow the name of a 1996 PBS documentary: *Triumph of the Nerds*, Channel 4/PBS, Apr. 14, 1996.

75 To be a nerd was to oppose: Benjamin Nugent, *American Nerd: The Story of My People* (New York: Scribner, 2009), 9.

75 There was one member of the nerdocracy: Alan Deutschman, *The Second Coming of Steve Jobs* (New York: Broadway, 2000).

76 "wants to be Madonna": Mark Singer, "Trump Solo," *The New Yorker*, May 19, 1997.

76 in '90s hip-hop lyrics: Allison McCann, "Hip-Hop Is Turning on Donald Trump," *FiveThirtyEight*, July 14, 2016.

77 In 1993, he published an essay: David Foster Wallace, "E Unibus Pluram: Television and U.S. Fiction," *Review of Contemporary Fiction* 13, no. 2 (Summer 1993): 151–94.

78 "The greatest humbug of all": P. T. Barnum, *The Humbugs of the World: An Account of Humbugs, Delusions, Impositions, Quackeries, Deceits and Deceivers Generally, In All Ages* (New York: Carleton, 1865).

79 Wallace's short story "My Appearance": David Foster Wallace, *Girl with Curious Hair* (New York: Norton, 1989).

80 Donald Trump appeared on Letterman's shows: Jason Zinoman, "The Misunderstood History of Trump on Letterman," *New York Times*, Aug. 15, 2017.

80 In a 1992 appearance: *Late Night with David Letterman*, NBC, May 21, 1992.

81 Neal Gabler writes in *Life the Movie*: Neal Gabler, *Life the Movie* (New York: Knopf, 1998), 170–71.

82 *The Art of the Comeback*'s story is a Hollywood story: Donald J. Trump, with Kate Bohner, *Trump: The Art of the Comeback* (New York: Times, 1997), xi–xx.

82 When Matt Lauer on the *Today* show asked him: *Today*, NBC, Nov. 3, 1997.

Episode 5: THE DARK SIDE

85 *Profit*'s creators were inspired by Shakespeare's *Richard III*: Harriet Winslow, "Risky Business," *Washington Post*, May 5, 1996.

86 "Its principal conceit": John Leonard, *Smoke and Mirrors: Violence,*

Television, and Other American Cultures (New York: New Press, 1997), 105.

87 **"Sex had become mainstream"**: David Friend, *The Naughty Nineties* (New York: Twelve, 2017), 2.

88 **In *Anatomy of Criticism***: Northrop Frye, *Anatomy of Criticism: Four Essays* (Princeton, NJ: Princeton University Press, 2000), 34–35.

90 **"Clean it up, deterge it"**: Laura Z. Hobson, "As I Listened to Archie Say 'Hebe'. . ." *New York Times*, Sept. 12, 1971, D1.

91 **CBS anticipated this before the show premiered**: Todd Gitlin, *Inside Prime Time* (New York: Pantheon, 1983), 36.

91 **"Dude, he's Archie Bunker"**: Jeremy W. Peters and Maggie Haberman, "Bannon Was Set for a Graceful Exit. Then Came Charlottesville," *New York Times*, Aug. 20, 2017.

93 **"an actor whom I've greatly admired"**: Trump, *Surviving*, 81.

94 **As Brett Martin notes**: Brett Martin, *Difficult Men: Behind the Scenes of a Creative Revolution: From* The Sopranos *and* The Wire *to* Mad Men *and* Breaking Bad (New York: Penguin, 2013), 13.

95 **"The object of all these shows in the past"**: Martin, *Difficult Men*, 287.

97 **"I like to believe there is some comeuppance"**: David Segal, "Art of Darkness," *New York Times Magazine*, July 10, 2011, 18.

97 **what the *New Yorker* critic Emily Nussbaum calls "bad fans"**: Emily Nussbaum, "That Mind-Bending Phone Call on Last Night's *Breaking Bad*," Newyorker.com, Sept. 16, 2013.

98 **This, critic Alan Sepinwall pointed out**: Alan Sepinwall, *The Revolution Was Televised: How* The Sopranos, Mad Men, Breaking Bad, Lost, *and Other Groundbreaking Dramas Changed TV Forever* (New York: Touchstone, 2015), Kindle edition.

98 **In a *New York Times* op-ed**: Anna Gunn, "I Have a Character Issue," *New York Times* Aug. 24, 2013, A21.

98 **On surveillance tapes**: James Poniewozik, "They Pull You Back In," *Time*, Jan. 9, 2000.

98 **Life imitated, or parodied**: Ian Crouch, "Of Course Roger Stone Thinks That He Lives in *The Godfather*," Newyorker.com, Jan. 25, 2019.

100 **One week in October 2001**: Nicholas Kristof, "An American Hiroshima," *New York Times*, Aug. 11, 2004.

100 **conservative essayist Michael Anton**: Michael Anton [as Publius Decius Mus], "The Flight 93 Election," *Claremont Review of Books*, Sept. 5, 2016.

100 **Five days after the attacks, Vice President Dick Cheney**: *Meet the Press*, NBC, Sept. 16, 2001.

101 **military officers had to deal with soldiers who now believed:** Jane Mayer, "Whatever It Takes," *The New Yorker*, Feb. 19, 2007, 66.

101 **In the 2008 primary debates:** Ari Melber, "The GOP's Ticking Time Bomb," *Huffington Post*, Dec. 12, 2007.

101 **In a 2016 debate, Donald Trump endorsed:** Tessa Berenson, "Donald Trump Defends Torture at Republican Debate," Time.com, March 3, 2016.

102 **Disney's *Davy Crockett*:** Olivia Waxman, "Fact-Checking 'The Ballad of Davy Crockett,'" Time.com, Aug. 17, 2016.

102 **One draft script had a detective smashing a coin box:** Gitlin, *Inside Prime Time*, 288.

102 **The creator, Shawn Ryan, had kicked around:** Sepinwall, *The Revolution Was Televised*.

105 **The outing recalled the scene:** Philip Roth, *The Plot Against America* (Boston: Houghton Mifflin, 2004).

106 **"I am Batman":** Thomas Lake, "'I Am Batman,' Trump Tells Boy on Helicopter Ride," CNN.com, Aug. 17, 2015.

Episode 6: MONEY MONEY MONEY MONEY!

108 **In this two-hour beauty-pageant-cum-meat-market:** James Poniewozik, "Fox's Bride Idea," *Time*, Feb. 20, 2000.

109 **His 1200-square-foot house in Encinitas, California:** Lisa de Moraes, "'Multi-Millionaire' Formula Goes Bankrupt," *Washington Post*, Feb. 22, 2000, C1.

109 ***Multi-Millionaire* was the brainchild of Mike Darnell:** Laura Bradley, "Meet the Mad Genius Who Invented Reality TV as We Know It," *Vanity Fair*, Apr. 24, 2017.

109 **Rockwell was revealed:** de Moraes, "'Multi-Millionaire' Formula Goes Bankrupt."

110 **The show's training of its audience was so successful:** Dustin Rowles, "The Time a Real Plane Hijacking Was Mistaken for a *Candid Camera* Stunt," *Uproxx*, Oct. 24, 2015.

110 **NBC's *Real People* valorized unsung Americans:** Brooks and Marsh, *The Complete Directory to Prime Time Network and Cable TV Shows*, 844.

111 **The third season, set in San Francisco:** Kate Aurthur, "Looking Back at *The Real World: San Francisco*, the Show That Changed the World," *BuzzFeed*, Jan. 7, 2014.

111 **In 1991, I sat in a packed crowd:** George Bush, "Remarks at the University of Michigan Commencement Ceremony in Ann Arbor," May 4, 1991.

112 **Reality fans might not know exactly how:** James Poniewozik, "How Reality TV Fakes It," *Time*, Jan. 29, 2006.

114 **"Everybody on the crew wanted Rudy to win":** Jeff Probst, "30 Epic Seasons," *Survivor: 30 Seasons: The Official CBS Collector's Edition*, Feb.–Mar. 2015, 20–21.

114 **Courtney Robertson, after winning *The Bachelor:*** Courtney Robertson, *I Didn't Come Here to Make Friends: Confessions of a Reality-Show Villain* (New York: It, 2014).

115 **For his 1975 essay "Travels in Hyperreality":** Umberto Eco, *Travels in Hyperreality: Essays* (New York: Harvest, 1990), 44.

117 **There were dating shows, quiz shows:** James Poniewozik, "Reality TV at 10: How It's Changed Television—and Us," *Time*, Feb. 22, 2010.

118 **It was there, on a tiki-beach set:** Marc Fisher, "Donald Trump, Remade by Reality TV," *Washington Post*, Jan. 27, 2016.

118 **After the *Survivor* finale:** Fisher, "Donald Trump, Remade by Reality TV."

118 **"He told me all the right things":** Donald J. Trump, interview by the author, Dec. 2003.

119 **The author Fran Lebowitz would later say:** Emily Jane Fox, "Let Fran Lebowitz Soothe All Your Election-Related Worries," *Vanity Fair*, Oct. 20, 2016.

123 **Producers designed the set:** *The Confidence Man.*

123 **Trump's often-repeated belief that success is genetic:** D'Antonio, *The Truth About Trump*, 326–27.

125 **"When I was a good girl":** Poniewozik, "How Reality TV Fakes It."

125 **as media critic Jennifer L. Pozner pointed out:** Pozner, *Reality Bites Back: The Troubling Truth about Guilty Pleasure TV* (Berkeley, CA: Seal, 2010), 164–67.

126 **Trump hired her to a $179,700-a-year White House position:** Elaina Plott, "No One Knows What Omarosa Is Doing in the White House— Even Omarosa," *Daily Beast*, Nov. 13, 2017.

127 **Was his instinct actually that unerring?:** A. J. Catoline, "Editing Trump: The Making of a Reality TV Star Who Would Be President," *Cinemontage*, Oct. 12, 2016, http://cinemontage.org/editing-trump -reality-tv-star-who-would-be-president/.

127 **Clay Aiken, a former *American Idol* finalist:** *Domecast* (podcast), July 8, 2017.

127   "Make Trump look good": Catoline, "Editing Trump."

127   "chipped furniture": Patrick Radden Keefe, "How Mark Burnett Resurrected Donald Trump as an Icon of American Success," *The New Yorker*, Jan. 7, 2019.

128   Braun described the music: Catoline, "Editing Trump."

131   This is an ancient, apocryphal tale: Snopes.com, "Trumped Up."

132   A 2006 *Time* magazine poll: Poniewozik, "How Reality TV Fakes It."

133   He fires Zervos: Brandy Zadrozny, "Apprentice Contestant Summer Zervos Slaps Donald Trump with Defamation Lawsuit," *Daily Beast*, Jan. 17, 2017.

135   "to exaggerate the unique part of themselves": Omarosa Manigault Newman, *Unhinged: An Insider's Account of the Trump White House* (New York: Gallery, 2018), Kindle edition.

136   Said Jim Dowd, NBC's public-relations rep: Kranish and Fisher, *Trump Revealed*, 217.

136   hanging up a fake cover of *Time* magazine: David A. Fahrenthold, "A *Time* Magazine with Trump on the Cover Hangs in His Golf Clubs. It's Fake," *Washington Post*, June 27, 2017.

Episode 7: THE PARANOID STYLE
IN AMERICA'S NEWSROOM

142   Shepard Smith, anchoring the afternoon coverage: "Fox News: Six-Year-Old Boy in a Runaway Balloon," *Studio B*, Fox News, Oct. 15, 2009.

143   Michaele and Tareq Salahi: Amy Argetsinger and Roxanne Roberts, "Who Are These People? The Climbers at the Gate," *Washington Post*, Nov. 27, 2009.

144   Republican representative Joe Wilson of South Carolina: "Wilson Funds Reach $1 Million After 'You Lie' Cry, Aide Says," CNN.com, Sept. 12, 2009.

145   On April 18, 1930, nothing much of note happened: "There Is No News: What a Change from 1930 to Today," BBC.com, Apr. 18, 2017.

145   "We used to believe there were only so many": Daniel J. Boorstin, *The Image: A Guide to Pseudo-Events in America* (New York: Atheneum, 1962), 8.

145   In *Amusing Ourselves to Death*: Postman, *Amusing*, 99–100.

146   He prepared a "doomsday tape": Michael Ballaban, "This Is the Video CNN Will Play When the World Ends," *Jalopnik*, Jan. 5, 2015.

146 **Reese Schonfeld, the veteran TV journalist:** Reese Schonfeld, *Me and Ted Against the World: The Unauthorized Story of the Founding of CNN* (New York: HarperCollins, 2001), 1.

147 **"For as long as the war held their interest":** Ken Auletta, *Three Blind Mice: How the TV Networks Lost Their Way* (New York: Vintage, 1992), 4.

147 **When she was finally brought out alive:** Lisa Belkin, "Death on the CNN Curve," *New York Times Magazine*, July 23, 1995, 18–19.

150 **Only later did researchers find:** "'Summer of the Shark' in 2001 More Hype Than Fact, New Numbers Show," *University of Florida News*, Feb. 18, 2002.

150 **Then came the clear blue morning of September 11:** Frank Rich, *The Greatest Story Ever Sold: The Decline and Fall of Truth from 9/11 to Katrina* (New York: Penguin, 2006), 21.

151 **the relaxed, improvisatory, and vaguely defined:** Marshall McLuhan, *Understanding Media: The Extensions of Man* (Cambridge, MA: MIT Press, 1994), 308–37.

151 **"The general public is just not sophisticated enough":** Gabriel Sherman, *The Loudest Voice in the Room: How the Brilliant, Bombastic Roger Ailes Built Fox News—and Divided a Country* (New York: Random, 2014), 40.

151 **Ailes sifted through Nixon's video clips:** Rick Perlstein, *Nixonland: The Rise of a President and the Fracturing of America* (New York: Scribner, 2008), 234.

151 **"It's a television show":** Joe McGinniss, *The Selling of the President: The Classic Account of the Packaging of a Candidate* (New York: Penguin, 1988), 65–67.

152 **A second slogan:** Sherman, *The Loudest Voice in the Room*, 199.

152 **"Viewers don't want to be informed":** Sherman, *The Loudest Voice in the Room*, 191.

153 **"Has P.C. changed our view of the Founding Fathers?":** David Brock, "Roger Ailes Is Mad as Hell," *New York*, Nov. 17, 1997, 35.

153 **A favorite Fox perennial was "The War on Christmas":** John Gibson, *The War on Christmas: How the Liberal Plot to Ban the Sacred Christian Holiday Is Worse Than You Thought* (New York: Sentinel, 2005).

154 **The divisive shorthand "blue state" and "red state":** Stephen Battaglio, "When Red Meant Democratic and Blue Meant Republican: A Brief History of TV Electoral Maps," *Los Angeles Times*, Nov. 3, 2016.

154   **dressed in skirts:** "Former Host Gretchen Carlson: Pants Were Not Allowed on *Fox & Friends*," *Media Matters*, Sept. 19, 2013.

155   **Fox was the first cable network to deal with the flood:** James Poniewozik, "The Tick, Tick, Tick of the Times," *Time*, Nov. 24. 2010.

156   **"The modern right wing":** Richard Hofstadter, *The Paranoid Style in American Politics* (New York: Random, 2012), Kindle edition.

158   **"Conspiracists," as Kurt Andersen wrote:** Kurt Andersen, *Fantasyland: How America Went Haywire: A 500-Year History* (New York: Random, 2017), 365.

159   **In 2007, the hosts spread a bogus story:** Matea Gold, "They're Having 'Fun' on *Fox & Friends*," *Los Angeles Times*, Oct. 21, 2008.

160   **"Would you fire [George W.] Bush?":** Donald Trump, interview by Howard Stern, *The Howard Stern Show*, Sept. 23, 2004.

161   **"Rita, I will say this":** Don King and Donald Trump, interview by Rita Cosby, *Big Story Weekend*, Fox News, Nov. 29, 2003.

161   **Trump became part of *Fox & Friends'* entertainment-news universe:** Descriptions of Trump's Fox appearances, here and throughout, are from video at the Internet TV News Archive: https://archive.org/details/tv.

163   **"I think you and I should have had a sexual relationship":** Michael M. Grynbaum and John Koblin, "Fox Settles Sex Harassment Suit as Another Anchor Abruptly Exits," *New York Times*, Sept. 7, 2016, A1.

164   **Since Obama had been elected:** David Crary, "New Burst of Attention for Old Doubts About Obama," Associated Press, July 23, 2009.

165   **"Our current president came out of nowhere":** Donald Trump, remarks at the Conservative Political Action Conference, Washington, DC, Feb. 10, 2011.

166   **Good Morning America introduced him:** Donald Trump, interview by Ashleigh Banfield, *Good Morning America*, ABC, March 17, 2011.

166   **To CNN's Anderson Cooper:** *Anderson Cooper 360*, CNN, Apr. 25, 2011.

167   **"He can finally get back to the issues that matter":** Barack Obama, "'The President's Speech' at the White House Correspondents' Dinner," May 1, 2011.

167   **"Every critic, every detractor":** *The Choice 2016.*

169   **A former aide said Trump was originally "indifferent":** Joshua Green, *Devil's Bargain: Steve Bannon, Donald Trump, and the Storming of the Presidency* (New York: Penguin, 2017), 111.

170   **The concept of the wall itself:** Julie Hirschfeld Davis and Peter Baker,

"How the Border Wall Is Boxing Trump In," *New York Times*, Jan. 5, 2019.

Episode 8: THE MOST OBJECTIONABLE PROGRAM

173 **"The problem with television is that the people must sit"**: Orrin E. Dunlap Jr., "Act I, Scene I: Telecasts to Homes to Begin on April 30— World's Fair to Be the Stage," *New York Times*, Mar. 19, 1939, 144.

175 **The news site The Outline**: Matt Porter, "Trump's First Real Tweet Was on July 6, 2011," Outline, Nov. 3, 2017.

177 **Ziering later appeared on *The Celebrity Apprentice***: Seth Abramovitch, "How *Sharknado* Casts Its C-Listers and Nearly Landed Trump as President," *Hollywood Reporter*, Aug. 2, 2017.

177 **Syfy did very little traditional advertising**: Amar Toor, "Twitter Twister: Why Did *Sharknado* Take a Huge Bite Out of the Internet?" *Verge*, July 12, 2013.

177 **who decades before had called up reporters**: Marc Fisher and Will Hobson, "Donald Trump Masqueraded as Publicist to Brag About Himself," *Washington Post*, May 13, 2016.

178 **After the tabloids obsessed**: Anne Helen Petersen, *Too Fat, Too Slutty, Too Loud: The Rise and Reign of the Unruly Woman* (New York: Plume, 2017), 136–49.

178 **New York magazine art critic Jerry Saltz compared her**: "Jerry Saltz: How and Why We Started Taking Kim Kardashian Seriously (and What She Teaches Us About the State of Criticism)," *Vulture*, May 20, 2015.

179 **"In the United States"**: Boorstin, *The Image*, 56.

180 **"The fragmentation of technology"**: Kevin M. Kruse and Julian E. Zelizer, *Fault Lines: A History of the United States Since 1974* (New York: Norton, 2019), 159.

180 **According to a study by Entertainment Weekly**: James Hibberd, "Favorite Shows of Republicans vs. Democrats." *Entertainment Weekly*, Nov. 3, 2014.

181 **They also really liked reality TV**: Josh Katz: "'Duck Dynasty' vs. 'Modern Family': 50 Maps of the U.S. Cultural Divide," *New York Times*, Dec. 27, 2016.

182 **an interview with GQ magazine**: Drew Magary, "What the Duck?" GQ.com, Dec. 17, 2013.

182 **identified by their neutral "TV accents":** J. D. Vance, *Hillbilly Elegy: A Memoir of a Family and Culture in Crisis* (New York: Harper, 2016), 79.

183 **"All mass culture under monopoly is identical":** Max Horkheimer and Theodor W. Adorno, *Dialectic of Enlightenment* (Stanford, CA: Stanford University Press, 2007), 95.

183 **"a cultural war, as critical to the kind of nation":** Patrick Joseph Buchanan, "Culture War Speech: Address to the Republican National Convention," Aug. 17, 1992.

184 **The president of Chick-fil-A denounced gay marriage:** "Chick-Fil-A Sandwiches Become a Political Symbol," Associated Press, July 26, 2012.

184 **"go 'against nature,' interrupting":** Dick Hebdige, *Subculture: The Meaning of Style* (New York: Routledge, 1979), 18.

185 **They wailed over a 2016 BBC history cartoon:** Sarah Zhang, "A Kerfuffle About Diversity in the Roman Empire," TheAtlantic.com, Aug. 2, 2017.

185 **"that political change follows":** Angela Nagle, *Kill All Normies: Online Culture Wars from 4chan and Tumblr to Trump and the Alt-Right* (Winchester, UK: Zero, 2017), 40.

186 **"Childhood ruined":** crazylegsmurphy, "Ghostbusters 2016: Childhood Ruined," Reddit, July 10, 2016, https://www.reddit.com/r/ghostbusters/comments/4s4vx3/ghostbusters_2016_childhood_ruined/.

186 **To Bannon, embittered online young men:** Green, *Devil's Bargain*, 146–47.

186 **Yiannopoulos rationalized the movement's ooze:** Allum Bokhari and Milo Yiannopoulos, "An Establishment Conservative's Guide to the Alt-Right," Breitbart, Mar. 29, 2016.

188 **Trump ordered printouts:** Bob Woodward, *Fear: Trump in the White House* (New York: Simon & Schuster, 2018), 207.

188 **"Every time Trump tweeted against amnesty":** Green, *Devil's Bargain*, 106.

189 **Fox invited *Celebrity Apprentice* contestant:** *Outnumbered*, Fox News, Oct. 24, 2014.

189 **Richard Dawkins's term for the basic unit of culture:** Richard Dawkins, *The Selfish Gene* (Oxford: Oxford University Press, 1976).

191 **"If @realDonaldTrump retweeted me":** Donald J. Trump (@realDonaldTrump), on Twitter, Mar. 29, 2014, https://twitter.com/realDonaldTrump/status/450099934617174017.

Episode 9: RED LIGHT

196 **If he sensed that it might blink off:** Philip Rucker and Marc Fisher, "Welcome to Washington's New Normal: One Trump Drama After Another," *Washington Post*, Nov. 22, 2016.

196 **The crowd was packed with actors:** Aaron Couch and Emmet McDermott, "Donald Trump Campaign Offered Actors $50 to Cheer for Him at Presidential Announcement," *Hollywood Reporter*, June 17, 2015.

197 **Foreign stereotypes were reliable:** Shaun Assael and Mike Mooneyham, *Sex, Lies, and Headlocks: The Real Story of Vince McMahon and World Wrestling Entertainment* (New York: Crown, 2002), 10.

198 **"Each sign in wrestling":** Roland Barthes, *Mythologies* (New York: Noonday, 1989), 16–17.

198 **"The 'winner' wasn't the wrestler whose hand was raised":** Lou Thesz, with Kit Bauman, *Hooker* (Gallatin, TN: Crowbar, 1995), Kindle edition.

199 **At the 2011 White House Correspondents' Dinner:** C-SPAN, Apr. 30, 2011.

199 **The fire marshal reported capacity:** PolitiFact, "Rachel Maddow Says Trump Exaggerated His Crowd in Phoenix," July 15, 2015.

201 **"designed to replicate the desert sky":** "Floor Plans & Specs," Phoenix Convention Center website, https://www.phoenixconventioncenter .com/floor-plans-specs.

201 **"What makes the circus or the arena":** Barthes, *Mythologies*, 15.

202 **Trump would don reading glasses:** Lara Weber, "Donald Trump Likes to Read 'The Snake' at His Rallies. The Author's Family Wants Him to Stop," *Chicago Tribune*, Mar. 17, 2016.

202 **Journalists at the rallies described attendees:** George Saunders, "Trump Days," *The New Yorker*, July 11 and 18, 2016, 50–61.

202 **Trump knew what wound them up:** Josh Dawsey and Nick Miroff, "The Hostile Border Between Trump and the Head of DHS," *Washington Post*, May 25, 2018.

203 **"Trump was able to take them up to the line":** Jared Yates Sexton, *The People Are Going to Rise Like the Waters upon Your Shore: A Story of American Rage* (Berkeley, CA: Counterpoint, 2017), 109.

203 **The New York Times caught it on video:** "Unfiltered Voices from Donald Trump's Crowds," *TimesVideo*, Aug. 3, 2016.

203 **That adrenaline would surge toward the journalists:** Katy Tur, *Unbelievable: My Front-Row Seat to the Craziest Campaign in American History* (New York: HarperCollins, 2017), 65.

203 In August, he mimed holding a rifle: Tur, *Unbelieveable*, 95.

204 "the fundamental metaphor for political discourse": Postman, *Amusing*, 126.

205 His two-minute closing ad was a rant: Team Trump, "Donald Trump's Argument for America," posted on YouTube, Nov. 6, 2016, https://www.youtube.com/watch?v=vST61W4bGm8.

205 CNN covered it for weeks: James Poniewozik, "Dear CNN: Sometimes Our Opinions Just Don't Matter," Time.com, May 7, 2014.

207 $5.6 billion in free media: Emily Stewart, "Donald Trump Rode $5 Billion in Free Media to the White House," TheStreet.com, Nov. 20, 2016.

207 "It may not be good for America": Eliza Collins, "Les Moonves: Trump's Run Is 'Damn Good for CBS,'" *Politico*, Feb. 29, 2016.

207 My *Times* colleague Amy Chozick: Amy Chozick, *Chasing Hillary: Ten Years, Two Presidential Campaigns, and One Intact Glass Ceiling* (New York: Harper, 2018), 131–32.

209 "Trump is fucking crazy": Michael Grunwald (@mikegrunwald), on Twitter, June 6, 2016.

209 he would request specific camera angles: Tur, *Unbelieveable*, 26.

209 After TV interviews, he would ask for a playback: Glenn Thrush, "What Chuck Todd Gets About Trump," *Politico*, Dec. 30, 2016.

210 "Reagan's experience as an actor": Leo Braudy, *The Frenzy of Renown: Fame and Its History* (New York: Vintage, 1986), 567.

210 Reagan's own assessment, to his biographer: Cannon, *President Reagan*, 32.

211 "My objective was": Manigault Newman, *Unhinged*.

211 Reagan had trouble separating movies from reality: Gabler, *Life the Movie*, 110–11.

211 he had never completely achieved "theory of mind": Jesse Singal, "Does Donald Trump Have a Fully Developed Theory of Mind?" *The Cut*, May 16, 2017; David Brooks, "When a Child Is Leading the World," *New York Times*, May 15, 2017.

212 "He didn't trademark it": Karen Tumulty, "How Donald Trump Came Up with 'Make America Great Again,'" *Washington Post*, Jan. 18, 2017.

213 "I'll defend you in court": Jose A. DelReal, "'Get 'Em Out!' Racial Tensions Explode at Donald Trump's Rallies," *Washington Post*, March 12, 2016.

213 it was to see nostalgia gone ugly: Donald J. Trump presidential-campaign rally, Sterling Heights, Mich., posted on YouTube, Nov. 6, 2016, https://www.youtube.com/watch?v=OAkt18Uw3Tk.

213 **"subhuman mongrel":** Manny Fernandez, "Ted Nugent Apologizes for Obama Insult," *New York Times*, Feb. 21, 2014.

214 **It was Sir Walter:** Mark Twain, *Life on the Mississippi* (New York: Harper, 1883), e-book edition.

216 **A 2014 poll found a thirty-eight-point gap:** Ezra Klein, "GamerGate and the Politicization of Absolutely Everything," *Vox*, Nov. 1, 2014.

217 **"a nation governed in the Anglo-American tradition":** Michael Patrick Leahy, "Why Coca Cola's Multicultural 'America the Beautiful' Ad Was Offensive," Breitbart Big Government, Feb. 2, 2014.

218 **"I can say Merry Christmas to anyone I want":** *60 Minutes*, CBS, Feb. 18, 2018.

220 **Trump's followers didn't practice:** Justin Wm. Moyer, "Trump Says Fans Are 'Very Passionate' After Hearing One of Them Allegedly Assaulted Hispanic Man," *Washington Post*, Aug. 21, 2015; Astead W. Herndon, "South Boston Brothers Plead Guilty to Brazen Beating," *Boston Globe*, May 16, 2016.

221 **When the fact-checking outfit PolitiFact:** "2015 Lie of the Year," *PolitiFact*, Dec. 21, 2015.

222 **The last real Republican challenge to Trump:** "Transcript of Mitt Romney's Speech on Donald Trump," *New York Times*, Mar. 3, 2016.

227 **"Someone unstable":** Barthes, *Mythologies*, 24.

227 **Ta-Nehisi Coates would later call Trump:** Ta-Nehisi Coates, "The First White President," *Atlantic*, Oct. 2017.

227 **Comic Dana Carvey once portrayed:** Brian Lowry, "ABC Abruptly Pulls the Plug on 'The Dana Carvey Show,'" *Los Angeles Times*, May 7, 1996.

228 **At the 2004 Republican National Convention:** John Tierney and Sheryl Gay Stolberg, "Terminator Talks Tough," *New York Times*, Sept. 1, 2004.

228 **psychological researchers found:** Eric Knowles and Sarah DiMuccio, "How Donald Trump Appeals to Men Secretly Insecure About Their Manhood," *Washington Post*, Nov. 29, 2018.

229 **"There is an Indiana Jones–style":** Rebecca Traister, "Hillary Clinton vs. Herself," *New York*, May 30, 2016.

229 **He had taken on Fox News's Roger Ailes:** Maggie Haberman and Ashley Parker, "Roger Ailes Is Advising Donald Trump Ahead of Presidential Debates," *New York Times*, Aug. 16, 2016.

231 **In September 1952, vice presidential candidate Richard Nixon:** Rick

Perlstein, *Nixonland: The Rise of a President and the Fracturing of America* (New York: Scribner, 2008), 36–42.

232 **"If anything"**: Maggie Haberman, "Donald Trump's Apology That Wasn't," *New York Times*, Oct. 8, 2016.

234 **One psychological study found that *Apprentice* fans**: Bert Gambini, "Reality TV Played Key Role in Taking Trump from 'Apprentice' to President," *UBNow* (State University of New York at Buffalo), Mar. 5, 2018.

234 **But what little polling there was**: Anna Giaritelli, "Trump Shuts Down Clinton in Poll of *Apprentice* Viewers," *Washington Examiner*, Feb. 24, 2016; Ryan Lovelace: "Poll: Viewers of *The Apprentice* Favor Clinton over Trump," *Washington Examiner*, June 30, 2016.

Episode 10: THE GORILLA CHANNEL

236 **Days after winning the election**: Emily Smith and Daniel Halper, "Donald Trump's Media Summit Was a 'F——ing Firing Squad,'" *New York Post*, Nov. 21, 2016.

237 **"Trump is an avid television viewer"**: Steven Perlberg, "How Donald Trump Launched a New Golden Age for Cable TV," *BuzzFeed*, Feb. 14, 2017.

238 **his executive assistant kept a trove of videotapes**: D'Antonio, *The Truth About Trump*, 153.

239 **"In the Huxleyan prophecy"**: Postman, *Amusing*, 155.

240 **Author Douglas Rushkoff described Trump**: "Why Donald Trump Is a Media Virus," *Digital Trends*, Dec. 17, 2016; see also *Media Virus: Hidden Agendas in Popular Culture* (New York: Ballantine, 1994).

241 **"Donald J. Trump is going to be the executive producer"**: *Cavuto Live*, Fox News Channel, Dec. 9, 2016.

242 **In her post–White House memoir**: Manigault Newman, *Unhinged*.

242 **a table stacked with manila folders**: Jonathan Lemire, "What Was in Those Folders at Donald Trump's Press Conference?" Associated Press, Jan. 13, 2017.

243 **"This is central casting"**: CNN transcript, Jan. 20, 2017.

244 **One obsequious North Korean anchor**: Ashley Parker, Josh Dawsey, Carol D. Leonnig, and Karen DeYoung, "'Why Can't We Just Do It?': Trump Nearly Upended Summit with Abrupt Changes," *Washington Post*, June 14, 2018.

245 **Trump later gave Paul Ryan:** Mark Leibovich, "This Is the Way Paul Ryan's Speakership Ends," *New York Times Magazine*, Aug. 7, 2018.

246 **Jim Dowd, who recalled Trump demanding:** *The Choice 2016*.

247 **In a speech to the VFW:** Alexander Mallin, "President Trump Defiant on Trade War in Remarks to VFW," ABCNews.com, July 24, 2018.

247 **"Not Stalin's and Hitler's skill":** Hannah Arendt, *The Origins of Totalitarianism* (New York: Harcourt, 1973), 333.

247 **"Ideological thinking":** Arendt, *The Origins of Totalitarianism*, 470.

248 **An overwhelming flood of information:** Zeynep Tufekci, *Twitter and Tear Gas: The Power and Fragility of Networked Protest* (New Haven, CT: Yale University Press, 2017).

248 **"In an ever-changing, incomprehensible world":** Arendt, *The Origins of Totalitarianism*, 382.

248 **the propagandists in Vladimir Putin's Russia:** Peter Pomerantsev, *Nothing Is True and Everything Is Possible: The Surreal Heart of the New Russia* (New York: PublicAffairs, 2014).

249 **"Truth isn't truth":** *Meet the Press*, NBC, Aug. 19, 2018.

249 **Trump told his staff:** Maggie Haberman, Glenn Thrush, and Peter Baker, "The President vs. the Presidency," *New York Times*, Dec. 10, 2017.

250 **When she was booted:** Avi Selk and Sara Murray, "The Owner of the Red Hen Explains Why She Asked Sarah Huckabee Sanders to Leave," *Washington Post*, June 25, 2018.

250 **"told colleagues he had no idea":** Jonathan Swan (@jonathanvswan), Twitter, Aug. 25, 2017.

251 **"Whenever there was a disagreement":** Manigault Newman, *Unhinged*.

252 **In May 2017, Trump took reporters:** Michael Scherer and Zeke J. Miller, "Donald Trump After Hours," *Time*, May 22, 2017.

252 **He became alarmed during a national security meeting:** Woodward, *Fear*, 102.

252 **"Not watching political television":** David Remnick, "Obama Reckons with a Trump Presidency," *The New Yorker*, Nov. 28, 2016.

252 **As CNN carried his first photo op:** *CNN Newsroom*, Jan. 26, 2017.

253 **Reportedly, there were three televisions:** Michael Wolff, *Fire and Fury: Inside the Trump White House* (New York: Holt, 2018), 84–85.

253 **"Tonight, I'm going to enjoy watching television":** *Lou Dobbs Tonight*, Fox Business Network, Oct. 25, 2017.

255 **"overtook the president's fight with CNN":** Philip Rucker and Ashley Parker, "Why Some Inside the White House See Trump's Media Feud as 'Winning,'" *Washington Post*, June 30, 2017.

255 a "BREAKING NEWS: TRUMP TWEET" graphic: Allahpundit (@allah-pundit), on Twitter, May 30, 2017; "CNBC Now Has a Breaking News Graphic for Trump Tweets," *NewscastStudio*, Jan. 27, 2017.

255 "Trump watches TV coverage of him": Josh Dawsey (@jdawsey1), on Twitter, July 24, 2017.

256 When Donny Trump was a little boy: David Smith, "Donald Trump: The Making of a Narcissist," *Guardian*, July 16, 2016.

258 "a self-made billionaire": *State of the Union*, CNN, Jan. 7, 2018.

259 "Am I like a baby to you?" Green, *Devil's Bargain*, 201.

259 "Rudy, you're a baby!" Woodward, *Fear*, 37.

260 "Two Minutes Hate": George Orwell, *Nineteen Eighty-Four* (New York: Harcourt, 1949), 13.

260 he had never cried: *The Brody File*, Christian Broadcasting Network, Jan. 19, 2016.

260 "Womp womp": *The Story with Martha MacCallum*, Fox News, June 19, 2018.

261 "their brilliant and witty praise": Arendt, *The Origins of Totalitarianism*, 330.

261 Trump started holding his rallies again: Charles Homans, "The Post-Campaign Campaign of Donald Trump," *New York Times Magazine*, Apr. 15, 2018, 24.

263 At the center of the chaos, invariably, was TV: Wolff, *Fire and Fury*, 22, 114, 159, 197, 247.

263 "Wow, this extract from Wolff's book": Ben Ward (@pixelatedboat), on Twitter, Jan. 4, 2018.

264 "Think what your brain would be like": Woodward, *Fear*, 299.

264 He directed his secretary of state: Donald Trump (@realDonaldTrump), on Twitter, Aug. 22, 2018.

265 "He basically has a desk in the place": Robert Costa, Sarah Ellison, and Josh Dawsey, "Hannity's Rising Role in Trump's World," *Washington Post*, Apr. 17, 2018.

265 "the great Lou Dobbs": Donald Trump, interview by hill.tv, Sept. 19, 2018.

265 "look like a loser": *Fox & Friends*, Fox News, Dec. 19, 2018.

265 thousands of dollars' worth of dental work: Joel Pavelski, "The Great White House Reporter Glow-Up," GQ.com, Oct. 1, 2018.

265 It was real that critics, lobbyists, and corporations: Ashley Rodriguez, "Lobbyists Have a New Tactic for Wielding Influence in Washington—Buying Ads on Trump's Favorite TV Shows," *Quartz*, Feb. 6, 2017.

265 White House officials would go on TV: Ashley Parker and Robert

Costa, "'Everyone Tunes In': Inside Trump's Obsession with Cable TV," *Washington Post*, Apr. 23, 2017.

265 **When Trump took a shine:** Jacqueline Thomsen, "White House Has Aides Go on Pirro's Show Every Week Knowing Trump Watches: Report," *The Hill*, Apr. 5, 2018, https://thehill.com/homenews/administration/381910-white-house-has-aides-go-on-pirro-every-week-knowing-trump-watches.

266 **Ann Coulter, conservative TV's perpetual font:** *The Next Revolution with Steve Hilton*, Fox News, June 17, 2018.

266 **"One of the ways to influence the president":** Astead W. Herndon, "What's Trump's Think Tank? Try Internet Message Boards," *Boston Globe*, Aug. 29, 2017.

266 **Maryland representative Elijah Cummings, seeking a meeting:** April Ryan, American Urban Radio Network, Jan. 25, 2017.

266 **An associate of his reported:** Jacqueline Alemany, "Trump Asked Source to Go on TV to Ask Him to Fire Robert Mueller," CBSNews.com, Apr. 13, 2018.

267 **What bothered Trump was his meekness:** Jeremy W. Peters and Susan Chira, "Court Pick Steals a Page from Trump's Playbook on White Male Anger," *New York Times*, Sept. 30, 2018.

Finale: THE IDEA OF A PRESIDENT

269 **The Trump White House cut back:** Anastasia Day, "How the White House Garden Became a Political Football," *Washington Post*, Apr. 3, 2018.

270 **"He gets out, walks two feet":** Rick Reilly, *Commander in Cheat: How Golf Explains Trump* (New York: Hachette, 2019), Kindle edition.

270 **alleged that he had not used condoms:** Gail Collins, "Trump's Birth Control Problems," *New York Times*, Jan. 31, 2018; Karen McDougal, interview by Anderson Cooper, CNN, March 22, 2018.

271 **"pee tape":** Naomi Fry, "When We Think About the Pee Tape," Newyorker.com, Apr. 18, 2018.

271 **Tom Arnold, the D-list actor:** James Poniewozik, "Tom Arnold's 'Trump Tapes' Blows Smoke with No Smoking Gun," *New York Times*, Sept. 17, 2018.

271 **The artist Jonathan Sun:** NBC News, Jan. 11, 2017; tweet from @tinycarebot to the author, Sept. 8, 2018.

271 **A fifty-three-year-old-man living on a pig farm:** Sam Dolnick, "The Man Who Knew Too Little," *New York Times*, Mar. 11, 2018.

272 **In *The Making of the President 1960*:** Theodore H. White, *The Making of the President 1960* (1961; repr. New York: Harper, 2009), 290.

272 **George W. S. Trow anticipated Trump's relativistic arguments:** Trow, *Within the Context*, 88.

275 **a fan of *The Wire*:** Michael D. Shear, "Obama's TV Picks: Anything Edgy, with Hints of Reality," *New York Times*, Dec. 29, 2013; Katie Zezima, "Presidents Have Favorite Television Shows, Too. Here's a List," *Washington Post*, June 27, 2014.

277 **The hall, with its "Audio-Animatronic" semblables:** Neal Gabler, *Walt Disney: The Triumph of the American Imagination* (New York: Vintage, 2007), 578–81.

277 **Today, the show begins:** "FULL updated Hall of Presidents 2017 with Donald Trump at Walt Disney World," Inside the Magic, posted on YouTube, Dec. 19, 2017, https://www.youtube.com/watch?v=nkxOdzVbrrs.

278 **The previous film:** "The Hall of Presidents," Attractions Magazine, posted on YouTube, Jan. 16, 2017, https://www.youtube.com/watch?v=KMn83d4tQp8.

279 **"The public is meant to admire the perfection of the fake":** Eco, *Travels in Hyperreality*, 44.

INDEX

Footnotes are indicated by *n* after the page number.

ABOUT THE AUTHOR

James Poniewozik has been the chief television critic for the *New York Times* since 2015. He was previously the television and media critic for *Time* magazine and a media columnist for Salon, and has contributed to publications and news outlets including *Fortune*, *Rolling Stone*, *Talk*, *New York*, *Bookforum*, and NPR. A graduate of the University of Michigan, he lives with his family in Brooklyn.